PIECES OF ROPE TOO SHORT TO KEEP

A Childhood in Back Country Vermont

Steven Holmsen Gardner

CONTENTS

ABOUT NAMES USED IN THIS BOOK

With the exception of the members of my immediate family, the actual names of persons appearing in this book have been replaced with fictitious names to respect their privacy.

ACKNOWLEDGEMENTS

My brother Paul David and sister Johanna were both a tremendous help to me in reminding me of the details of many of these stories and reading and critiquing the text. Many other friends read draft versions and made helpful comments, but special thanks go to Paul Eichen and Susan Flieder, who caught many significant errors. Thanks also to Mike Yorkey, who provided encouragement and technical help on how to get the book into print.

For Mary.
It's to my great good fortune that no one told her about all of this before she said "til death do us part".

1 PREFACE

As a young adult I never thought there was anything remarkable about the childhood I spent in an old Vermont farmhouse two miles out a dirt road from a town of a couple hundred people in the 1960s. But over the years as I swapped stories about growing up with friends I worked with in my engineering job in Southern California and witnessed their amusement and astonishment at stories like Oscar the pig getting drunk on rotten apples, or my father rising at daybreak to shoot an annoying woodpecker off the roof just a couple feet above where I was sleeping, I came to realize that not being from suburbia was different and unusual and in a way maybe even a little exotic. I gradually became aware that there was something I should value in those memories, and I began fitfully capturing some of the stories during periods of late night boredom while folded with my computer into ergonomically destructive coach class seats on airline flights returning me to San Diego from east coast business trips. This proved to be an ineffective way to write a cohesive book, but it was a start, and now with the additional time of a retiree, but a correspondingly duller memory, I've been able to tie it all together in a finished story.

I don't feel selfish in saying that what is written here is primarily for my own entertainment. In my view that's not necessarily a bad thing. In similar fields like music or film, something is lost when the creator focuses on satisfying the audience rather than self-expression. But I can imagine that some people might find limited amusement reading about what it was like to be a kid in a small town in rural Vermont during the 1960s. And that's alright with me. I've enjoyed the process of writing this all down, re-living the memories of a way of growing up that's often romanticized but not really known or understood. It was unusual then, and it's even more rare today.

My older brother Paul David and younger sister Johanna still live in Vermont and might very well disagree with my perspective, but I always say that Vermont is a good place to be from. It was hard to get in serious trouble growing up, so there was a better chance of surviving childhood without a rap sheet, an unwanted pregnancy, or a drug habit than in other places (although with our highly interconnected world this is unfortunately not so much the case today). Childhood then was spent outdoors, close to nature. There was less material gratification than in much of the rest of the country, and you learned how to make do with less. But compared to the city it could be a hard place for adults – at least economically. Fortunately many Vermonters feel amply rewarded in other ways, and compared to people living the fast lane city life they are more likely to not just believe, but to actually live, the old saying that money isn't everything.

However, as a kid there were times when I'd had enough of Vermont and its isolation. I can still remember with striking clarity looking at a map of the United States in one of those big atlases most homes had before the internet age. The city of San Diego was in the far southwest corner of the country and although I was only ten years old I thought: "That's as far as I can get from Vermont and still be an American. I'd like to go there." It was a moment of prescience, since for reasons completely unrelated to that vision, I've lived in San Diego most of my adult life.

I suspect I wasn't unusual among children in thinking that

upon reaching adulthood any normal individual attained the state of a mature, all-knowing, all-seeing, emotionally balanced person, prepared to weather any crisis and to act with reason and justice in all circumstances, and I had little tolerance for departures from that expectation. My parents, alas, proved to be actual human beings and like most people they struggled with their relationships with each other, with their children, and with the mental baggage that came with their own upbringings. Having reached my sixties I am only now at the age my father was when I was ten and I'm keenly aware that there is no stage of life where anyone really "gets it" completely or even mostly, and that it was grossly unfair that I expected this from my parents. For me the gradual arrival of this understanding has been one of the joys of aging, and now I can look back and remember with fondness the unique childhood I experienced, and I see humor in a lot of things that I didn't used to perceive that way.

Those looking for an orderly, chronological narrative will be disappointed, I fear. In my own head the stories just don't fit on a timeline anymore. They happened in a distant past over a span of ten or twelve years, and they are all jumbled together, with part of one event serving to remind me of another that might have happened either earlier or later. To me the odd interconnections are almost as entertaining as the events themselves, so I've organized the telling around these linkages.

I have to add that I'm no longer completely certain that all these stories happened just as I've described them. Now and then I've discussed some of these memories with Paul David and he has reacted with puzzlement, saying, "Gee, I don't remember that at all". (He also says it was *he* who built the boat that sailed once, whereas until he objected to my version of the story I hadn't anticipated that there could possibly be any question that I was the shipwright. Well, let the reader choose between us when he gets there.)

But I also notice that the things he remembers the least are the stories that show him in the best light. And there are a lot of these stories, because in Paul David I was blessed with one of those older brothers who was patient, kind, and good (but, as he emphatically insists on me saying, not by any means a saint), and who would not only put up with an ultra-competitive and often annoying pest of a younger sibling, but would actually be his best friend.

I'm sorry to say that there are far fewer stories involving our younger sister, Johanna, and at times she may seem almost absent from the narrative here. This is largely my own fault, since as a self-absorbed adolescent male I was uninterested in any involvement with a girl five years younger than me. For her part, it must have been especially lonely without a close sibling relationship to carry her through the sometimes solitary existence we led. Ironically, today she still lives in our old house, just past where Wardsboro Road turns to dirt at the third bridge over Smith Brook, and has raised three children of her own through what has probably been at times a very similar set of experiences to those recounted here.

Perhaps the biggest surprise in writing this book has been how much enjoyment I've had in recalling the details of the various anecdotes that I've tried to capture. At times I've felt like I'm almost experiencing them all over again. If that sense of pleasure and flat-out fun comes through in the telling, then this story will have been a success.

2   A BOX OF DEAD FATHER

It was the light that woke me. My first reaction was confusion – the bed was all wrong – stiff and hard compared to home. But then I saw the doctor standing by my father, and yesterday came flooding back. I felt guilty for having slept. I felt worse when the doctor said softly "He's passed on". It made me feel slightly sad, but even though the outcome wasn't really a surprise it seemed like a proper person should be feeling more emotion than I was. I didn't cry, and that made me feel guilty, too.

I'd come in from the west coast the night before and Papa (being of Scandinavian stock on our mother's side, we were taught to call our parents "Mama" and "Papa") was awake and alert. He asked me about my job and I tried to explain it to no avail. It was all so confusing to him to understand what it was I was doing on the other side of the country, but he seemed vaguely proud of it. He was lying on the bed, looking vulnerable and weak, something I wasn't much used to seeing even after he passed ninety years of age. He was a stubborn old goat, my father, and even though he wasn't born in Vermont, he'd lived there long enough that he'd picked up a lot of the crotchety behavior patterns that form the caricature of the classic Vermont farmer.

A few days earlier Papa hadn't answered multiple phone

calls so Johanna's husband Bahman drove by to check on him. He found Papa fallen on the cold autumn floor of the house he'd been in for most of the past sixty plus years. His hip was broken, and he'd been lying there in agony for most of a day. He'd had an emergency alert device, but he'd taken it off and left it on a table he couldn't reach.

Pneumonia was taking him by the time I arrived at the hospital, and deciding that it wasn't worth fighting it, he'd refused the antibiotics that could have kept him alive. It didn't surprise me that he'd turned them down. A long stretch of recuperation under the dictates of medical authorities was not something he would suffer gladly.

When I arrived in the evening Paul David and Johanna had already spent the whole day sitting by his bed at the sleepy little hospital in Townshend, some ten miles from Newfane. They were tired and back at their homes their families were waiting for them, so I'd sent them off, promising to watch over Papa that night. I'd sat by his bed for several hours, watching as he dozed fitfully. He slept the agitated sleep of the dying, with his hands jerking involuntarily and his breath struggling. I ran my hand through his thinning hair to comfort him. Me comforting my father! The thought of it alone seemed like an improper act. Overt displays of affection or compassion had never been a family strength.

Midnight passed and Papa's sleep grew broken, with his breath becoming ragged. He spoke: "Don't leave me", he pleaded. "Please don't leave me!"

"I'm here, Papa", I replied softly. "I won't leave you". I squeezed his hand and rubbed his shoulder. And he slowly passed into a quiet sleep, while I sat and watched for another hour or so, holding his hand. Then my own eyes grew heavy and the bed next to his beckoned. I loosened my hand from his and lay down. Instantly sleep took me, and in what seemed like no time at all I was awakened by a light switching on and then the doctor's voice.

It was dawn, and the morning that followed would be

surreal. Paul David and Johanna arrived while the rest of Townshend was still asleep, and we made arrangements with the little town funeral parlor. No casket for Papa; he'd asked for cremation. No tombstone or graveyard; he'd asked instead that we scatter his ashes in a brambly glade behind the barn that oddly struck him as a place of beauty.

Paul David, Johanna and I went to the home where we'd grown up and we sat in the rickety old kitchen chairs and talked about Papa for a while. But the needs of young children don't wait long even when their grandparent has just died. Soon my brother and sister left me alone at the table where I'd eaten and argued and played all the years of my childhood, its wood soaked with the milk I'd spilled and permeated with the grease from the deep fat fried donuts Mama used to make and which I had ingested by the hundreds.

I looked around. The place was filthy, and things were piled everywhere. A product of the Great Depression, my father saw value in everything and he kept everything, stashed in utter chaos in grocery bags and cartons rescued from rubbish piles behind grocery stores, stacked from floor to ceiling with only little pathways between groupings of boxes that made little sense. Everything was piled up everywhere, from rinsed out plastic milk bottles to junk mail to cans of food to newspapers and magazines. It had been bad when we were children and Mama was still alive. Her Scandinavian sense of order and neatness was repelled by the overwhelming volume of rubbish collected by my father. And although she didn't win all of her battles, she had won enough to keep the living areas of the house in a presentable state. But it was worse – much worse – since she had died sixteen years earlier. Without her the only thing that restrained Papa was the fact that age had sapped him of the energy to acquire as rapidly as he once had. No matter, he had still proven capable of nearly filling the house.

To me the boxes were appalling. I remembered like yesterday the bitter fights my parents had over my father's unceasing accumulation, and though I'd had plenty of my own rows with my mother, this was a place where I sided with her completely. Now here I was, alone in the house, with my father's watch over his collection at a permanent end, and nothing else to do. I set to work.

Two days later, I'd cleared three rooms of their most completely valueless contents. It was a task that required some care, since there was no clue what was in a given box. A carton would come off a stack. *Heinz Ketchup* might be the marking it bore, signifying its original purpose of bearing condiments to the Grand Union grocery store in Brattleboro some thirty years previous. If through an act of monumental foresight it had instead been printed with the contents that it actually held for the vast majority of its service life, it might instead have declared *books, broken model railroad cars, loose change in a cat food tin, newspapers, machine tool parts, a lamp cord,* etc. Each of these boxes required quick sorting, with decision making of the most merciless sort determining whether an item would be dispatched to the dump (nine times out of ten) or placed in another box with like objects for later and more thorough evaluation. After ten consecutive boxes yielded nothing worth keeping I might grow careless, but then a treasure would suddenly appear; a photo of the grandfather who died twenty years before I was born, an insurance policy, or an envelope full of old coins from the twenties.

A rumbling and crunching of gravel down the driveway through the field announced the UPS truck. I met the driver and signed for the package. It was Papa's ashes from the crematorium delivered in a cube shaped cardboard box of eight inches on a side. Not at all anxious to open it, I placed it atop the refrigerator. It seemed appropriate, since my father had always used the refrigerator as a place for important things that were to be used in the immediate future, and it briefly occurred to me how unusually normal it was for people well over six feet tall, as Papa was and I am, to find the top of the refrigerator to be a useful kitchen surface.

Then I went back to work, unconcerned whether the ashes might be annoyed that in these few days my efforts had undone several years of careful selection and saving.

Later that afternoon, Paul David and Johanna arrived with their families. It was a typical late fall day in Vermont. The leaves had surrendered weeks earlier and fluttered to the ground, and now the bare trees blanketed the hills in a dull, dead grey that Dickens would have admired. The sky was blue and clear, but the air had a cold bite. We took the box from the top of the refrigerator and opened it. To our surprise there was nothing but a plastic bag holding its contents, which bore as much likeness to Papa as the scrapings from the bottom of the fireplace in the living room. It might have been anyone in that box. It might not have been anyone at all.

We carried the box to the appointed spot between the barn and stony Smith Brook, the length of which we'd splashed throughout our youths. Not knowing exactly what to do, but recognizing that decorum required us to manage to make at least a few minutes of ceremony, we determined that each of us should scatter a portion of the ashes. Little Emmet punctuated the pretentiousness of the scene by kicking the ash and leaf mixture so that the dust blew all over us, just like the scene in the movie *The Big Lebowski*.

Both parents were gone now, and although in reality I hadn't counted on either of them to provide me with much of anything since I'd left for college at seventeen years of age, there is something about knowing that for the first time in your life you're truly performing without a net of any kind, even one that you knew you'd fall right through if you actually needed to use it. I was forty-one and my childhood was most definitively over.

3 A MAN'S HOME IS HIS CASTLE

Papa was eighty-eight when he had first met Mary three years before his passing. I knew I had to introduce her to him. We planned to marry soon and prospective spouses need to meet the parents of their beloveds, no matter how awkward. By now I was old enough to realize that a rational assessment of the facts would not assign *me* the personal responsibility for my father's strange mode of living. But I still felt a nagging requirement for some explanation why a son would live in prosperity in a city about as far away as could be managed while his father languished in companionless solitude in a decrepit house whose paint peeled off in sheets like writing paper and where the indoor temperature in mid winter rarely topped sixty degrees.

It wasn't like we didn't try to help, my siblings and I. My brother had tried it first, living with my father through several years after college. It wasn't easy. There was little that could be done that Papa would appreciate unless it was his idea to have it done, and even then, it was unlikely that the thing could be done in the way he envisioned. And if Paul David – named, from my own selfish perspective, in an act completely lacking in foresight, for *both* of our grandfathers at once – thought on his own of something that needed to be done and undertook to do it, well, I could be assured that in my next phone call home Papa would complain bitterly about how my spendthrift older brother was painting the house with *the* most expensive paint that money could buy, whereas *he* had always bought paint at Railroad Salvage and then extended it by adding paint thinner to save useless expense. No matter that this cheap, diluted paint would inevitably be peeling again in a year. The point was that throwing money around like some millionaire's debauched playboy son was not the way things were supposed to be done.

And later when Paul David had married and moved into the comparatively urban town of Brattleboro, Johanna took her turn, moving in with Papa along with her Iranian husband Bahman. Papa loved the granddaughter they brought him, but despite the regular meals they cooked and the company they provided at the dinner table there was always reason for complaint. There was too much rice, and he couldn't sleep after he ate rice. The pots were not kept where he wanted them. They used too much hot water when they washed dishes. They wasted electricity, leaving two lights on in a room where one would be enough. They ran the heat too high in the winter. Eventually he asked them to leave, and they did. And of course he then couldn't understand why they'd gone to that house ten miles away.

Me, I kept my distance by staying far away in California. I sent him money, but that wasn't really much of a burden compared to the emotional but not-measurable-in-dollars contribution of my brother and sister. But money was something Papa could appreciate. Money never aggravates anyone except by its absence. It seemed to me that my father viewed this contribution to his well-being with more gratitude than just about anything that had ever been done for him, but in my view it was a cop out. Writing the check was easy compared to the sacrifice of actually living with him that both Johanna and Paul David made for several years each.

I had tried to explain all this background to Mary as we drove up from Boston. But words can never make this sort of situation make sense. Because what she saw was an old

11

and lonely man sitting by himself in a rocking chair in a dimly lit, filthy, cold kitchen whose cabinets were spattered with years of food and grease. Right out in the open next to the kitchen sink was the hot water heater, placed there because my father was convinced that it would save him money if the hot water only had to flow through three feet of pipe to get to the kitchen faucet. It certainly was a mournful scene. When he spoke he seemed eccentric, but in a charming sort of way, and he welcomed her graciously. Who could feel anything but empathy for this man?

But I saw something completely different; a man who could still probe for old wounds with the precision of a neurosurgeon. We didn't converse, we dueled. Any topic could easily flair into a full scale shouting session. The only real change from my youth was that I was pretty confident I wouldn't end up getting a thrashing.

So it happened again with Mary there to watch, and for no apparent reason pretty soon we were at each other, just like old times. Him telling me I didn't care about anything that mattered and me telling him he was irrational.

Back home in San Diego it was so much easier. I'd call him every few weeks and put him on the speaker phone while I did little tasks around the house. This worked perfectly since it allowed him to lead the conversation as he preferred and I could walk past the phone now and then and make a brief remark to acknowledge that I heard him. But I rarely told him much news of my own life. Existence in a modern city was too hard for him to comprehend and he lost interest quickly.

At the end of the evening while driving back to our motel room, I tried to explain the dynamic to Mary. It wasn't easy, but at least I think she understood that the situation was complicated. She gave me sage advice – to try to block out all the past history and just deal with my father based on today. It seemed like a pragmatic idea. Just not an easy one.

The following afternoon we were due to have a barbecue at Paul David's house. Mary and I went to pick up Papa for the fifteen mile drive along the West River to Brattleboro. But of course, he didn't want to be driven. Driving for his generation of young men was like being adept at computers today. It had been a source of pride for him for as long as I could remember. When I was young he would tell me repeatedly how he got his first driver's license by paying a dime in a drugstore and had never had to take any kind of test for it in his life. He would regularly explain bits of automotive knowledge that he felt would be critical for me to know and then drill me to be sure I remembered. Never forget, for example, that the right way to start a car with a hand cranked engine is to place the palm on top of the handle with the thumb on the same side as the fingers so that a backfire throws the hand up and off it rather than whipping the crank around and breaking the thumb, or worse yet, the forearm.

Every car trip was a non-stop discussion of present day road hazards and the driving experiences from the past that could be applied to surviving them. And without fail, when the trip began, Papa would assign us the task of remembering the odometer reading so that he could track the distance we covered. The fact that he'd been driving these Vermont roads since 1932 and knew the mileage to three decimal places was irrelevant. For all we knew, tectonic plate movement might have changed everything the previous night, and if this was true, we needed to know it.

Even at the age of eighty-eight, Papa was determined to show that he was still the master of the turnpike. Informing us that he wanted to have the freedom to come back when he felt like it, he insisted on taking his car. I failed to dissuade him, so I asked Mary to drive our rental and I rode with Papa.

Mary went first and soon disappeared out of sight ahead of us. Having checked the odometer, we followed at about half the speed limit down the curving, narrow road. Cars might back up behind us, but my father thought it would do them good to slow down just for once and he said so loudly. But then, as he began down the steep hill towards the junction of the West and Rock Rivers, something in his pants cuff began to annoy him and he leaned over to tug at it. This failed to produce the desired result, and seemingly forgetting that he was behind the wheel he bent even further to see more closely what was going on. As he did this, he pulled the wheel slightly to the left and the car began drifting over into the northbound lane and heading towards the guardrail and a steep embankment on the other side of the road.

At my sound of alarm he looked up and just in time pulled the car back into his lane. But rather than apologizing, he mocked my concern and said flatly that there had never been any danger. And for the last time in his life he reminded me of the number of consecutive years he had driven without an accident, concluding triumphantly that it was longer than I'd been alive. It had always been like this.

Our house was a two mile trip up Wardsboro Road from the village of Newfane. This road was all dirt until the early sixties and pavement was extended to within a few hundred yards of our driveway only later in the decade. To this day the road past the house is dirt, with a simple pair of compressed and parallel tire tracks divided by a center strip of loose gravel. It's a further nine miles of jaw rattling, vehicle destroying, choking dust washboard to Wardsboro, a town that made Newfane seem positively metropolitan by comparison.

Reaching home, you'd cross the third bridge over the Smith Brook and then turn left onto Grout Road. Our place was on the left, set a hundred yards back from the road in the middle of a gently sloping field, with Newfane Hill rising steeply to the south behind it. At the corner of Grout and Wardsboro Roads was a small house that at one time was a tiny school but during our childhood was occupied by the Bensons, a large family of classically native Vermonters. As a schoolhouse it had been a few hundred yards further up the road, but it had been moved and re-purposed as a residence at some time in the past. I don't know when. In my youngest days they had almost no running water in that house. I say "almost" because there was a thin pipe leading from a trickling spring up on a hillside across the road that brought them a small amount of cold water, but it would have taken amazing patience to fill a tub with it, and that was usually managed that by hauling buckets from Smith Brook instead. If hot water was needed, it was prepared by boiling a kettle on their gas stove.

As a traditional farmhouse, our own home was much bigger, but it had plenty of its own quirks. Like many Vermont houses, it had originally been a small structure of just a couple rooms, but succeeding generations had tacked on more rooms as well as woodsheds and outbuildings so that over the years it gradually became something much bigger. The oldest part of the house had been built in the 1790s. It was a typical frame house whose structure was provided by eight-by-eight beams, with sills and posts joined in the classic colonial-era mortise and tenon style. All the major frame members were held together not by iron spikes or bolts, but with oak pegs hammered into holes connecting adjoining timbers, one of which would have a tongue cut in it that fit into the slot of its neighbor. The house was originally built to be right on the side of a road that went to the top of Newfane Hill – so close, in fact, that a man could have stepped from a wagon on the road onto the front porch of the house without his shoe touching the dirt.

In those days the village in the township was on top of Newfane Hill. The site was chosen because during the French and Indian War in the mid 1700s, Indians came down the West River in canoes to attack towns in Massachusetts along the Connecticut River Valley. Given relatively recent horrors like the Deerfield Massacre, establishing a village anywhere near the water seemed like a bad idea, regardless of the superior fertility of the soil along the river valley and the longer growing season provided by the lower elevation. But when the Indian threat receded, the townspeople decided to disassemble their hilltop buildings and cart them to present-day Newfane Village where they established a new town.

This task was relatively simple: pry the wall boards off the studs, knock the pegs out of the joints in the beams, and load the lot onto wagons for the four mile journey down the hill. Put down a stone foundation and reassemble the pieces on the new site. To this day it's not unusual for people to buy two hundred year old Vermont barns *in-situ* and move them using the same techniques.

But without a village at the top of the hill, the road by our house lost its purpose. Now getting to the village required going in a completely different direction, so a new road was created running several hundred yards away and following (more or less) the line of Smith Brook. Our house now found itself with its backside facing the new road, and to this day it still faces the wrong way. Meanwhile the old road is now the driveway, and was the driveway for all of my childhood as well. It runs up onto the hillside south of the house where traces of it can still be discerned in the midst of the forest covering.

After the village moved, our house was expanded on several occasions, so that by the time I was a child it had two tiny upstairs bedrooms, two downstairs bedrooms, a living room, a dining room and a kitchen. A cellar was below the living room and dining room, but not the rest of the house. The cellar had been excavated after the house was built above it, and at one end the digging encountered a boulder in the dirt the size of a compact car. Since there was no getting this boulder to move, it established the boundary of the cellar wall in that direction.

The cellar was cool even in the middle of the summer, but in the spring it routinely flooded to a depth of several feet when the melting snow made the water table rise to a level considerably higher than the floor of the basement. In one corner of the cellar was a coal bin, which was filled by shoveling coal off a wagon (and later a truck) and tossing it through a three foot high door into the basement. The coal was burned in a furnace to provide heat. When I was about eight my parents installed an oil furnace, but the coal furnace still provided a backup for times when the power was out and the burner and blower of the oil furnace stopped.

The coal furnace got plenty of use, since heavy snows and ice storms regularly downed tree limbs across electric lines. A winter without many days of power outage was a rarity. The time until electricity was restored after an outage was a function of how many lines were down throughout the county. It was said that the power company arranged repair priority based on how many customers were impacted by a particular downed line. I can believe it, since I remember one winter when the several hundred yard long line from the road to our house went down, affecting us but no one else. We had to heat with coal for two weeks that winter, and we used plenty of candles for light.

It took real skill to operate the coal furnace. There were no thermostats or blowers in it but through careful control of the airflow settings one could make it burn ragingly hot or damp it down to a slow red glow that made a shovelful of coal last through the night.

An electric pump tried valiantly to keep the water out of the cellar each spring, but it required power and there were many springs when the water flooded both the oil and coal furnaces. Then we would use logs burning in the fireplace to maintain some degree of heat.

Like many Vermont houses, ours was deficient in right angles. Nothing was straight, no surface was flat. One Thanksgiving dinner I was sitting on the uphill side of the dining room table and spilled my glass of milk. The milk ran quickly across the table, splashed over the edge, and flowed straight across the wood floor into the living room, cats chasing after it to try to lick it up before it disappeared down some crack. No one was the least surprised.

Plumbing was added after the house had been in existence for over a century. Water pipes were attached with brackets to the walls of rooms, out in the open for all to see. Where they plunged under the floorboards we kept them wrapped in heating tapes that we plugged in during the winter to prevent freezing, since nothing is worse than a broken pipe spraying water in a sub-freezing crawlspace under a house. Until the mid sixties our water came from an old stone-lined well about ten feet deep. It was covered by what looked like the second story of a miniature house having a couple rows of clapboards on the ends and a shingle roof. At times we'd lift the cover and there were almost always garter snakes hiding under it. Upon being exposed they'd slither off to safety in the nearest thicket of tall grass.

In the summers this well would go dry at times, and in a winter cold snap it could freeze. When I was eight or nine we had a deeper well dug – about fifteen feet. This well didn't go dry, but one especially cold winter the feeder pipe from it froze between the house and the well. There is just no way to thaw a frozen pipe embedded in frozen ground, so until the ground warmed up in the spring enough to let it unfreeze we had to get water by drawing it in buckets that we lowered into the well with a rope. This was fine for a few days, but over time the spilled water around the well created a hill of ice that had to be ascended to get more water. This situation is the very definition of a vicious cycle, since slipping and skidding down an ice slope with full pails of water in hand is a fine way to spill more water and thus create bigger and steeper ice slopes that are that much harder to navigate with full pails of water in hand. Eventually we had to chop it away with an axe to be able to get close.

And of course, a well needs a pump to bring water into the house, and for years the pump was under the kitchen sink. It had a small motor with a very little pulley on the end of its shaft and this turned a belt driving a large cast iron wheel to rotate the pump shaft. The pump would fill a bright red tank of a few gallons and then shut off automatically. There was enough pressure that water could run for a few seconds without the pump, but as soon as the pressure fell off it would start up, making a repetitive wheezing sound as it sucked water from the well. Obviously dependence on an electric pump meant that a power outage was also a water outage, and we'd be back to buckets and ropes for a few days whenever the lines were down.

Like the plumbing, much of the electricity in the house was also routed on the outside of the walls. Until the mid 1960s the wiring all went to a single fuse in the basement. Since there was just one circuit it was easy to blow the fuse; a few too many lights on, the toaster going and then the pump starting because someone flushed the toilet, and then a quiet darkness would descend over the house. I made many frightened trips to the basement holding a flashlight and a new fuse, and it was a truly hair raising experience to screw that fuse into its socket while standing in water nearly to the top of one's rubber boots in the springtime.

In the living room was a stone fireplace. Papa always said that he had built the fireplace sometime in the thirties with the help of a neighbor from up the road. The arch of the fireplace opening was supported by the upside-down leaf spring from a Model T Ford, which you could see clearly until just a couple years ago when Johanna had the fireplace removed because its cement was falling apart and the chimney was in danger of collapse. It was an early "Heatilator" design, meaning that vents on the left and right of the fireplace circulated cold air from the floor around the firebox and emitted it via convection near the top, nicely heated.

In the winter we constantly burned logs in the fireplace. An arm of the house pointing southward contained a woodshed, and inside were stacks of logs and kindling wood that we'd accumulated the previous summer. Our firewood mostly was cut from elm trees or from dead apple tree limbs. Elms were stately trees that towered above almost every other species. There were several along the banks of Smith Brook, and many others back in the woods. On breezy days their leaves rustled with a soothing roar almost like the surf in California, but with less bottom end and more treble. Like the sight of millions of stars on a moonless, black night, the sound of the wind in the trees is one never experienced in urban settings, and elms used to be one of the biggest contributors to this foliage concerto.

But unfortunately the Dutch Elm disease killed them all in just a few years in the first half of the 1960s. We'd have a professional cut the trees down as they died and then we would cut them into firewood ourselves. But it was a lot of work. Some trees are easy to cut up. Birch, for example, has nice straight grain that saws easily into logs. Splitting birch logs is actually fun if you have the right technique. Set the log on a chopping block, swing the splitting axe down onto it and give your wrists a little twist just as you make contact, and if your blow is accurate the log explodes into two pieces in a way that's almost as satisfying as hitting a pitched baseball right on the meat of the bat.

Elm is another story altogether. First of all, just getting it into the form of logs is a major effort. The lower part of the tree can be three or four feet in diameter, and even the upper branches that are only a few inches wide are as tough as steel cables. Whereas a branch emanating from the trunk of a birch tree can be stripped with a single stroke of an axe, elm branches nearly all have to be sawn off because an axe blow simply bounces off the tough, rubbery wood. And unlike a lot of Vermont families, we didn't own a chainsaw since Mama and Papa regarded it as too dangerous, so all this kind of work was done the same way it had been done two hundred years earlier, with sweat and brute force.

There were two towering but very dead elms along the west bank of Smith Brook and we paid to have a man cut them down with a chain saw when I was about nine years old. The main trunks of these, between three and four feet in diameter, lay out in the field for years because we didn't have any saws big enough to cut them up. But we would cut anything less than eighteen inches across into logs by lifting the limb up onto a sawhorse and going at it with a bucksaw.

Elm grain is fibrous and wiry. Attempting to split an elm log with a hard swing of the axe onto its end is more likely than not to result in the axe head being irretrievably stuck. If you are either lucky or very good with the axe, the first blow creates enough of a crack that you can put the blade of an iron wedge into it. Hammering at the head of the wedge with a sledgehammer opens the crack wider. Following the first wedge with a second one and more sledgehammer blows breaks the crack open wider. After repositioning wedges several times and employing an iron pry bar when the separation is nearly complete, the log finally splits apart. But splitting just one log can easily take ten minutes and a few hours of this work results in blistered hands and total exhaustion.

Since we had at least ten old apple trees around the house and they were constantly in need of having old branches thinned out, apple wood was the primary alternative to elm. Reducing apple limbs to firewood might even be worse than working with elm. Elm trees at least have the merit of growing straight, so an elm log has a cylindrical shape. Apple trees grow in all directions, and it's hard to find an apple log of more than eighteen inches length without it having an elbow or a fork in it. Splitting such a log is another nightmare of wedges and sledgehammers.

One day when I was fourteen or fifteen and everyone else was away on a shopping trip to Brattleboro, I got the bright idea that I should try cutting down a hundred fifty foot tall dead elm that was on the south end of our lawn. It was nearly three feet in diameter and I went at it with an axe, cutting a wedge down low on the side where I wanted it to fall and then hacking through it a foot or so higher up on the other side. I was pretty strappy at that age and could swing an axe for a long time if needed, but this was a much more difficult proposition than I'd envisioned and it took well over an hour of swinging and sweating before I began to hear the sound of grain cracking and tearing and saw the tree start to gradually tilt. A couple more well placed blows and it went down with a *whump!* that made the ground shiver. There was a fleeting sense of pride when it fell right where I'd planned it, but then it gradually began to dawn on me that as long as it had taken to cut through it once, to cut this huge tree into firewood was going to take hundreds of hours with a buck saw and axes.

I was dreading the reaction I'd get at the mess I'd made when Mama got home, but she was surprisingly accepting of it. I suppose she'd been thinking herself about how to get that tree down, so it didn't bother her as much as it might have.

In the first part of the sixties kindling wood had been much easier to accumulate. A lot of our kindling came from decaying farm buildings, which in those days we had in abundance. Good, dry kindling was important because our normal process of building a fire in the fireplace was to stuff crumpled newspapers under the grate, stack some kindling on that, and top it all with a couple logs of eight to twelve inch diameter. A match would light the newspaper, the kindling caught fire from the burning paper, and when the kindling developed enough heat the logs would follow. If the kindling gave few minutes of good intensity and the logs were placed with a couple inches of spacing between them they developed a strong draft and burned gratifyingly hot for an hour or more.

Since our place had been a functioning farm in the 1800s it had most of the out-buildings that would naturally be required for Vermont style agriculture. This means not just big barns for cows and horses, or for storage for carts and wagons, but also a henhouse for chickens, and an icehouse. We didn't have one ourselves, but many farms also had a sugar house used to boil maple sap down to syrup and sugar during the spring thaw.

In today's world not having electric-powered refrigeration is so unimaginable that most people are unaware that not very long ago the winter was a time for harvesting ice from lakes and ponds. Ice was cut with saws into big blocks and stored away in the icehouse, a structure like a miniature barn and usually sited in a cool place under trees where the surrounding hills maximized shade. The ice blocks were packed around with straw or sawdust that helped both to insulate them from melting in the summer heat and to keep the blocks from freezing together in a solid mass. Ice was commercially harvested in Brattleboro and other places with large areas of standing water, delivered locally to homes without their own supply by an ice man driving a heavily loaded horse-drawn cart, and even stored for summer shipment by train to Hartford, New York City, and beyond.

In the place of a refrigerator the well-equipped kitchen of those times had an icebox, an insulated storage box with a compartment at the top where you put a fresh block of ice, and the cold filtered down into the storage area. When the ice melted, you drained the water out of the ice compartment and replaced the block. But the arrival of inexpensive refrigerators made icehouses redundant, and the roofs of both our icehouse and our henhouse had collapsed under heavy snows in past years. So we put the ruins to the axe and cut their wallboards, roofs, and timbers into kindling which we stacked in huge heaps in the woodshed. This wood was so combustible that you could almost light it directly from a match, and even if a couple sheets of crumpled *Brattleboro Daily Reformer* were needed for encouragement, it would be only a minute or two from striking the match to feeling the warmth.

One of the dreaded rituals of winter was the twenty-below-zero January night when the fire ran low and we had no more logs in the woodbin by the hearth. Mama would then choose either Paul David or me to go out to the woodshed for more. I was too impatient for the ordeal of putting on all my outdoor clothes, so more often than not I'd run out hatless and in shirtsleeves in the Arctic air and grab an armload of wood: two or three ice cold logs and a batch of kindling all cradled against my chest. I'd come racing back into the house huffing and puffing against the cold and the fire would feel fantastic as it warmed me up again.

One night after I had lit a fire in the fireplace and was sitting back in a chair with our cat purring in my lap, three or four mice came out of the vent on the side of the firebox, driven by the heat. They stood on the hearth full of uncertainty where to go next. I tried to make the cat recognize their presence, but she was oblivious until I cupped her head in both my hands and turned it to face the mice. When finally she saw them she tore off in pursuit across the hardwood floor. The mice ran under a low standing bookcase, which the cat, unable to brake on the slippery surface, collided with head on. It was one of the few graceless acts I can recall seeing from any cat, and good for a huge laugh.

In the early sixties we had a black, cast iron, coal-burning cook stove in the kitchen, and it made the kitchen piping hot even on the coldest winter days. When we came in from outdoors we'd hang our wool socks, hats and mittens to dry all around it. Wool accumulates hundreds of little ice balls around the fibers at the wrists and ankles and anywhere else it is exposed to snow during play or work. It was impossible to knock these all off your clothes until they began to thaw, so we would hold our frozen things over the stove to speed up the process. The ice balls would drop off and jump and sizzle on the stovetop like they were alive.

When the coal burned low, we'd shake down the white ashes using a crank handle on the side of the stove. This moved interlocking fingers of the firebox grate back and forth against each other so that the fine ash would fall through into a catch bucket, while the unburned coals mostly stayed in the firebox. We'd carry the ash outdoors, and after cooling it we'd run it through a big wood framed sieve to recover any pieces of coal that might still have something to burn in them. These would go back into the coal bin, while we put the ash into re-purposed five gallon buckets that originally carried roofing tar. Filled ash buckets went into the trunk of the car to provide weight for better rear end traction in winter, or, if we were truly stuck, to be shoveled under our tires and create grit on the ice.

Later Mama remodeled the kitchen and the coal stove was

sacrificed to provide more room, but it was a big part of things until then, and it meant that in addition to containing everything for cooking, our kitchen also housed boxes of kindling and buckets of coal and ash.

Between the house and Newfane Hill to the south were two large barns. In the days when the place was actually a farm, one barn was meant for cows and the other was a carriage barn for horses, harnesses and carts. Vermont cow barns are generally designed to house cows on the first floor and to store hay on one or two upper floors, and ours was no different. But in the early 1960s no cows had been in the barn for at least fifty years – instead it was filled with things accumulated by Papa and by his parents before him. He used to say that when his parents first arrived from New Orleans in the early thirties they brought barrels filled with household goods and stored them in the barn. Some had never moved since, and from my limited experiences looking inside them, it was clear to me that my father didn't have to leave home to learn his collecting skills.

The exterior of the cow barn was covered with bare boards weathered gray and nailed vertically onto a peg-and-post frame, but the carriage barn had actual siding on it and was painted red. In the Second World War, Papa had run a machine shop making metal parts for the war effort, and the first floor was of poured concrete and covered with benches supporting lathes, milling machines, drill presses and other heavy equipment. All that metal acted as a huge thermal reservoir and made the shop cool even on the hottest summer days, and freezing cold in the winter. Upstairs was heaped with boxes filled with books, magazines, tools, and all kinds of other things. There were so many boxes that only narrow passages existed to pass from room to room.

In between the gray barn and the red barn was a small garage. This in no way resembled the sorts of garages seen in suburban homes. The floor was dirt, and each bay was enclosed not by a roll-up door, but by two large hinged doors that swung to the left and right. The roof was attached to the red barn about fifteen feet up on its end wall, and sloped downwards from there to a height of not more than six feet, so that on the right side of the garage the roof was far out of reach above you, while on the left my father would frequently whack his head on the roof supports.

This garage was originally meant for horse carriages but had space sufficient to park two or maybe even four cars. In our youngest days there was a decrepit black 1940 Plymouth in one bay. We used to play in it and pretend we were Chicago gangsters from an Al Capone movie. The second bay had an assortment of dead lawn mowers, wheelbarrows and other mostly non-functional yard maintenance equipment. In the back was an area that had been a coal bin for the heating of the machine shop, but which had subsequently been used to save every issue of the *New York Times* from mid-war until the beginning of the fifties. Paul David and I used to go down there now and then and read stories in the sports pages from the days of Ted Williams and Joe DiMaggio. To us these were clearly far more significant than the relatively minor and uninteresting articles in the news pages that we discarded, such as pieces about the invasion of Normandy, the testing of the hydrogen bomb, or the Communist takeover in China.

With the exclusion of school, that was the environment in which we spent the vast majority of our time: an old farmhouse, two brooks, two barns, an open pasture, a tree-covered hillside and a sparse network of roads that were mostly dirt. It was enough to keep us more than busy. But now it's time to venture into deeper waters.

4   FISHY STORIES

Fishing was a major pursuit for Paul David and me back then. Given the puny little brooks that ran within the scope of our pre-teenage world, it was an activity that required a strong element of imagination to be truly satisfying. But imagination was something we never ran short of, so there are lots of fishing stories to be told. In hindsight, it's not at all clear why fishing mattered as much as it did. I certainly had no aptitude for it. Fishing required patience and planning, and my attention span was far too mercurial for me to be any good at it. But that didn't stop me from trying.

Trout fishing season started in early April while the brooks were still running high from snow melt and rain. For several weeks prior to that Paul David and I would be checking our fishing gear to make sure everything was in shape. Whenever we could get in on a shopping trip to Brattleboro with Mama we'd try to get her to go into either Galanes Sporting Goods store or the Giant Department Store and we'd head straight for the fishing equipment. We had almost no money for any of the things on offer, but we'd gawk at the sophisticated reels, lures, tackle boxes, bait boxes, wading boots, fishing hats, nets and gutting knives and we'd dream our big dreams of how we'd be kitted out when we were older and more flush with cash. Surely if we only had all that gear the fish would leap out of the water and into our catch bucket without hesitation.

Improved fishing gear was just one reason we were always looking for ways to get our hands on money. Mama and Papa would get us things for our birthdays and for Christmas, but it was pretty much pot luck whether their gifts would actually be something we wanted. On a comet-like schedule some crucial present like a bicycle would arrive for a birthday. For gifts of this magnitude it made little difference if it was for Paul David or for me, since if it was for him, I'd get his hand-me down, and that was always a big upgrade on whatever I had. Of course, for Paul David, me getting a new bicycle was meaningless since he would keep on with whatever he had. But these were events on a scale of once in five years anyway.

Anyone born in December or January will appreciate that my mid-summer birthday conveyed two outstanding advantages. First, the year's two crucial gift days were far apart and the thinking of what to give me on my birthday wasn't colored by what I got for Christmas. Second, presents suited to summer activities were always the most useful, and they were far more likely to be given in the summer than in the winter. Summer presents were things like snorkel sets, swim fins, baseballs, bats, gloves, soccer balls, and fishing gear. The good stuff.

With birthdays three days apart in early December, Paul David and Johanna were both shortchanged by comparison. Their celebrations were little more than a dress-rehearsal for Christmas, and they were likely to get dreaded gifts like sweaters, boots, mittens or hats. From my perspective these kinds of subsistence items were completely inappropriate as presents. One might as well be given a plate of eggs and toast wrapped in a bow. But it was inevitable that a winter gift event would produce more than a few of these kinds of presents.

Outside of birthdays and Christmas, from a very early age, our expectation was that if there was something specific you wanted, you'd figure out a way to save the money for it. Even without this constraint, the choice of something like a baseball glove or fishing reel was a highly personalized decision and it would be foolish to expect an unsupervised parent, especially a Norwegian one like our mother, to select something suitable. You simply had to finance it yourself.

But getting money was a challenge. Papa had an allowance program for us that started at age six when you got ten cents a week. Each year on your birthday this increased by another ten cents until it reached a dollar at age fifteen. When you hit sixteen you were expected to have personal finances figured out and allowances stopped altogether. I suppose that as a child-rearing strategy it worked, since well before that age both Paul David and I had learned to get enough paying odd jobs that it made the allowance irrelevant.

It was no good complaining about this by pointing out how some other kid was given a dollar a week by their parents. First, many children in Newfane got no allowance at all. And Papa would always come back with a story about how during the war he had paid the men working in his machine shop twenty-five cents an hour, and they had supported their families on this wage. Did we really think that it was not a marvelous thing for an eight year old boy to be getting an allowance that was more than one of these grown men made for an hour's work?

It did help that things were a whole lot cheaper then. For example, in the late 1960s a gallon of gas was twenty-nine cents in most places, and if you looked hard (which Papa always did) you could find it for twenty-seven. A bottle of soda was a dime in the machine in front of the Texaco station in the village. Still, a dime didn't go very far, and it took many months of saving your thirty cents a week before an eight year old kid's bankroll got to where it could buy something really useful. You'd have to hope to augment this by getting a couple dollars in a birthday card in order to accelerate the next key sporting goods item you were saving for.

Another impediment to building a nest egg was that Mama was a devout Lutheran and a strong believer in giving ten percent of what you made in each week's offering. We went down to Brattleboro for service at the Lutheran church every Sunday. She'd give us each a couple of coins to put in the plate, but we were expected to put in a share of our allowance as well.

This financial situation taught me a level of frugality that would have been well received in Japanese culture. For example, not many children ever had more of a sweet tooth than I had growing up, but I would have just as soon set my allowance money on fire as spend it on a piece of chocolate. Buying edibles was just too transient an experience. I wanted to spend my money on things with permanence.

Fishing gear had permanence. A rod and reel could last for years and be a central element of existence during that time. Critical to a satisfying fishing experience was the reel. The cheapest reels were nothing more than a spool on a little axle with a handle on the end of it. It was impossible to cast with a reel like this. With a spool circumference of only three inches or so, to play out twenty feet of line required the spool to turn about eighty times, which created so much resistance that you could only cast if you used a sinker heavy enough to knock a trout unconscious on impact. And reeling the line back in was equally arduous work. This was simply no good in the small streams we were dealing with.

On the other hand, a good spinning reel let you cast and then quickly bring in the line because it was geared with a pickup that could turn the line around the spool five or ten times for every turn of the crank handle, making retrieval of a hundred feet of line a piece of cake. These things were beautifully inventive contraptions. You'd flip the line pickup out of the way and give the pole a little flick over your head and just the weight of the worm impaled on the end of the hook would send the line sailing off the spool. Even if you never got a nibble, the act of casting and reeling in felt almost as good as hitting a baseball.

So Paul David and I would stand in the sporting goods section gaping at rows of spinning reels with prices that started in the range of five or ten dollars and rose to a point that was more than most of our family cars cost, and we'd dream about buying one. And eventually, we did, but inevitably what we got was the cheapest, most poorly made, bottom-of-the-line selection. No matter. Fitting even the cheesiest spinning reel to our pole and heading out for a day of trout fishing made us feel that we were at the pinnacle of luxury and professionalism.

Other items were coveted but less critical. A tackle box was nice to have to carry supporting gear like extra hooks, a spool of extra line, a knife for cleaning fish, a screwdriver for repairing the reel if it started falling apart, and maybe some sinkers or bobbers. But carrying a tackle box while fishing was cumbersome, and we tended to use old toolboxes that Papa had in plentiful supply, so purpose-made tackle boxes were not much of a necessity.

Bait boxes were always important. Standard issue was a box made with a couple of slots in it that you could pass your belt through and wear on the hip. The top was hinged so you could quickly flip it open and reach in for a worm. You'd fill it with damp topsoil and worms before heading out in the hope that the worms would maintain some spark of life in them until you were ready to use them, since as everyone knows, trout expect their dinner to be served alive and wriggling.

Worms were most often obtained by grabbing a spade and going out into the unmowed part of the field where we'd turn over a shovel full of sod and knock the dirt loose from the clump of grass. If the soil was moist, you might find a couple of worms in a clod. Otherwise you'd keep turning.

Later we found that if you turned over rocks along the brook there were often big night crawlers under them, especially when the rock was on the margins where some soil appeared and not in the gravel closer to the water. But you had to be quick – as soon as the rock was flipped the night crawler would zip back down the tube he'd cut into the gravel for himself, and once he got a quarter of the way in, you couldn't get him without breaking him.

Other kids told us that they got night crawlers by sticking a pitchfork into the ground at night and then wiggling it back and forth. Delusional though it seems to me today, this was alleged to make the worms think it was raining and they would then come out of the ground. (Looking back, I wonder why darkness was supposed to be significant. Worms lack eyes for one thing, and they're underground for another. The whole idea seems fraught...) But armed with a flashlight, you could supposedly harvest an Eldorado of bait by this technique. Whatever the merits of the scheme, the foresight and planning involved in acquiring worms the night before fishing was sufficient that I only tried it once or twice and I don't remember having much success at it.

Anyway, once you had worms, you had to go to where the fish were, or failing that, to where there was sufficient water that you could convince yourself that fish were there. Our only realistic candidates were the two brooks that ran near the house. Smith Brook was by far the more appealing of these. It began four miles up the Wardsboro Road in a string of muddy beaver dams, but after that it ran briskly downhill alongside the road in a bed that was all big rocks and clean gravel – the dream environment of any upwardly mobile trout. In the spring the snow melt made the water level high enough that there was no way to cross the brook other than on road bridges, but in the summer the level dropped until it was no more than ankle deep in any place that the water was moving with any speed at all. This made it possible to use the brook as a walking path, hopping from rock to rock. Mobility in the brook bed itself was important, since in many places trees and nearly impenetrable undergrowth covered everything for a strip forty to fifty feet in width on either side of the water. Getting through that kind of vegetation was a fight you didn't want to take on, especially when carrying all your fishing gear.

With several years of practice we became able to move at nearly a running pace up and down stream. This needed good anticipation and an ability to read the character of the next rock in an instant. Was it firmly anchored in the gravel, or would it tip over when you landed on it? If it was wet, would it be slippery? Was it in a place where the next rock could easily be reached from it? Over time, these decisions for the most part became instinctive, but inevitably I'd miss a sign now and then and the result would be a good foot soaking or worse, a painful fall, like the one where I landed on a stone with my new cast aluminum spinning reel absorbing the impact and smashing tragically into pieces.

Kenny Brook was the other choice, but it was disadvantaged in almost every way. At its lower end where it emptied into Smith Brook, it often ran completely dry in the summer. Further up it ran through that cool deep ravine of pines, but there were too many standing pools that bred mosquitoes and horseflies. And unlike Smith Brook's appealingly clean rocks and gravel, in many places Kenny Brook had the kind of mud that, assuming you were silly enough to wear any sort of shoes while fishing, would suck them right off your feet. There were rarely good sized fish in it, at least in its lower stretches. And if the underbrush was bad along Smith Brook, much of Kenny Brook felt like something out of Conrad's *Heart Of Darkness*.

The problem with the traditional bait box was that somewhere in all this rock hopping and fighting through underbrush I'd eventually end up slipping and taking a fall. When this happened the lid of the bait box would inevitably fly open and I'd be showered with dirt and half dead earthworms, which I'd then have to scramble to find so I'd have bait for the rest of the day's fishing. So often as not I'd just carry a used soup can with the label torn off. This probably got spilled even more frequently, but at least it wasn't attached to my belt and in an ambulatory mishap I didn't end up with worms in my shirt pocket and wet dirt in my underpants.

Fishing was fraught with peril. So many things could go wrong and all of them did at one time or another. Fishing line has an amazing ability to get itself tangled into the most impenetrable knots. Most of the time these were easily cut away, but sometimes they'd happen right in the reel and then it was a hellish thing to unsnarl. You'd be reeling in a little too enthusiastically and a piece of branch would get into the pickup mechanism, the line would pop over the reel seat and get trapped in the handle, and before you knew it everything was bound up so tight that there was no way to release the pickup to let line out.

But there were lots of other things that could go wrong. You'd be standing on a slippery rock innocuously baiting the hook and suddenly you'd lose your balance and fall and the next thing you knew the hook was embedded in the meat of your index finger with the worm still on it wiggling away right in the middle of all the blood that was streaming out of you. Or you'd flip over a forty pound rock looking for a night crawler and land it on your bare foot, giving yourself a black toenail that would hurt like hell until it came off in a couple weeks. Or you'd put a two inch slice in your palm trying to close the jackknife you used for cleaning fish and have to tourniquet the wound shut so that Mama wouldn't find out and make a big fuss.

Grout Road went along the north side of our field and up into the hills to the west. There were usually two hard packed tracks where everybody's car tires compressed the dirt, and in the center and on the sides was a smattering of loose rocks and pebbles that got kicked up by the traffic and scattered away from the packed dirt. The packed part was smooth enough that you could walk comfortably on it with bare feet, and since we went pretty much shoeless all summer long this was important. If there'd been consistent rain for a few weeks the center strip would sometimes have a light bearding of green grass. Right after a rain we'd sometimes find salamanders with a brilliant orange color out on the roadway, but within hours after the rain they'd all vanish.

34

Every few weeks the road crew would scrape the road with a big metal rake hauled behind a truck or attached to a grader to break up the potholes and washboard that inevitably developed in the surface, and then there'd be stones everywhere. For a few days the road would be painful to walk on and impassible with a bicycle, but after some rain and a week or so of passing cars the surface re-packed and got back to where we liked it.

The first couple hundred yards of Grout Road passed on a flat stretch between our neighbor's fields, but then it climbed up into the woods with Kenny Brook down an embankment on the left.

Right where the field ended was a concrete dam that must have been made sometime in the forties or even earlier. Apparently built to make a swimming pool in its day, or maybe a last gasp attempt at a water powered mill, the dam formed a pond behind it that had long ago filled in with silt, rotting leaves and pine needles. The concrete wall of the dam ran along two sides, with thick bamboo pushing its way right up to the edge on its landward side. On the pond side a mere six or seven inches of water covered the detritus filling the pool.

At times we'd try to work our way along the top of the concrete wall to the deeper parts of the pool where we might drop a fishing line. Once while trying to push my way past the thicket of bamboo crowding up to the edge, I fell off the wall into the water at its side. There was about five inches of water standing above what looked like a floor of decaying leaves and mud, but where the water ended was by no means the bottom and I sunk to my chest in a disgusting muck. When I finally extracted myself I was smothered head to foot in rotting and foul smelling vegetation, and had to walk a quarter mile in this covering to reach the cleaner Smith Brook where I could wash up.

There were never any big fish in this water – maybe a feisty four inch bullhead, but not much more.´ And it was a struggle getting by the bamboo. In flower, the bamboo was

35

loaded with bees, and at the best of times, the pond was infested with dragonflies, horseflies and mosquitoes. In retrospect, given the potential for a disastrous fall, it is perhaps hard to see why anyone would want to go there. But there's no understating the allure of being able to scoop up pails full of frog's eggs, polliwogs and tadpoles to a young boy.

Tadpoles were the best. Early in their metamorphosis they were just a green-grey head with a tail whose simple waggle sent the two inch beast at an amazing pace from open water into cover. You had to be quick to grab them, and a successful catch was something to be savored.

Later in the summer, the tadpoles sprouted a pair of back legs, and a little later, another smaller pair in the front. The tail started shortening, and soon the tadpole looked more like a frog with a little stubby tail. By August, there were no tadpoles, but there were lots of frogs. The prizes then were the big bullfrogs. If you were lucky enough to catch one, you held it by its hind legs with the body and head flopping forward.

A good sized bullfrog had a body that was way bigger than a seven year old kid's hand. Its stomach was smooth and glistened white, and you could see the blue veins through the skin. The stomach color turns to yellow, then light green, and then much darker green as your eye progressed around to the back. Some bullfrogs had really dark backs, and others were lighter.

All bullfrogs had the sort of tightly set jaw that would make a football coach proud. Their mouth was a hard line with no lips, and although we always wanted to see what their teeth looked like, no frog would ever open up, even for a moment. Digestion was inevitable for any fly entering this lair.

Earlier in the spring there were what we called frog's eggs, but maybe they were toad's eggs – chains of transparent gelatinous outer material with a black center in each link. The centers eventually hatched out into little polliwogs – like black tadpoles but way smaller. I leave it to the biologists to say what the polliwogs grew into, since unlike the tadpoles I never saw polliwogs transition into their adult stage. We'd see them grow to have four little legs to go with their tail and then we'd stop seeing them altogether.

Water skippers darted around in a living demonstration of the principle of surface tension. Looking like an aquatic daddy long legs spider, a water skipper stands on the surface of the water as though it's frozen solid, and a simple twitch propels him a foot ahead in the blink of an eye, way too fast for a boy to catch.

Under the surface were minnows by the hundreds, tiny fish less than a couple inches in length with a black horizontal stripe running the length of their body. They spend their careers vacuuming algae off the stones with a mouth patently designed for suction.

Above the pond, Kenney Brook ran in a dark, cool little gorge below the roadside. On a hot summer day, it was a pleasant and refreshing place to go fishing, hopping from rock to rock and dropping a worm-baited hook into each little pool. Not often, but not never, you'd get a surprise. I pulled a trout nearly nine inches long out of a pool on this stretch on one memorable afternoon. Not much by Hemingway standards, but a veritable monster to me.

My brother and I would walk up the road past the pool to the Fifty Cent Bridge, where we'd then drop down to the brook side and fish our way down to the pond. The Fifty Cent Bridge was little more than a culvert, and why it had the dignity of a three word name, we were never sure. In hindsight, I suspect that the town assessed a half dollar tax on all its residents one year to pay for its construction, but as kids we always had a picture of a distant time when there was a toll booth in the woods where the unfortunate people living up the hill had to fork over a handful of dimes to get home.

On many of those fishing excursions, Paul David and I would walk with our bait boxes full of worms strapped to our belts, carrying our fiberglass fishing poles, and rambling on about last night's Red Sox game or other events of lesser international significance. At times, we'd put the tip of the rod on the packed part of the road surface, and with the handle of the rod against the palm of our hand, would push the tip so it slid along the road in front of us as we walked. Although the hard packed part of the road was mostly smooth, it still had small stones embedded in it, and the tip of the pole would sometimes catch a little on a stone. When this happened, the pole would flex until the tip popped loose, making the pole jerk up in the air momentarily. There was something very satisfying about the way the pole popped and stuttered as you walked along like this.

Naturally, anything that could be done to exaggerate this effect needed to be experimented with, and it quickly became apparent that by an appropriate snap of the hand at the point where the tip of the pole popped free, the pole could be made to jump several feet in the air, almost like it had a life of its own.

So it was inevitable that one day when we were walking along, with me snapping and popping my pole as though I suffered from a rare neurological disorder, I would push things too far. The pole popped well over my head and half out of my hand. The release of the reel came off, and the hook flew out of the end of the rod. By the time I had regained control of everything, I found that the hook had come to a rest – snagged in my brother's eyelid.

Nothing that happened to Paul David ever seemed to perturb him much. Take our fungo games for example. The driveway through the field in front of our house was littered with small rocks. Paul David and I used to each grab a stick, toss a rock up in the air, and hit it fungo style across the field. Half a football field away was a row of trees along Smith Brook, and we played by a set of rules in which a stone hit into the base of the trees was a single, more than half way up the trees was a double, and a towering shot that carried over the trees was a home run. We'd play imaginary major league baseball games – always the Red Sox against somebody else, like the Minnesota Twins with Cesar Tovar, Rod Carew, Tony Oliva, Harmon Killebrew, Rich Reese and all those guys.

One day, my brother grabbed a stick out of the barn with two big nails sticking out of it. The nails were folded over, and Paul David figured that if he gripped the stick well, the nails would be no problem.

On his first swing he tossed the stone up, took a prodigious swing, and clobbered his rock into the upper deck at Metropolitan Stadium. I was still admiring the blast when I heard his calm voice saying "Gee, this is bad. I don't think I'm going to be able to play anymore." He held out his hand to show me one of the nails going right through the tips of his three biggest fingers. As I watched in horror, he slid the nail back out of the punctures, which then immediately bled like a river. His reaction was simply to clench his hand into a fist and head for the house and medical treatment from Mama. No screaming, no crying, nothing. Just: "I'm not going to be able to play anymore."

So now, here he was with a fish hook lodged most inconveniently in his eyelid. Cool and focused as always in an emergency, my brain quickly rallied to the critical task of thinking up an alibi to get me out of the thrashing I knew was likely to be my fate. Of course, my brother's impending blindness did nag at the back of my thought process as possibly a secondary issue worthy of consideration, but even at a young age I exhibited a profound ability to prioritize and attend to what truly mattered.

I'm sorry to say that I don't remember at all how this story concluded. I only remember walking back down Grout Road, holding my fishing pole with a respectful bit of slack in the line and my brother gingerly grasping the filament it to prevent any further pulling on the hook. No doubt, my mother started with her usual exhortation of "Steven, you have to be more careful!" rendered in her sing-song Norwegian accent. And no doubt, once the hook was extracted from my brother's eyelid, swift and well deserved punishment was meted out to the guilty.

The legal limit for a keeper trout was six inches. Our rule was that six inches was the distance from the tip of the middle finger to the bottom of the palm, a pretty generous guideline on a boy of ten years old or so. It was rare to catch a trout much above the limit. I'd guess there were five six-inchers for every one seven-incher, twelve six-inchers for every one eight-incher, and forty six-inchers for every nine-incher. I might have caught one ten-incher in my life. This was not championship fishing.

With fish this small, it took a good number to make a meal. But we did indeed eat them. We'd come back on an especially good day with a string of fish hanging on a Y-shaped piece of alder branch where one arm of the Y was threaded through the fishes' gills and out their mouths. We'd then clean them with a jackknife, cutting off their heads just behind the gills first, slitting open their stomach, and stripping out the intestines and other organs. Then we gave the remaining carcass a good rinsing and Mama would lay them in a plastic container that a half gallon of ice cream had once come in. She'd run enough water over them to cover them and then stick the container in the freezer. Next time we caught more, she'd layer them on top of the previous catch. When there were enough to feed the five of us, she'd thaw the whole pan out and then fry them up in some butter with potatoes. Despite being fairly boney, they tasted delicious. We especially loved the tails and fins, which came out crispy but with a nice salty and buttery taste.

Needless to say, Paul David could take credit for at least eighty percent of the catch. My own experiences were far too often similar to the one where I hooked a nine-incher in the pool below the bridge at the Wilkinson's house on Smith Brook. This pool had a nice big boulder you could stand on while fishing and the water right at your feet was three feet deep or so even in midsummer. I threaded my bait onto the hook, pushing the barb straight in at the end of the worm and then sliding it down through the body so that the worm was firmly in place. You didn't want to leave a lot of worm hanging free off the hook or the fish would just eat off the loose part. But you had to leave some to make the presentation appealing – a little bit to wiggle and appear to have some life in it.

Next I tossed the line into the running water upstream from the pool and guided the hook to float down under the rock. Received wisdom was that fish expected food to flow into the pool from above and would cunningly reject bait offered via direct entry from the sky above. My brother, whose ability to think like a fish far surpassed my own, would regularly stand upstream from any pool and let his line float down into it naturally. My own need to be in the center of the action prevented this sort of tactical thinking. I wanted to see the fish take the hook if at all possible.

So I watched with deep pleasure as the worm floated in front of my boulder and a fish of epic proportions emerged from underneath to take the bait. Bracing myself for the heroic struggle that was sure to come, I pulled hard to set the hook. But my enthusiasm apparently overcame my touch with the pole, and this maneuver resulted in the fish rocketing out of the water and soaring into the tree above, with the line wrapping itself about eight turns around one particularly inconvenient branch some ten feet above my head. In the blink of an eye my fish had gone from an aquatic denizen to a creature inhabiting airborne heights well out of the reach of any sportsman unaided by aluminum extension ladders.

My first thought was that if I gave the line some slack, the weight of the fish would cause it to slide down on the other side. No luck – the line was wrapped too tightly around the branch. I then tried getting a branch from another tree to try to knock the fish down, but it was too high up and I couldn't do anything other than whack at the fish like some kind of undersized trout piñata. This merely made it swing back and forth. My mood fouling, I then threw rocks at it for a few minutes before cutting the line from my pole to the tree and returning home, defeated.

It would have been different for Paul David. He knew how to handle these situations. My favorite example of this is the day we decided to fish Smith Brook all the way to Newfane village. The brook follows the Wardsboro Road closely for the first mile but then turns and goes through a deep ravine while the road curves along the hillside and makes its way to the village over the east shoulder of Newfane Hill. The brook emerges from the ravine a mile further down and rejoins the road. But in between was a stretch that to us seemed incredibly wild and remote – the sort of place I assumed that Lewis and Clark could have enjoyed if there were only more buffalo. There were boulders so big that we couldn't climb up on top of them, and some of them were loaded full of garnets as big as golf balls. Having picked up the flow from several smaller springs and side streams, Smith Brook was noticeably bigger here than near our house and pools were more frequent and deeper than we were used to. Surely there must be fish to match.

In the deepest part of the ravine we came across a beautiful spot where granite ledges sloped out into the brook on the east side and on the opposite shore was a gravelly little beach. The trees grew tall overhead and they combined with the closeness of the ravine to block out most penetration by the sun, so it was cool and shadowy.

There were two pools in succession here, with the lower pool being the bigger. Between the pools was a short stretch of current where the water quickly dropped to the lower level. In this spot the ledge actually overhung the water, which ran both underneath it and around it at a depth of half a foot or so. A stone the thickness of a softball was wedged under the overhung ledge, forcing the water to squeeze by under the ledge on one side or around the ledge on the other.

As usual on these trips, I was ahead of my more patient brother and I quickly headed for the bigger pool, running down the beach side of the brook. A good sized rock stood in the shallow water near the west shore, and I jumped up onto it to look into the clear depths in the center of the stream. I couldn't see any fish, but I threw my line in regardless. Nothing.

Meanwhile, Paul David's line came floating down the stream from up above. It passed through the upper pool untouched, and as he walked down the beach it floated over the drop between the two pools and into a rippling stretch of water. And then a trout hit it and took off with the hook in its mouth with a speed and power that we had almost never seen. For a moment I saw the trout shoot past me like a torpedo. It was a green-black blur, moving so fast I couldn't guess its real size. But it was big – really big. And it snapped my brother's line like it was made of paper.

That was it for us. We knew that in this pool was the fish of our dreams and we had to have it. But a fish with a hook in its mouth was not going to take another one, and besides, my brother, who rightfully viewed the fish as his, didn't have another hook. I certainly wasn't about to give him mine. Although I didn't see what would persuade the fish to take a hook from me, it seemed that it was try this or nothing.

Paul David had bigger ideas. While I continued to run my line down the pool over and over, he went to work. At the lower end of the big pool, he piled a series of rocks with spacing big enough for the water to run through but small enough that his trout couldn't make it. Then he did the same upstream from the upper pool. His idea was to chase the fish to the upstream pool and trap it in the shallow water.

Nearly half a century later detailed memories of what happened next are hard to recall with certainty. I remember us splashing about in the water chasing our fish. We'd lose track of him completely for a while and then we'd stand up on the ledge letting the water surface become still so we could see in. Then we'd spot him and we'd wade in and try to get him to swim upstream. We were completely soaked, splashing around in water half way up our thighs. This went on for a long, long time, maybe an hour. I gave up and sat on the shore, but Paul David kept at it. Then he got his break.

43

STEVEN HOLMSEN GARDNER

The trout came to rest under the section of overhanging ledge between the two pools. And Paul David was standing on the ledge right overhead. The space beneath the ledge was small and constricted – in my recollection it was maybe four inches high and six inches from the stone to the back. Very slowly he dipped his two hands into the water at the same time, one just upstream from the stone and the other just below. The trout didn't move; it just continued to tread water in the current. Cautiously, Paul David closed his two hands closer together, and then he suddenly grabbed for his fish.

It seems impossible now – in fact, it seemed impossible then – but he got the trout by the head with his right hand and by the tail with his left. Incredible! But how to get it out? A trout is a slippery thing, and holding on to one that's underwater by one end is not easy to do. But to get the fish out from under the ledge he would have to let go of one end of it to get it past the stone. He hesitated for a minute, and then he forced the index finger of his right hand into the trout's mouth (no easy task since a trout has a jaw with a grip like a vice) and out its gill, closing his grip by pressing his thumb against the tip of his index finger. His fish was doomed now. He could let go of its tail and just lift it out of the water.

We stared at his catch, which was easily a foot long and the biggest trout I ever saw in Smith Brook. I know now that the weight of a fish varies roughly as the cube of its length, so by weight this fish was eight times as big as our usual six inchers. A veritable monster of the deep.

With no chance of topping this outcome, and my brother with no hook anyway, we turned and headed for home. To this day I've never been to that pool again. I must do it some time to convince myself that it wasn't a dream.

Another of my favorite stories involving my brother's relentless, take-no-prisoners approach to fishing happened at the beaver dams at the source of Kenney Brook. Below the Fifty Cent Bridge the water flowed reasonably quickly and the

44

beavers didn't care for the surroundings much, but on the upstream side of the bridge was a series of dams. Reaching these dams through the surrounding jungles of alder trees and shoulder high scrub brush was a challenge to match Henry Stanley's opening of the Congo.

One day we climbed into the woods high up behind the big ponds formed by the dams to where the uppermost dam was located. This dam was fed by several little springs coming in from steep ravines. Since these streams were all too insignificant to dam, the beavers had left them alone. But the upper dam was the biggest by far of all the dams in the chain. It was impossible to approach the deepest part of the water from the shoreline because of all the vegetation crowding against the water, but we were able to fight our way to the dam itself. We walked out to its center and looked down into the depths of the pool formed behind it.

A diversion to talk about beaver dams is probably in order, since the average reader may have little or no experience with them. Beaver dams are of course built by beavers, but they are the most reclusive of builders imaginable and it's rare to see one. Like the California Highway Department, they do most of their work at night, so the best time to catch the construction action is at dusk. But even that requires a high degree of stealth, because they're shier than Howard Hughes and can seemingly hear an out-of-place noise from three townships away. I've never seen a beaver on land. It's always been swimming across the pool behind the dam, and usually almost as soon as I realized what I was seeing I'd hear the *ka-thwap!* of their flat tail smacking the water as they'd dive under and disappear.

Beavers display much of the same sense of architectural aesthetics that people typically associate with the designers of oil refineries. Their dams are a tangled mess of denuded branches and mud, but they are amazingly water tight. A big beaver dam can easily hold a head of ten feet even when the source of water is a small stream providing just a trickle of flow. In the spring when the brook is in flood, water might run over the top of the dam, but in mid-summer the only water that gets downstream seeps through the dam itself. The thickness of an older dam at its base might be ten to twenty feet, which obviously is not built in a day. Like a European cathedral from medieval times, a big dam is a decades-long project built up by generations of beavers working like, well, like beavers, all night and every night.

It was a great diversion for us to tear open a hole in a beaver dam in order to create a small flood in the brook below. We'd walk out onto the dam and start pulling branches out and digging away the mud with our bare hands. It wasn't easy work. Each branch would be buried deep in mud and tangled with other branches, usually skillfully chosen from a stringy, elastic tree like an alder so that breaking it was next to impossible. If you couldn't somehow manage to pull a branch free from the dam it was going to stay there. But eventually we could sometimes tear an opening in the dam a foot deep or so and we'd have water roaring out of the pond and creating a minor flood downstream. At times we'd do this in the evening and then sit and wait to see if a beaver would appear and commence repairs. Our patience was never rewarded, but in the morning without fail the breach would be mended and everything would be back in place.

Inevitably as the water rises behind the dam it floods the surrounding land and kills whatever had been growing there. Trees spared by the rising water level are often regardless destroyed by the beavers themselves, who kill some trees by chewing the bark around their base and fell many others, dragging the more tender branches into the pool where they weight them down with mud for winter food while hauling the tougher and less tasty wood to the dam for construction material.

They'll also build a house from a pile of branches and mud, usually on an island if their pond has created one, but otherwise on the most unapproachable piece of mainland. The beaver house is built with the same sticks and mud technique as the dam and is as difficult to break open, and its only entry is via water through a tunnel cut from the depths of the pool under the ground into its center. As a result, a beaver's sleep is uninterrupted by fears of burglary, solicitation, or the delivery of junk mail.

Although the beaver lifestyle makes the area surrounding its dam into a scene of environmental devastation, it also creates a habitat for all kinds of interesting life forms. The standing water makes a haven for all sorts of flying insects, so approaching the area without a lathering of bug repellent is not advisable. There are frogs everywhere. Turtles sun themselves on fallen logs. The insects attract small birds, and small birds attract big birds like hawks. The air surrounding almost any beaver pond is filled with a symphony of sounds from buzzing insects, croaking bullfrogs, and chirping birds. In the summer the humidity and heat always seems worse near a beaver dam, and by the time you've fought through the brush to get to the dam you are a filthy mess of repellent flavored sweat caked with mud and infused with golden rod pollen. Every inch of unprotected skin is covered with bug bites and abrasions from being lashed by the branches you've been trying your best to push aside, with all these injuries stinging like the dickens from the salty sweat that's smearing into them. Little biting flies crawl into your ears or up your nose into your sinuses where you can feel them crawling around somewhere near where you imagine you keep your brain, giving you no way to get at them, or they get into your eyes where your blinking crushes them lifeless, and their drowned black corpses drift on tears into the corner of your eye by your nose, smarting like mad. Terrifying monster dragonflies that seem big enough to sever a forearm and carry it away hover briefly by your head and then fly off to other business.

In short, a beaver dam has everything a young boy could possibly want.

The water in the middle of the pond behind the Fifty Cent Bridge dam was deep enough to be well over either of our heads and it was clear as a window right to the bottom. Forty feet from the dam we could clearly see ancient submerged tree stumps, and swimming around the protective cover provided by these stumps we could see what we'd come to see. Trout. BIG trout. They were a long way off, and it was hard to be sure, but it looked like there were loads of nine and ten inch fish out there. Maybe even some twelve inchers.

Neither of us had a pole, and even if we did, we didn't see much chance of landing a hook with a worm on it that far from shore. But something had to be done. We'd discovered the mother lode and we needed to plunder it.

So we headed back home, and Paul David conceived of a plan. The previous summer he'd gotten a blue plastic boat as a birthday present. Made from the kind of material used in milk bottles these days, it was a little wider than a bathtub and about as long. It was small enough to fit in the back of our Rambler station wagon, and was equipped with a single paddle for navigation. He'd been using it on the West River to fish for bass when we went down to Brookline, and he'd had some luck. But to get to the river was simple matter of carrying the boat from Mama's car down a broad, sandy path about a hundred feet long. To get it to our beaver dam we had to carry it a half a mile up Grout Road and then even worse, we had to pull it through the underbrush for another quarter mile to get to the beaver dam.

After a story about catching a trout barehanded, the reader is probably prepared to expect that these obstacles would not stop Paul David, and the reader would be correct. Scratched and whipped by countless branches and preyed on by horseflies whose bites felt like they were being delivered by rattlesnakes, we found ourselves once more atop the dam. Paul David, who even past sixty years of age today is wiry and lean and who as a pre-teen was about eighty percent legs and arms, gingerly folded himself into the boat with his knees doubled up in front of him to the height of his chin, tackle and bait boxes on the floor of the boat between his legs, fishing pole protruding out over the bow, and paddle in hand. A few strokes sufficed to position the boat over the stump

48

where the serious action would soon begin.

It was all over in less than a minute. The ripples created by the boat prevented visibility into the water from my vantage point on the dam, but I remember Paul David baiting the hook and dropping it overboard. He spooled out about eight feet of line, and then something took the hook and ran straight out from the bow. Adrenalin surged through Paul David as though someone had dropped a hairdryer into his bathwater, and he pulled backwards on the line for all he was worth. Too much so! For the delicate balance of his blue boat demanded movements of a more subtle character. Right over backwards he flipped, crashing into the water and dropping his pole, which went to the bottom. In another moment, so did the boat, since once it filled, it lost its buoyancy. Swimming to the dam, Paul David dragged himself spluttering out of the spring-cold water onto the mud.

Gradually calm returned to the surface and once again we could see to the bottom. There was the boat, the tackle box, the bait box, and the fishing pole, all neatly laid out on the bottom like they'd been placed there by hand. The fish were all gone, the one that had taken the bait apparently having broken the line or spat out the hook. The paddle was floating placidly out on the surface. The usual telltale signs of shipwreck.

Now we had a real job to recover everything. We were passable swimmers when it came to getting across the West River, but this required diving in water that was deeper than we were accustomed to and also a heck of a lot colder. As if this was not enough, rather than just swimming downwards and floating back to the surface on our own buoyancy, here we had to lift things from the bottom that wanted to stay at the bottom and then get them to shore.

The most difficult of these was the boat, since it presented a huge amount of resistance to movement when submerged. But getting the boat was the key, since if we floated it we could then put the other things into it once we brought them up. So we went at it first. We quickly found that it was impossible to bring it straight to the surface, so instead we'd dive down, grab the edge of the boat and pull it towards the dam a little, and then pop up for air. Then we'd go back down and move it again. Three or four feet progress for every freezing dive. It seemed we'd never do it, but after fifteen or twenty dives we'd gotten it up onto the slope of the dam and could stand and drag it. Once we floated it, we then swam back out and dove for the other gear. Tackle box, bait box, pole and paddle recovered, we swam back to shore. By now we were half blue from cold and there was no question of trying for fish again. Defeated, we trudged home. I don't know if Paul David ever tried fishing that beaver dam again. I know I didn't.

I can't tell the story of the blue boat without being reminded of Paul David's Christmas watch. In our day a wristwatch was a uniquely adult thing, and getting one meant you were really moving along in the world. I'm not sure what year it was or how old Paul David was – probably eleven or twelve – but Mama bought him a watch for Christmas. I was envious as hell, of course, and he was equally proud of the watch and valued it like a treasure. Of course this was a pre-digital, pre-battery powered watch, so you had to wind it every day. And it was most certainly not water resistant.

A few days after Christmas we were out on the ice of the beaver dam on Kenny Brook down behind our house. There was nothing quite so intriguing as figuring out what might be lying below the ice on a brook in winter. We routinely ventured out on the ice, stomping on it until it cracked and leaping from the slabs as they broke lose just before they tilted us into the water. Sometimes we were too late and fell in – usually just a boot under water, but on one very cold day I remember going in up to my neck. I dragged myself out of the water and went straight home – a mere hundred yards or so – but by the time I placed my hand on the door latch I was so cold I could hardly move my legs to walk or my fingers to lift the latch. If it had been twice as far I might not have made it.

Other times one of us would try to break the ice that the other was standing on. This would backfire as often as not, but it made the whole situation that much more hair-raising to be unaware that a break was imminent. Strangely enough, on a recent visit to see Johanna's family at Christmas I witnessed my niece and nephew engaging in exactly the same ice-breaking warfare with each other, some fifty years after the time I'm remembering here. Before I die, I hope to read how some Nobel prize-winning geneticist has isolated the segment of DNA responsible for this behavior.

On the particular day of the wristwatch affair, we were trying out ice fishing. There was far more water behind our little beaver dam in winter than in summer when the flow in the brook nearly stopped, and on this day the water reached the very top of the dam. There had been a cold snap and the ice was far too thick to break by stomping on it. Paul David brought an axe with him and chopped a hole through to the water. Worms being unobtainable in winter, he baited his hook with some now-forgotten piece of household food, dropped his line, and, like Jonah, waited for his fish.

But not much happened, so he decided that he needed some motion to provide enticement. He began to move the pole up and down, making a clear demonstration of what an attractive piece of bait was on offer. Even this level of marketing didn't yield a fish, but unfortunately it did result in the hook setting into a submerged tree stump. Paul David pulled left and right and front and back, but the hook didn't free up and in fact only caught harder into the stump.

Without ice, freeing a snagged hook by pulling the rod in different directions works a pretty good percentage of the time. But when the line is dropped though a hole in the ice that's only a few inches wide, it's hard to get much variation in the angle the line makes with whatever it's stuck on. So Paul David decided that if he reached his arm down into the water, he could pull the line at a much sharper angle and maybe free it. Looking down through the hole and the crystal clear, ice cold water below, we could see right where the line went, even though we couldn't see the hook. It was pretty deep, but maybe a sideways pull would get the hook out.

At this point Paul David displayed a level of foresight that I never would have been capable of. He remembered he was wearing his Christmas watch and that sticking his arm in the water would ruin it. So first he took off his coat, then, shivering in the cold, he rolled up his shirt sleeve, unstrapped the watch and put it in his chest pocket. Then he reached his bare arm down into the water to grab the line.

And in that instant the watch slipped out of his shirt and right down the hole in the ice. Straight to the bottom of the pond it went, where it lay glistening on the mud. The mental anguish of such a tragedy can hardly be imagined in these times of plenty. Paul David was stunned, but he still knew that if there was any chance of recovering that watch he had to act fast. So he quickly broke the line snagged line, attached another hook, and set to work to use the hook to snag the clasp of the watchband. Which he did in short order, so soon the watch was up in the free air. But already there was moisture inside the watch face, and sure enough the watch stopped, never to run again, another example of the sacrifice a good fisherman must at times make.

Most of the fish we caught were trout, but occasionally we'd hook what we called either hornpout or bullhead. These were a sort of miniature catfish, black in color with long mustache-like whiskers hanging off their cheeks, and sharp, spiked fins pointing left, right and straight up from just behind the head. Their heads were wider than their body, and they'd fight like madmen, wriggling frantically back and forth. A four inch hornpout fought harder than a nine inch trout.

We never ate hornpout, so when we caught one we'd want to throw it back. But they'd thrash around so violently that those spiked fins would often puncture your hand multiple times before you could get a good enough grip to pull the hook out. And they seemed to always really get the hook set well, so removing it wasn't easy. Sometimes they'd swallow the hook completely, and the only way to get it out was to pull hard, which generally ripped the entire digestive track out of the poor fish, killing him in the process.

Once in a while you'd catch a hornpout that was over eight inches long, and then you really felt like you had a fish. When you landed him, the fins were fearsome, and often we'd just leave him out of water gasping until he lost most of his strength.

Today neither Paul David nor I have any interest in fishing at all. It's hard to connect the dots to understand what changed, thinking back to the joyous anticipation of the first day of the season each spring. It was usually a cold, raw morning when the water in the brook was too high and too muddy from melting snow and rainwater runoff for the fishing to be any good. Yet we went out anyway, and the next day in school we'd listen to the stories of the exploits of the other kids who were out on their stretch of the brook. Invariably someone had brought in a big fish on the first day, while Paul David and I usually caught nothing, and we used to imagine what it would be like to be the kid who could tell that story. I suppose the only real difference now is in the dreaming.

5 THE LAY OF THE LAND

The fact that our father was born in 1905 had a lot to do with the seemingly strange way that he saw the world. He was in his late forties when he married Mama, was fifty when I was born, and fifty-five when Johanna arrived. In many ways the situation was more like being raised by a grandfather.

Papa's father David had been a doctor, but he died over twenty years before I was born so of course I never met him. Papa didn't usually talk all that much about him, probably due as much to my all-too-apparent lack of interest as anything. But I know that David was born in 1871 of Nantucket whaling stock, that he worked as a baker to pay his way through Boston University medical school, and that shortly after the turn of the century he married a woman ten years younger than him named Nettie Morgan.

David seems to have had a high degree of intellectual curiosity. Around 1910 he and Nettie took an "around the world" trip that had them riding camels at the pyramids in Egypt and visiting China and Japan in the days prior to air travel when international tourism was nothing like the ho-hum event it is today. Home for them was in many different places, among them New Jersey, upstate New York, Governor's Island in New York City, and New Orleans. In the closing days of the First World War David served as an army field doctor in France, and when I was a kid I found his uniform, gas masks and medicine bags among all the stuff in Papa's carpenter shop. I wore the belt from his uniform all through high school, not out of any sense of family heritage but because I thought it looked cool.

Most doctors in that time were generalists and applied whatever branch of medicine was needed for a given case, but when the war ended David worked for the Veteran's Administration and gravitated to psychiatric treatment and also to the medical use of X-ray, an odd combination by today's standards but very cutting edge for the time. He was also interested in the new wireless radio technology and when we were kids we used to play with his old radio equipment out in the barn: huge tuners that could, if, unlike us, you knew what you were doing, receive shortwave transmissions from around the world.

Near the bottom of the Depression in 1932 David decided to retire and bought the Vermont house along with its seventy acres of land for a price of about two thousand dollars. What made him choose Newfane is a complete mystery, since he had no known connection to anyone or anything in the region. But less than two years after arriving from New Orleans he died from cancer that Papa always said was the result of excessive exposure to X-ray radiation before proper safety precautions were understood. Nettie found herself a widow in the strange state of Vermont at just past the age of fifty. Papa was twenty-seven.

Papa was an only child, and while his father had four siblings, they were considerably older than David and family ties were not very close. Papa never spoke about his mother's relatives, and by the 1960s he had lost track of all but one cousin on his father's side. I met this cousin once during the 1964 World's Fair in New York, and that may well have been the last contact Papa ever had with any of his parents' relatives.

Papa graduated from the University of Pennsylvania in

Philadelphia in 1927, majoring in old English literature. His life for the next several years was a confusing trek through a number of colleges as both a student and instructor. An MA degree in English grammar at Emory in Georgia in 1929, three years teaching at Georgia Tech from 1929 to 1932, and then work on a doctorate at Johns Hopkins that was interrupted by his father's death. For two years he lived with his mother and his maternal grandmother in the house in Newfane, but in 1936 he got a job teaching at the University of Colorado at Boulder. He used to tell us that that ended when the administration accused him of being a communist because he had organized a student housing co-op in a Boulder house. Housing for students was expensive, and by creating a co-op it was possible to have some bargaining power to drive the cost down. At the end of the 1800s, Colorado had lived through a nasty and turbulent period of conflict between mining interests and labor unions, and this sort of organizing was still not appreciated. So he returned to Vermont to live with his mother.

The thirties were bad economic times for everyone in Vermont and for a young newcomer brought up in cities and far better versed in Chaucer than cheese making, a career path was not evident. But he had a good mechanical mind and somewhere along the line he started buying metal working machinery and making things with it.

His new skills served him well when the Second World War started. He was thirty-five in 1940, young enough that he probably could have served, but the fact that he was taking care of his now elderly mother coupled with his ability to make equipment for the war effort meant that the government preferred him to stay at home. He got contracts to make machine gun parts, and he remodeled the carriage barn into a full-fledged machine shop, hiring several residents from the town and training them to run the machines.

He poured concrete on the ground floor suitable for supporting the weight of the machines, and the upstairs was used for storing raw materials and all the different tools and accessories required for making a wide range of gun parts. A coal furnace was installed in one corner of the barn for heat in the winter, and windows were cut to provide light and outside air in the summer. The windows were designed so that a section of the outer barnboard wall could be swung up and out of the way to let light in, but when they were closed the barn looked like it had solid walls. I never saw them opened when I was young, and inside the barn it was always dark and depressing. The machines were still there, but things were piled haphazardly on top of them. Bare light bulbs with little pull chains to turn them on provided only a dim sense of what was in there. But during the war the place had been humming with activity.

Mama was born in Trondheim in Norway in 1920, the eldest of five siblings. She was delivered by her mother's father, a prominent Trondheim surgeon. Her father was a mining engineer, as his own father had been. Norway in those times was one of the poorest countries in Europe, but at her birth her family seems to have been reasonably prosperous. In the 1930s, times got harder and her father rode the Trans-Siberian Railway across Stalin's Soviet Union to take a job in mining in imperial Japan for a couple of years, sending money home to the family. In mid-decade Mama enrolled in a Norwegian school for hotel management, and completed her degree just before 1940 when the Nazis invaded the country. The re-united family then moved to Oslo and Mama took a job working in the Norum Hotel in the western part of the city.

If the depression years were hard in Norway, living through the occupation was worse. All kinds of essential food items were either rationed or could not be had at all. For five years there was no coffee, tea or sugar. Flour for bread was available, but it usually had sawdust mixed in with it. Despite Norway's long heritage in fishing, even the fish markets rarely had anything as most of the catch went to the Germans. Many families would plant potatoes wherever there was a patch of space and they'd eat meals made out of potatoes in every possible form day in and day out.

But these were minor hardships compared to the fear of the Nazis. As in all the occupied countries, Norway had its own concentration camps, and Norwegian Jews were transferred to Auschwitz and murdered in the gas chambers. Mama's family wasn't Jewish, but a wrong step or suspicion of support for the resistance could still result in incarceration in the local concentration camp. And at times RAF planes from England bombed Oslo, sometimes targeting the Gestapo headquarters that were less than a mile from the Norum Hotel, so there was always fear of being caught in collateral damage.

Many members of the German high command for Norway stayed at the hotel or ate in the restaurant. Mama didn't speak much German, but somehow had to keep peace when the drinking became loud and belligerent.

After the war, Mama had jobs as a nanny and au pair in London and Paris, and in France she became friends with the daughter of the politically influential Norwegian Trygve Lie. A socialist, Lie had been a significant figure among left leaning parties in Norway in the 1930s and held several ministerial level positions under the country's pre-war Labor government. During the war he was the Foreign Minister of Norway's government in exile based in the UK. When the United Nations was founded after the allied victory, the choice of the first Secretary General was a contentious battle, with the Soviet block refusing almost any candidate from a western country and the western countries flatly refusing a communist candidate. As a westerner with a strongly leftist perspective and an acceptably high profile, Trygve Lie was eventually chosen as a suitable compromise.

Lie's new calling in 1946 meant that he had to go to New York, and his daughter recommended Mama to be his household manager. So she embarked for the United States, which she viewed as a big, rough place. Lie was managing the creation of the United Nations from the ground up and was constantly meeting with major leaders of the day. So Mama's new position found her frequently working in the presence of many high profile political figures. She used to tell a story of serving melting ice cream at the end of lunch on one very hot August day and having some of it spill out of the bowl and onto Eleanor Roosevelt's lap. When she told some of her more rightward leaning friends about it one of them asked: "And what was wrong with her head?" which Mama, being politically inclined more like her boss, felt was quite uncharitable.

After the war Papa's experience helped gain him a job for Pratt and Whitney aircraft in Connecticut, his first experience as an employee in over fifteen years. Although he lacked formal training, he worked in Hartford in various positions as a machinist, draftsman, and engineer, returning to Newfane to be with his mother most weekends.

Our parents were always very coy about how they met. The story we were told is that they met in a club for people over six feet tall in Manhattan. Mama was really a quarter of an inch too short to qualify, but she came with several taller girlfriends who escorted her in. How Papa came to be there is a mystery, but he was and they met. Beyond that their story is obscure.

In 1952 Mama became pregnant with Paul David and she and Papa married. Things didn't go well almost from the start. Mama tried to return to Norway the following year, but apparently her marital problems made her something of a disgrace to the family and she eventually came back to America. I was born in 1955 about a month before Papa's mother passed away, and Johanna was born in 1960. During this time they lived in Connecticut during the winter and school year and in the summer they'd go to Newfane. Since I arrived in July, I became the only member of our family who was actually born in Vermont.

Those trips from Connecticut had the feel of an African safari in colonial times. There was a certain inevitability about the process. Today it's a simple ninety minute drive north on the interstate to Brattleboro and then twenty minutes up a modernized, high speed Route 30 and you're in Newfane. Back then the freeway was only partially built between Hartford and Springfield, Mass, and beyond Springfield it was the two lane Route 5 through a dozen western Massachusetts towns on the Connecticut River before Brattleboro. That was followed by twelve miles of the treacherous, winding old Route 30, a road that snaked along the contours of the hills above the bed of the West River.

Route 30 from Brattleboro in those days had no proper guardrails. Instead there were huge rectangular blocks of granite spaced at regular intervals along the roadside. On summer days when you drove with the windows open, the noise of the car reflected back off the blocks but not the gaps, so you'd hear this continual *whoosh-whoosh-whoosh* sound that's somehow ingrained in my memory.

For any unfortunate whose car might choose to leave the pavement, it was not at all clear whether it would be better to shoot the gap between blocks and land in the river below or to hit a block head on. The latter approach would stop the car instantly, and in this era before seat belts, would in all likelihood send the driver hurtling through the windshield and into the river anyway. During our high school days a classmate driving home in a Volkswagen beetle missed a curve while trying to get cigarettes out of his glove box. The unoccupied passenger side of the car hit a block, ripping away most of it. The other half of the car went through the gap into the river, taking the driver with it. He survived with only some bruises, but had there been a passenger that day would certainly have been his last.

Where there were no blocks, in places trees grew with their trunks sitting right against the pavement. Once on a warm spring day our school bus was driving north after school. All the windows were down to let the cooling breeze blow through the bus. Upon meeting an oncoming truck loaded with logs, our bus driver pulled a little too far to the right and smashed the right side rear view mirror on a tree. Shattered glass flew in through all the windows and showered all the riders with shards. Amazingly no one was seriously hurt.

Route 30 finally rolled into the village of Newfane, a characteristically quaint Vermont town whose charm was accentuated by the fact that its position more or less in the center of the county had earned it the distinction of being the county seat or "shire town". As a result, in addition to the usual Congregational Church and Grange Hall, Newfane's commons also boasted the very elegant Windham County Courthouse and a combined sheriff's office and jail that Andy Griffith would have found welcoming. The all-brick Vermont National Bank building exuded the inflexible confidence of an era when deposits were backed by canvas sacks of shiny Morgan silver dollars stored in the vault.

Morse's General Store provided everyday grocery necessities like bread and milk at the highest prices that could possibly be asked without convincing the prospective shopper to drive to Brattleboro instead. The Newfane Inn sat opposite the courthouse and served a clientele of out-of-staters in a style well beyond the means of most of the town's inhabitants. A Texaco gas station, a library, a tiny post office, and a two room school building rounded out the major buildings, and these were complemented by a few dozen homes, all painted white in time-honored New England style with either black or dark green shutters, and a few with red barns or woodsheds in the back. And up and down all four streets were rows of maple trees that turned flaming red on autumn days if the mornings were icy cold and the days had calm blue skies.

To get to our house from the village, you made a left off Route 30 onto West Street just in front of the courthouse. After two short blocks of thickly settled area, the road bent to the left and put the village behind it, turning to dirt in those early days and becoming the Wardsboro Road. After two miles of listening to the random hammering of rocks kicked up by the tires and smacking the wheel wells, we'd cross a bridge with nothing for guardrails but two decaying logs lying on the sides of the road, turn left onto Grout Road, and there was our destination, a hundred yards back from the road and facing away from it in the middle of a field of hay three feet high.

The strategy for traveling from Connecticut always called for us to start preparations a couple days ahead and to leave for Vermont early in the morning, but despite the best intentions something would always push departure late into the afternoon. Tires had to be checked and possibly replaced. Oil might have to be changed, or at the least topped up. The proper tools to deal with breakdowns had to be in the trunk. The house had to be prepared to stand vacant. Dishes, pots, pans, bedding, towels were stuffed into the car, leaving just enough space for the passengers to squeeze in surrounded by all these supplies. Necessities difficult or impossible to acquire in Vermont had to be procured and packed. Somehow more than half of these things seemed to be thought of only just before it was time to go, and then there was a blind panic while Paul David and I sat around impatiently choking back our excitement to be on the road.

As the timely member of our family, Mama would start off fairly close to plan in our two-tone green 1950 Chrysler New Yorker and sometime later in the day, possibly much, much later, possibly even the next day, Papa would follow in his grey 1948 Plymouth. Before one of our last trips in the spring of 1963 we'd gotten a German shepherd puppy that Mama named King. Mama was behind the wheel with Johanna, then barely more than an infant, in the front seat next to her. Paul David, me, and King manned the back seat, surrounded by boxes of linens and clothes and bags of groceries. It was a hot, muggy day, and of course cars then had no air conditioning, so the only relief was rolled down windows. King was whining and whimpering incessantly as we were driving, and somewhere before Holyoke the explanation for his fussing manifested itself as he crawled up on the shelf under the rear window and created a huge pile of what young dogs are inclined to create when they aren't let out of the car with sufficient frequency. Mama stopped and heroically cleaned it up, but the heat and the smell accompanying us the rest of the trip is not a memory that has left as quickly as I'd prefer.

We always seemed to arrive at the house with about thirty minutes of light left. We'd thread our way down the driveway, the old road to the village on top of Newfane Hill. The bushes on either side were so overgrown that they'd scrape along the car no matter how you tried to avoid them. At the entry to the driveway were two gateposts made of stones cemented together and topped with one big flat rock crowned by a second, nearly perfectly spherical one to add a touch of bourgeois class. One of these gateposts had broken in half and the top had fallen over, but the other was still proudly standing.

We'd stop at a point that was either the front or the back of the house, depending on whether the old or the new road served as the reference point. Usually what we'd see would be mostly a jungle of Japanese bamboo, imported to Vermont at sometime in the distant past and as impossible to get rid of as black flies in the spring. You could uproot every plant in an area, break up all the soil in which it grew with a pitchfork, take away every last bit of root that you could find, and the next spring it would all grow back just as though you had never been there. What was worse, wherever you had dumped and burned the uprooted bamboo the previous year there was now a proud new stand of it growing, too. In the spring the bamboo blossomed with clusters of little white flowers, which attracted hundreds of bees. We had to fight our way through this jungle to get to the front door.

In those days if you stood back from the house after the bamboo was uprooted what you'd see on the left was a classic New England porch facing to the warm sun at the south and fronting the part of the house that dated from before 1800. In the center of this section was a big solid door supported by heavy cast iron hardware and to the right and left a pair of typical farmhouse windows of four big rectangular panes each. A rusty metal roof above sloped at a pitch that could be walked on for the width of the porch, but became very steep up to the second story ridgepole above a big attic. Behind the big door was a large room that Papa called the library, more because it had some book shelves in it than due to the presence of any sort of collection of literature. To the right of the library was a small bedroom. Both these rooms were floored with wide pine boards that had been walked on for so long that knots rose up around the softer and more compressible surrounding wood. Being on the west side of the house they didn't receive sun until the afternoon, which meant they were ice cold in winter.

At some point the house had been extended with a wing that branched to the south at a right angle. This added two good sized first floor rooms. In our time the first of these was a dining room and the second was the living room. There were two different stairways up, both treacherously steep and narrow by modern standards. One stairway from the dining room went to a large attic above the library and dining room. The other stairway went from behind the living room to two small bedrooms tucked under the eaves and a second, smaller attic. At the top of each stair was a ceiling mounted light fixture with a bare bulb and a pull chain switch. Papa rigged up a way of controlling the switch from the bottom of the stairs by tying a string to the pull chain and threading it through a series of eye screws twisted into the wall. The last eye screw was at the bottom of the stairs and the string beyond it terminated in a large metal washer too big to pass through the eye and heavy enough to take up all the slack in the string. So at any point on the stairs you could just grab the string and turn the light on or off. As kids we were always tearing up and down the stairs, plunging each other into darkness by yanking on the string and nearly ripping the light fixture out of the ceiling in the process.

South of the living room was another small bedroom, and beyond that the southward wing of the house became more of an outbuilding. Except for a wall of lattice work, a large woodshed was open to the outdoors on the west side and had a floor of dirt. A rough staircase led to yet another attic above, and we piled firewood under these stairs. The rest of the space was littered with wheelbarrows, lawnmowers, saws, axes, sledgehammers, iron stakes, and an assortment of garden tools.

The last space in the south wing was a carpenter's shop. We thought that was the coolest room in the house. You'd step up from a small concrete entry pad just inside the woodshed onto a roughly finished floor. On the right was a double set of wide doors that rolled open on a rail under the eaves, and the step down to the ground was about two feet. When you sat in the opening with the doors rolled aside you could imagine that you were a hobo riding in a boxcar on the Vermont Central with the wind blowing in your face and heading for Canada. And when it rained you could sit dry and comfortable in the doorway as the water poured off the roof right in front of you. An opening in the ceiling made it possible to drop things from the attic onto unsuspecting victims below.

The back of the carpenter shop had a big workbench and all sorts of carpentry tools hanging on the wall behind it. Wood of all kinds was scattered everywhere, from scraps to long boards and pieces of eight-by-eight beam. From very early on Paul David and I both had our own carpentry hand tools including saws, hammers, screwdrivers, drills, clamps, squares, rulers, rasps and sandpaper. There was always wood available to make just about anything we wanted to.

The most recent addition to the house had taken place a little before the First World War when a square-ish kitchen was added in the space between the two main wings. The roof of this kitchen had an alarmingly flat pitch for a Vermont house where many feet of snow could easily accumulate in just a few days of storm. Before we started living in Vermont year round, there was a small entry porch at the south end of the kitchen with a chimney for the coal stove next to it. Arriving from Connecticut, our first job was to get through this door, forcing our way through the bamboo and bees, hoping that the key ring that had been lying neglected at the bottom of a drawer in Connecticut since last fall still had the right key for the padlock holding the solid wood storm door in place, and finally praying that the lock hadn't rusted to the point where even the right key couldn't open it.

Having negotiated these perils, we'd step into the kitchen while our noses grew accustomed to the musty aroma of non-occupancy. It was an odd place. In our Connecticut house we were not a family who had the latest of everything, but most of what was in this Vermont kitchen had been acquired at least thirty years earlier. Dishes, pans, utensils, and kitchen tools all were relics of a pre-war time. There was an electric range for cooking, but the original coal cook stove was still in service as a reminder that in this place electricity wasn't something to be counted on. Even the few wall mounted light switches were completely different from what normal houses had.

In the bathroom was an old style washing machine with a big tub and an electric wringer, a pair of rollers that squeezed the water out of clothes. Washing with this contraption was a highly manual operation. Mama would close the drain valve at the bottom of the washer and then fill the tub with water from a spigot in the wall above it. Then she'd add detergent and dirty clothes, and turn on the motor. The washer would laconically slosh the tub clockwise and counterclockwise until she intervened to turn it off. The drain valve had a length of hose connected to it and she'd put the end of that in the floor-standing claw footed cast iron bathtub standing nearby. Then she'd open the valve and let the soapy water out. She'd feed the clothes one item at a time through the wringer to squeeze out as much soapy water as possible. Then she'd throw the whole load back in the tub, close the drain valve, and refill the tub with rinse water. After four or five cycles like this, she would have most of the soap rinsed out and she'd put the load in a wicker basket and haul it out under the apple trees, hanging the washing to dry on lengths of cotton rope tied from tree to tree. This laundering process was less work than going down to the brook and beating clothes clean on a rock, but not by a lot.

There were still many farms in Vermont that made money, but most of these had land along the river valleys where the soil was richer, the hillsides a little less precipitous, the exposure more to the sunny south, and the elevation low enough to buy a couple more weeks of growing season before frost struck. These qualities were all in short supply at our place, and it had gone out of business as a farm around the end of the nineteenth century.

The seventy acres of land that came with the house lay mostly on the steep north face of Newfane Hill. The stonewalls surrounding and sub-dividing the property were evidence that at one time it had all been cleared for pasture, but in over a half century of neglect trees had reclaimed most of their rightful place. The only open land remaining was at the bottom of a bowl surrounded on all sides by steep hills, with the exception of the narrow valley cut by Smith Brook and followed by Wardsboro Road. In the winter the sun's southeastern rising and southwestern setting were intercepted by these hills with the result that the sun was actually visible in the sky for several hours less than the official sunrise and sunset times would suggest, and on any but the warmest of days when the sun's afternoon path was eclipsed by the hill to the west the temperature dropped like someone had thrown a switch.

The topsoil was only a few inches thick and below that were many feet of gravel which had been dumped there 12,000 years previously by the receding glaciers of the last ice age and whose principle component seemed to be stones of diameters on a scale that began at an inch and terminated at the size of an asteroid. The ten or so acres of relatively flat land that was still mostly unforested slumped gradually from Grout Road towards Kenny Brook at the base of Newfane Hill. Near the road the soil was so poor that hay would hardly grow, and near the hill it was so sodden as to be nearly a swamp. It was a place that only the truly desperate would try to farm.

This was the scene when Mama and Papa decided that we should abandon Connecticut and live year round in Newfane starting at the end of the school year in 1963. It was quite a project. Aside from the effort of moving, no one had lived in the house in the winter for over ten years, and a lot of improvements were needed to make this possible. Nettie had died in 1955, and the expectations of modern living had moved on. Refrigerators without freezers: *not acceptable*. Coal furnaces: *passé*. Wringer washing machines: *nyet*. Rusty clawfoot bathtubs: *out!*

And so Mama embarked on a fury of home improvement that continued for the rest of her life. And she had a bigger target in mind than just fitting the house out for a family of five. She was going to put her hotel management skills back to work and turn this ramshackle farmhouse into a bed and breakfast inn that she called Trollhaugen Farm, a name she'd co-opted from the Bergen residence of the composer Edvard Grieg. This might have been a fitting title for the estate of the man responsible for the iconic *In The Hall Of The Mountain King*, but attaching this appellation to a decrepit New England farmstead could only have been an act of utter homesickness. During the composition of his masterpiece (written to accompany performances of Henrik Ibsen's *Peer Gynt*), Grieg had sent a letter to his friend about it, saying: "I have composed a piece to go with the scene in the hall of the mountain King – something that I almost can't stand listening to because it completely stinks of cow shit, excessive Norwegian patriotism, and the narcissism of trolls! But I suspect that the irony will come through." And perhaps Mama felt the same way about applying the name to our home.

The term sweat equity hadn't yet been coined, but Mama was about nothing if not sweat equity. When it came to improvement she was a force of nature. If she could do something, she did it. If she couldn't she'd cobble together the money to hire people who could. She rented a huge belt sander and stripped the paint (and the knots) off the pine floorboards in the library and adjoining bedroom herself. She hung wallpaper, sewed curtains, tiled bathrooms, re-finished and re-upholstered second hand furniture, and painted door frames and windows in visually jarring Norwegian colors of burnt orange and olive green. And she enlisted my brother and me to work with her to paint the outside of the house red and the shutters bright white the way a proper Norwegian farmhouse would be painted. When the traditional white clapboards were finally all red, the place looked totally different.

A German carpenter named Mr. Hemmenger was one of her favorites. His English was so thick with echoes of his home country as to make him nearly unintelligible. I remember Mama standing out in the driveway with him discussing re-doing the roof and as they were looking up our now grown King mistook the Prussian pant leg for a fire hydrant. "*Gottverdammt!*" was his immediate response when he realized what had happened.

Mr. Hemmenger built a new bathroom in part of the small bedroom by the library and closed in the porch, making a bright sunny room of it. I regretted that, since I'd always loved sitting out there when a muggy August afternoon turned to thunderstorms, reaching my hands out into the rainwater streaming off the roof above. Inside the house it would still be hot, but the porch was cool and comfortable.

But when this work was complete, Mama could launch her American hotel career. It was more than just bed and breakfast since she also served very fancy dinners inspired by the Norwegian concept of how an inn should be operated. She hit on the scheme of placing small ads in the back of the New York Times or magazines like the Nation so that she could attract professional and interesting people from the sort of urban environment she'd been used to, and she hugely enjoyed making conversation with them after meals.

It cost each guest $10 a day to stay at Trollhaugen in those days; not a lot given that Mama was manager, accountant, concierge, chef, waitress, maid, laundress and the maintenance department all in one person. But she plowed every penny she made back into expansion so she could bring in more and more guests. The business grew as Paul David and I got older and more able to help out, and by the time we were in high school it was not that unusual at the peak of winter ski season to have so many guests that meals were served in two shifts. Paul David was always more presentable and more helpful than I was and he'd make salads, set tables and wait on the guests. But both of us would wash dishes in marathon sessions of cleaning up formal place settings for as many as twenty people and all the accompanying pots and pans, done in a kitchen with sink and counter space not much greater than people today expect in a Winnebago. At times we wouldn't finish until after 11:00, and Mama would collapse in bed knowing she had to be up at dawn the next morning to start breakfast.

Within five years the woodshed, carpenter shop and all the attics upstairs had been turned into guest quarters, and if there was snow at Christmas time, our family crammed itself into the minimum possible space and the house was turned over to the tourists. Mama was charming with the guests, and despite our accommodations being considerably outside of industry norms many families came repeatedly for both summer and winter holidays.

Our guests often traveled the surrounding region far more widely than we ever did. The area of interest to us was constrained to places that had practical value, and we rarely departed from a few well trodden paths. Going up and down to Newfane village was a near daily event, especially in the school year. Before we started high school a Brattleboro trip down Route 30 happened twice a week, once to get the week's groceries on Wednesday and the other to go to the Lutheran church on Sundays, but of course Mama did the Wednesday trip unaccompanied during the school year. In the summer we'd go to Brookline to swim in the West River in a place with a deep pool under the iron bridge, or we'd go to Townshend where a flood control dam with a swimming area had been built in 1961. Once a year or so we'd go to Wardsboro or to Grafton to watch parades where Papa would play drums with the Grafton band. In all, probably 99% of our sojourns took place on a total of less than fifty miles of road.

Our winter guests were there to ski, but in the summer they came to see things, and they'd drive all over the state to do it. If my behavior was suitably ingratiating and the people were nice beyond the call of duty, they'd sometimes take me along. One of the best such scenarios happened the summer when I turned thirteen. A college girl of about twenty drove up in a red Ford Mustang convertible and took a room during the slow part of summer. I can't remember her face now, but I know I thought she was gorgeous beyond belief. Amazingly, she was in Vermont because she was a rock collector and was looking for sites to find interesting specimens. Although I could contribute nothing of any value about the subject, I had always been fascinated by odd looking rocks. But in truth I have to confess that this pro-rock position was an extremely distant secondary consideration. No one could have possibly responded in the affirmative faster than I did when she asked if I wanted to come with her as she drove all over the surrounding hills with the top down and her hair blowing back while we traced out the instructions and maps she had obtained to lead us to old granite quarries, abandoned fluorite mines, and river banks loaded with concretions. I was seriously smitten, and it's probably a good thing she left after a week or I'd have considered robbing the local bank to get money to buy an engagement ring.

Another couple were butterfly collectors looking for fields loaded with specimens that they trapped in their nets, poisoned in jars filled with cyanide powder, and then pinned to framed slabs of corkboard. Others would come to do gravestone rubbing, tracking down abandoned 170 year old cemeteries far out in the woods and making likenesses of the dolorous, fading inscriptions on them by taping a big sheet of paper to the stone and smearing a sponge dampened with black ink over it. But most would just go off exploring over the country roads, looking for quaint towns and covered bridges, which you could hardly spit without hitting in those parts.

Because of Mama's business we had a lot of exposure to what many Vermonters would disparagingly call either *out-of-staters* or *flatlanders*. A lot of locals couldn't fathom how a person who couldn't get their car to start in the winter, couldn't negotiate an icy road without ending up in a ditch, and had no idea how to get from Saxton's River to Bellows Falls could possibly have so much money that they could buy lift tickets for their whole family for two entire weeks, and when they talked about flatlanders the conversation was often thick with resentment. Our family was a little more understanding since we'd been through the transition ourselves, albeit in reverse. It's not that far from New York to Newfane, but in New England seventy miles changed everything in both climate and culture.

Vermont in those days was a very parochial place. Families were tightly knit, and a slight against one family member was often taken as a slight against the whole family. Some families hadn't talked to each other for months or years over some arcane transgression. And marriage ties created broad webs of relationships that made these situations even more complex.

Even though Papa's father had bought our house in the 1930s, we were definitely considered out-of-staters. Papa was born in New Jersey and had lived in New Orleans. To our townsmen, the Big Easy was as good as a suburb of Caracas. As for Mama being Norwegian, well, she might as well have been an intergalactic traveler. Being born in the same hospital in Townshend where pretty much everybody else in the town had been born gave me no points in this evaluation.

The child of space aliens is clearly also a space alien.

It wasn't just out-of-staters that could come in for abuse. People in Newfane thought people in Brattleboro were soft because it was a few degrees warmer there and people could live out most of their lives without driving onto dirt roads. The power went out less often in Brattleboro, and when it did go out, it came back on in Brattleboro first. And of course, when I went to high school in Brattleboro, some of the kids thought that people from the outlying towns were yokels. We *were* yokels, but it still hurt.

Many Vermonters scrapped to make ends meet, as they still do today. Most worked at jobs where they provided manual labor. Common trades included carpentry, house painting, plumbing, masonry, automobile maintenance, working for the road crew, or logging, a particularly dangerous career. There were still a few farms big enough to provide a decent living, and these hired seasonal help. Many people did nothing but seasonal work. They might operate a ski lift in the winter and do odd jobs in the summer.

People would augment meager salaries anyway they could. In the spring they'd tap maple trees and hang sap buckets to make syrup and candy. In the summer they might cut and split massive heaps of firewood to sell to people with less land in the fall and winter. They'd grow big vegetable gardens to offset their grocery bill and raise pigs or calves or sheep for meat. They'd keep chickens for eggs. If they had fields they'd cut the hay and bale it to provide feed in the winter or to sell to neighbors with livestock, and if they were too old to do the work themselves, they'd let someone else do it if they'd pay a little cash for the hay. They'd buy dead cars and repair them for resale, hoping to turn a profit.

Our family was certainly not wealthy by urban standards, but my impression was that we were situated well in the middle of the pack in Vermont. We could keep the heat on all winter, and although we raised a lot of it ourselves we always had good food on the table. We might have gone barefoot all summer and worn shorts made from cutting the legs off last year's patched blue jeans, but just before Labor Day Mama would always take us to Brattleboro and buy us clothes for the school year, which although they were expected to last until next summer no matter how much we grew and came from the discount store, were nevertheless still new. We went to the dentists for check-ups and if we got sick we went to the doctor.

By contrast, many of the kids we went to school with lived in places that weren't much more than shacks covered with tar paper to keep the winter wind from blowing between the wallboards. When it was twenty below zero outside, their homes were freezing inside unless they had a good woodstove and access to firewood. Their cars were worse than ours, and often the poorest people lived the furthest out the dirt roads so they had the most miserable times getting to town for school or groceries when the weather was bad. Many houses lacked running water and proper sewage: there was no town water or sewer system of any kind for anyone, but a decent house had a septic system and leach field far enough away from the well to avoid contamination. Many poor people didn't have even this.

A lot kids came to school in badly fitting and worn out clothes purchased at rummage sales. They'd have teeth nearly rotting out of their heads because their parents didn't know enough to make them brush and they never saw a dentist. And very few of the kids had parents like ours who were educated well beyond high school, had been places, thought seriously and critically about the outside world, and could inspire us to think beyond the narrow confines of our little town.

Down Wardsboro Road toward the village was a tiny little yellow cabin tucked under pine trees. It couldn't have had more than three small rooms, and there was a couple with two small children living there. They'd get on the bus in the morning and stay totally to themselves, sitting quietly dressed in their dingy, patched clothes. Their father was a logger, and one day we heard that he had a bad accident in which he'd cut deep into his leg with a chainsaw. A mishap like that was a financial disaster for a poor family, but these kinds of things happened all too frequently.

Even without injury, doing physical work in the cold outdoors is not a job for the elderly. Those of us past our fifties who are fortunate enough to work in climate controlled offices and come in on Monday morning complaining about how our muscles ache because we spent a couple hours on a nice day doing yard work would do well to reflect on what it means to run a chainsaw or work a shovel in winter weather for eight hours a day at that age.

But many Vermonters did exactly that when I was a kid, and many of them are still doing it today. Mr. Benson always walked with a bad limp from an injury, but he still worked pouring concrete until he looked as old as the hills. I used to catch rides up from the village with Marvin Winston, a widower well past sixty who went to work in a furniture factory every day and came home pungent with the mixed aromas of sawdust and sweat. I don't think Marvin ever said much more than "hello" and "goodbye", but he worked hard and he was as reliable as the sun coming up.

I do believe the loggers had the worst of it. Much of the logging was on private property. If you had a good number of trees on your property, which with almost sixty acres of forest we did, you could contract with a logging crew to cut trees suitable for timber and they'd pay you a pre-negotiated amount based on the value of the trees at a saw mill. The foreman for the crew would come and walk your forest, make an estimate of how many good trees you had, and present you with a bid. If you accepted, they'd show up with chainsaws, bulldozers and log trucks and go to work. It was a good way to bring a couple thousand dollars of welcomed cash into the family budget without having to expend a lot of effort, as long as you didn't mind your property looking like Verdun in 1917 for the next twenty years after they'd left.

Logging certainly made a frightful mess of things. The logging roads tore the forest floor to pieces and left a muddy channel that was welcomed by spring runoff from snowmelt carrying silt down to the brooks below. Monstrous heaps of branches too small for timber value were left everywhere. There were lengths of rusting broken cable that had snapped when too heavily loaded. Empty oil cans for lubricating chain saws and bulldozers were abandoned wherever they had been used. The loggers cut only the biggest trees and left the smaller ones standing, but when a big tree is cut in the middle of a stand of small ones, all too often its fall severely damages its neighbors, breaking off major limbs and sometimes completely snapping off the trunk. These smaller trees were just left to recover maimed or die depending on the severity of their injury. And when the logging took place in the winter the forest would be left with big stumps at a height determined by the depth of the snow at the time of cutting. Some of these stumps would stand five feet above the floor of the forest in summer.

Typically a section of forest would be logged once every forty, or fifty years. Mama and Papa contracted to log our place around 1964, and Johanna just had it done again in 2017. The crew for the 1964 cutting arrived in winter, and their first step was to make a road into the woods. This was helped to some extent by the fact that the Napoleonic era road to Newfane Hill was still in some evidence and pointed the way to start, even if it did have trees up to two feet in diameter growing in the middle of it in places. The logging road required making a bridge over Kenny Brook, which the crews did by laying five or six stout tree trunks side-by-side across its banks at a narrow spot, nailing heavy planks cross ways to the trunks, and then laying a couple more planks in the direction that a vehicle would move and spaced so that tires would ride on them. There were no guard rails, and the bridge was no wider than it absolutely had to be, so the driver had to be careful. A truckload of logs spilled over the edge makes for a significant problem.

Further up in the woods, they chose a place where their road had a steep embankment on the right side, and against this they built a platform called a skidway out of more logs. The skidway was designed so that you could park the log truck on the logging road next to it and the tops of the side rails mounted to the truck bed would still be a little below the level of the platform. The process from tree to truck began with loggers cutting down a big tree somewhere back up in the woods. Although the loggers were magicians at getting a tree to fall in whatever direction they wished, with such dense forest the tree almost never fell all the way down to lie flat on the ground. More commonly its descent might stop at a thirty degree angle with its upper branches hung up in a tangle of neighboring tree tops.

The tree always fell before it was completely cut through, but the only way to get it completely onto the ground was to complete the cut. This was one of the most dangerous parts of the job, since breaking the attachment from the stump was a little like releasing a stretched rubber band. At some point just before the cut was finished the trunk would break free of the stump and the springy branches holding the top of the tree would propel its base forward and sometimes sideways. At this moment a logger had to be especially alert and agile to avoid getting hit and crushed.

If separating tree from stump didn't make the tree fall onto the forest floor, the loggers would then wrap a huge chain with massive heavy hooks on either end around the bottom of the tree's trunk and attach it to a length of cable coming from a winch on a bulldozer parked as closely as possible. They'd then drag the tree until it came down.

Once it was lying on the ground, the men could saw all the small branches off the tree and then the bulldozer would drag the part that was useful for timber through the forest to the top of the skidway. Here it was cut into logs of a length that would fit on the truck. The loggers used a tool called a log jack or a peavy to maneuver and roll the logs. The peavy has a long hardwood handle fitted with a heavy iron point at the business end. About a foot above this tip is a hinge that supports a curved hook. The hook and tip combination can be used in multiple positions to get a firm grip on a log and the handle gives the leverage needed to move it. Typically two loggers would work in tandem to move one log, with each man positioned about halfway between his end of it and the middle. They'd use their peaveys to maneuver the log to make it lie parallel with the truck bed at the top of the skidway and then roll it towards the truck until it dropped off the platform and into the bed with a big crash. If the log didn't lie straight after falling they'd have to clamber up onto the pile of logs in the truck and use their peaveys to straighten it.

When the truck was full, they'd strap chains across the top of the load and pull them each tight with a come-along, a sort of manually operated ratcheting winch attached to two ends of chain. With its logs secured the truck would then crawl down the log road, across the bridge, through our yard, and out onto the road.

Each departing log truck was always loaded as heavily as possible, and a full truck was a top heavy monster that terrified any driver who met one on the narrow Vermont roads. The load would sway from left to right as the truck made its way around curves or over frost heaves in the road, completely filling its lane and often crossing well over the single center line painted down the middle of the wider roads. Having the unfortunate timing to arrive at the same time as an oncoming log truck on one of the narrow bridges built after the floods from a 1927 hurricane had destroyed most river and brook crossings on Route 30 would send a driver's heart into his throat and turn his knuckles white.

Given the many opportunities in logging work for serious injury or even death, it would clearly be in the interest of the crew to work deliberately to ensure safety. But caution in the interest of safety was sadly counterbalanced by the goal of getting as many logs out of the woods as quickly as possible to maximize earnings. Experienced loggers can size up most situations rapidly and make wise judgments, but it only takes one moment's careless act in a lifetime of otherwise good decisions to sever a limb with a chainsaw or crush a leg under a log, and after that a man's career is over and he is usually condemned to a life of poverty.

When I first started school in Newfane it was quite a change entering the third grade with kids from this kind of background. I've never forgotten the shock of playing soccer in my first recess at the start of third grade and hearing the other kids swear like sailors. My Connecticut friends from first and second grade were almost all from middle class white collar families, and a nasty word rarely passed their lips. I'd only ever heard bad language from Papa, and my understanding was that he had a note from his doctor that made it OK. It certainly wasn't OK for Paul David and me. And now I was out on the playground hearing phrases that combined the topics of procreation, religion, and the lower digestive tract with a creativity and panache I'd have never dreamed possible. I had a lot of catching up to do.

In our Connecticut school recess had mostly consisted of hanging around and playing a variety of gambling games with baseball cards. In Newfane it was mostly sports as long as the field by the school was clear of snow; soccer in the fall, baseball in the spring. Despite the love of playing baseball among the other boys, there was no interest in baseball cards. But marbles served an equivalent function in Newfane to our baseball card games in Connecticut. There were two main games, neither of which required a huge amount of skill. In one game you grabbed a bunch of marbles out of your bag, which to be acceptably stylish had to be made of thick velour-like cloth or soft leather that could be closed tight with a drawstring. You hid the marbles in your fist, held it out to a school mate, and asked *odd or even?*, referring to the number of marbles. If he took the challenge, he'd make a guess. If he was right, he got what you held, and if not, he had to pay you the number of marbles in your hand. There was a code of honor in paying back that would have been appreciated by Stagger Lee, the guy who shot his cheating neighbor in a card game in the old blues song. If you welched on a game with a bigger kid you'd probably get a good beating and your marbles taken from you, but even if someone failed to pay a smaller kid, word would get around and no one would play with him anymore, which was a form of social death too shameful to bear.

The other game was based on rolling marbles into a hole in the ground. You'd make the hole with the heel of your boot, kicking at the ground to start a small indentation and then twisting your heel around in a circle to carve the hole deeper. You'd then clear all the surrounding area with the same care that the groundskeeper at Augusta applies to tending the putting greens. You'd agree with your opponent on a number of marbles to shoot and you'd stand back and toss them one by one at the hole, alternating between players. The player with the closest shot would then use his index finger to try to flip the other marbles into the hole. He kept shooting until he failed to get a marble into the hole, and then it was the other player's turn to shoot. The player who put the last marble into the hole won the lot. Games would often come down to one marble a long way outside the hole with neither player willing to make a serious attempt to put it in, since a shot that was only close to the hole was death. Many altercations broke out over questions of whether a marble was actually in the hole or sitting just outside on the shoulder.

Once on the bus home when I was in fourth grade, one of the kids held out his whole marble bag and asked *odd or even?* to anyone who would take the bet. He gave an annoying sort of smirk of self satisfaction at having the audacity to do this, feeling certain that no one had the stomach to take him up. But I was a reckless sort and I stepped up to the challenge. When it turned out I was right, the poor kid first wanted to hold out, but when he realized there was no backing down he burst into tears and gave me the whole contents of the bag. That was quite a conquest, but I have to confess that even at this early age I had enough of a conscience to feel a guilty sting from cleaning this poor kid out. But that didn't mean I gave him his marbles back.

Marble playing stepped up in wintertime when the school's fields were covered in snow so that soccer and baseball were impossible, but after fifth or sixth grade kids outgrew it. The only other recess diversion in the winter was playing King Of The Mountain, a game that endangered life and limb for all participants. The principle requirement for a game was a high snowbank, and the plow that cleared the school parking spaces generally provided just what was needed after each snowfall. Once the snowbank was selected, you'd try to fight your way to the top past everybody else. If you could hold the top you were the king. Since it was the lone guy on the top against everybody else, not even the toughest kid ever held the peak for long.

But that didn't mean he couldn't wreak a lot of havoc during his abbreviated reign. One time I made it up to challenge the top guy of the moment, a kid who was a couple grades older and considerably bigger than me. He grabbed me by the wrist, swung me around in a big arc and hurled me headlong off the mountain. I crashed face first into the forehead of an unfortunate classmate who was storming his way up the snowbank after me. Whether or not he was killed by the violence of the collision I'm not sure, because the impact rendered me momentarily senseless, shattering all the cartilage in my nose, blood flooding from both nostrils like the Tigris and Euphrates in the rainy season. Mama was duly telephoned to ferry me to Grace Cottage Hospital where they stuffed my face full of cotton balls, said nothing was broken, and asserted that I'd be fine eventually. "Eventually" turned out to be thirty-eight years later when I had sinus surgery to repair the deviated septum I'd incurred.

From an academic perspective, school wasn't really designed to challenge us much. There was a lot of filler time. The school was small and often had more than one grade in a room, and the same teacher instructed us all day. There were lots of art and music classes. Art was especially fun on days when you got to turn your desk around and butt it up against your classmate's desk behind you to work on a joint project.

On one such occasion I was paired with my friend Jimmy Rivers. He wasn't feeling really well that day, and all of a sudden his mouth opened wide and he heaved his entire stomach onto the desk in front of him. I watched in horror as the sheet of paper he'd been coloring floated up on a tsunami of vomit rushing across first his desk and then mine straight towards me. Although I'd been feeling fine up to that point, my immediate reaction was a sympathetic hurl of my own and the two of us ended up drenched in each other's puke, which poor Mrs. Jones had to clean up. They really don't pay teachers enough.

Music was another avenue for consuming classroom time. The teacher would pass out sheet music and words for some traditional piece of musical Americana and invariably ask us what key it was in before we'd sing it. No one had ever explained to me how you could read the key from the sheet music or even what the significance of the key was, so I had no clue, but there was always a bright spark of a classmate who'd howl out "C-flat" or some such thing. The teacher would then blow a pointless note on a pitch pipe and we'd all start braying like a paddock full of donkeys until she couldn't take it anymore and brought the lesson to a halt.

As if music class in school wasn't enough of a waste, like many parents Mama decided that it would be a terrible thing if one of her kids proved to have the latent ability of a Mozart or a Bach and she failed to provide the opportunity to bring it to fruition, so she signed us up for piano lessons with a fossilized dowager named Mrs. Hanes, a musician of such depth and breadth that she felt that contemporary music was anything first performed after the Reformation.

I have failed to mention that in the living room of our house stood a massive grand piano that had been brought there by Papa's father in 1933 and quite likely not been tuned since, not that this was in any way the limiting factor in the performances that Paul David and I inflicted on it. We were both completely lacking in musical talent and we augmented the absence of latent ability by regarding practice as a form of punishment and lessons with Mrs. Hanes as something even worse. The only upside was that just one of us could sit at the piano with Mrs. Hanes at any one time, and the other was then free to roam down by the brook below her house, one that was a lot bigger than our Smith Brook and had lots of nice sized fish swimming close by for us to dream about catching.

In school we had reading, penmanship, history and arithmetic but very little in the way of science. It was all pretty easy stuff. There was no homework, and I can recall being terrified at the thought that once I started high school I would actually be expected to do schoolwork outside of classroom. The very anticipation of the oppression from the high school teaching cadres seemed far too much for any person to bear. But when I began sixth grade in a classroom that was shared with the seventh grade, I managed to move ahead a year by the simple expedient of paying attention while the seventh grade material was taught instead of reading books about Lou Gehrig or looking out the window daydreaming like my other classmates did when it wasn't the sixth grader's turn.

My school experiences in Newfane set a pattern of starting behind the curve everywhere and gradually catching up as time went along that seemed to stay with me for the rest of my life. After Newfane's tiny grade school system I floundered the first year of high school. It was intimidating moving from room to room every hour and being with a completely different group of strange kids for each new class, and my Newfane education had left me way behind in science and math where Brattleboro's K-8 school system was much stronger. After high school when I went to college in Massachusetts it was the same thing. My new classmates had taken much tougher high school courses than I did and keeping pace was a big challenge. Finally, when I ventured out into an engineering career, the other new grads I worked with were from top tier schools like MIT or Stanford and had worked summer internships at technology companies, while

I'd been emptying garbage cans and swinging a scythe at the flood control dam in Townshend to earn money for tuition and books. Moving from a place like Newfane into the larger professional world took perseverance and much more old fashioned luck than most people are ever blessed with.

A rural township of a thousand mostly working class people clearly can't afford a high school, so there are a couple ways of dealing with the situation. One method is to work out an arrangement with one of the larger towns in which the small town sends their students to the high school operated by the large town and pays them an agreed-upon fee for each child. Another is that they form a union with a number of the other small towns surrounding them and pool their resources to build and run a single school for the whole union.

At the time I went off to high school, our town had arrangements with two schools – a small school in Townshend called Leland and Gray, and a bigger school in the hub town of Brattleboro called Brattleboro Union High School, or BUHS. At the time Leland and Gray was generally considered more of a vocational school that would turn out students who could repair a snowmobile, fix a frozen septic line, or milk a cow, but they didn't produce a lot of college bound graduates. BUHS was bigger, with graduating classes of over a hundred students, and it was also a much bigger leap for someone out of the tiny Newfane school system. Most Newfane kids went to Townshend, but Paul David and I went off to Brattleboro with about ten others from our town.

In my freshman year (when Paul David was a sophomore), Newfane joined a union with Townshend and several other towns north of us to build an enlarged Leland and Gray. It was agreed that students currently going to BUHS could continue there until they graduated, but all students after my class had to go to Townshend, and the bus service to BUHS was terminated.

I was over my head at the start in high school in

Brattleboro, but to give credit where credit is due, two things really saved me. After a freshman year of mostly B grades, I began sophomore chemistry by getting a D on the first exam. For the most part neither of my parents really seemed to pay much attention to my report cards, but Papa hit the roof at a D, and he laid down the law: I had to spend a full hour studying chemistry every night after dinner before I could do anything else. Strong medicine, but it worked, and I aced every test the rest of the year. The second blessing was my good fortune in getting a great geometry teacher, Mr. Stephens, who could make any problem seem so clear and logical that it was almost impossible not to get everything right. After that high school was as easy as grade school had been.

With one exception: English. I had loved to read from as early as fifth grade, and I read books the way most kids watched television. But before high school it had never occurred to me that psychoanalysis of the author was part of the reader's responsibility. So when we'd be asked to submit a paper explaining why we thought John Steinbeck wrote *The Grapes Of Wrath*, I would come up with an angle like saying that he did it for the money, since he was an author by profession and writing was how he put food on the table. Then I'd write what seemed to me to be a detailed and fairly expressive tract expounding on this idea. Inevitably these submissions would send the teacher into a towering rage since, far more than just a poorly written paper with no obvious effort behind it, this kind of subversive thinking posed a truly existential threat to their positions as the masters of meanings and metaphors. It would be less than candid for me to pretend that I didn't take a perverse enjoyment from finding that I could provoke such a reaction, and my first success led me to keep finding similar perspectives for subsequent papers.

This began a trend in which I would hand in a paper and a few days later be sent to the principal's office as punishment for my bad attitude. To me the pretense that these courses fostered creative thinking seemed fishy, since as long as you acted out the charade of analysis in the approved manner you could get a good grade, but the moment someone gave an answer that was outside the accepted bounds they were treated as an object in need of discipline. So after the end of the school day I'd take my place quietly outside the principal's door for forty minutes with the other kids serving time for high crimes and misdemeanors such as smoking in the bathroom or beating up one of the smart kids. And at the end of the quarter I'd come home with a report card bearing a C in English.

The head of the English department especially annoyed me. He reeked of pretention, shaving his beard in an artiste's goatee and walking around with his head tilted back like some misplaced aristocrat who felt that he had patently demonstrated the qualifications to teach at Oxford or Cambridge but, through an egregious clerical error that surely would soon be discovered and rectified, he had been condemned to expound on the arts to a rabble of future farmers and salvage auto part specialists in Brattleboro. Across the front page of one of my papers I can still remember him writing "I wish you would stop stumbling around in a quasi-illiterate stupor and write what you are capable of writing." I didn't know what "quasi-illiterate" meant, so I asked my sympathetic Latin teacher, Mrs. Williams, to explain it. I can still remember her laughing softly and with a slight shake of her head muttering in a bemused sort of way: "*He* said that?" When she explained the Latin root of the modifier "quasi", I remember feeling that it was really a complement. The head of the English department didn't actually think I *was* illiterate. He just thought I made it *appear* as if I was. In my view the exact reverse of this description suited him, so that was good enough for me.

I don't know if this kind of teaching went on in other schools or if it still happens today, but I think nothing could be done to destroy a student's interest in reading more than forcing this kind of labored deconstruction. Moreover, although I couldn't have articulated this idea then, I think that great writing is inherently too subtle for most high school students to analyze, because really first rate literature conveys the author's message and alters the way the reader thinks without the reader even noticing that anything has happened.

The adolescent who feels traumatized by his outsider status is such a cliché that in all probability it was the tiny minority of insiders who formed the true outsider group and all the others were just unaware of it at the time. I don't think I was particularly different in feeling that I didn't fit. But I did have something going for me: for the most part I didn't really care. I was used to being on my own or just with Paul David. We'd grown up together learning how to make life interesting without the involvement of a lot of other people. We knew how to retreat into our own imaginations and think about things that were far away when life where we were seemed dull or uncomfortable. My classmates in high school only included a couple other Newfane kids and these were mostly from the southwest part of the township outside of bicycling range. I didn't know them well and didn't hang out with them. Because I was a good student I'd have normally been a target for the school toughs, but even though I was a year young for my grade and had yet to go through a real growth spurt I was fairly scrappy from years of competing with my older brother and at school I got less grief than most kids.

The lack of a thirst for companionship meant that I only made a few close friends at school, and the friends I did have usually got there because they were so personable that it was impossible to avoid liking them. One was Leonard Timmons, who once gave me a great lesson in how words could be used to control a situation. Leonard was one of the really smart kids. He did well academically in everything and was also a gifted musician, playing trombone in the school band and drums at home. But he wasn't particularly athletic and his thick horn rimmed glasses marked him.

One day the two of us ran into a couple of older tough guys hanging around behind the school for a little smoking. It was at the end of an outdoor gym class and we were late getting back in the building to shower so most of the class had gone in ahead of us. One of these boys began hectoring Leonard and ultimately said something to the effect that he was going to punch him in the face and break his glasses. In an example of under-reaction that I'll never forget, Leonard responded in a dead level voice dripping with sarcasm: "Oh, yeah, like beating up a guy like me is going to show anyone what a big *man* you are." The two older boys just skulked off, defeated by nothing more than the combination of what Leonard said and the tone he used in saying it.

For the one year we rode it, the high school bus was a lot tougher than the school. That bus trip was a real ordeal by fire. Mr. Swenson was one of the only people who would drive down Wardsboro Road on the way to work at seven in the morning every day, and Mama arranged for him to give Paul David and me a ride to the village. So we'd run out and stand by our bridge ten minutes ahead of time to be sure we didn't make him wait. He'd then take us the two miles to the village Texaco station where the bus driver Tommy Wilkinson worked during the day and parked the town's big yellow school bus when he wasn't using it. We'd get there half an hour before the bus was due to leave, and we'd hang around goofing off. On January mornings when it was twenty below zero we'd both cram ourselves in the phone booth at the corner of the parking area for protection from the wind and for the slight temperature increase that the trapped heat escaping from our bodies would produce. In our poorly insulated green rubber boots our toes would throb from the pain of the cold, and ears would hurt like bee stings.

When it seemed like we couldn't take another minute of freezing Tommy would arrive and start up the bus. Tommy was a friendly young man of probably twenty-five years age at the time, but like a lot of Vermonters he never said much beyond "Morning!" or "It's a cold one today, *ayup*." He'd fire up the eight track tape player he'd installed in the bus in order to drown out the screams of the little monsters destroying each other behind him, and he'd pop in one of his two tapes: it was either *The Best of Johnny Cash* or *The Best of Country and Western*. I much preferred Johnny Cash and I think Tommy did, too, since he probably played it four times for every once the other tape played. The first track, *Ring Of Fire*, is seared into my memory forever, probably because the idea of being in a situation where it was actually too warm was so appealing.

Tommy's job was to take us and two or three other schoolmates about four miles down Route 30 to a place called Williamsville Depot before he began his more complicated grade school run. There had once been a station here for the West River Railroad, a never-profitable feeder line spanning the thirty-six miles from Brattleboro to Londonderry that had been built on speculation during the rail building bubble of the second half of the nineteenth century. The railroad had gone bust in the Depression and its rails and bridges had been torn up for scrap value, but the rail bed and many stone or concrete supports for bridges crossing the river are still clearly visible all along its banks. Williamsville Depot had been a stop for people heading up the Dover Road, which trailed off west from Route 30 along the Rock River until it met Route 100 at the spine of the state. But by the time of our school journeys all that was left of the depot was a flat open area next to the road that had probably been used first by waiting horse carriages and later by cars. Tommy would let us out there, and for the third time we'd wait in the cold, this time for a bus coming from Dover.

As far as I was concerned the Dover kids were the absolute last scrapings from the bottom of the barrel of humanity. Most of them were in what was called vocational course work, meaning they were learning trades like carpentry or auto repair. Those studying agriculture all wore a blue corduroy jacket with an emblem for the *Future Farmers Of*

America. Now I have nothing against tradesmen, blue collar workers, and farmers, and I'm certain that taken as a whole they are every bit as upstanding as any other segment of society (and quite likely more so given the behavior of many people who should know much better), but for this particular lot it is my considered opinion that on the jackets they should have replaced the word "farmers" with "inmates". I suppose this was not done because the principal felt that the Dover students might find such realism to be de-motivating.

Our stop was the final one before arrival at the school, which was still ten miles away, and when we'd step aboard we'd look down the bus at rows of grim, stony faces. Wherever there was a seat with only one of these hoodlums in it, he'd be sitting at the aisle with his legs braced against the seat in front of him. If you asked to sit by him, he'd act as if he couldn't either hear or see you. The bus driver would peer into the rear view mirror and holler at you to sit down, but the only way to get a seat was to choose the one with the most vulnerable looking defender and enter a pitched battle to either move him to the window seat or fight over him to get there yourself. As the youngest kid on the bus and often carrying a pile of books, homework papers and lunch in a paper sack that I had to maintain control of while fighting, I had a pretty hard time of this, but it wasn't easy for Paul David, either.

A lot of times you'd have to brace your back against the guy you were trying to move, put your feet on the sides of the seatbacks across the aisle, and push with your legs for all you were worth. Sometimes you'd be putting forth every ounce of strength you could muster and the guy would suddenly let go, and you'd go crashing on the bus floor with your books and papers everywhere. Often we'd be halfway to Brattleboro before finally resolving the issue and getting seated.

But that didn't mean the fight was over. The boys behind you would slap your head, steal your hat, and fire paper clips at you with rubber bands. If you had taken the aisle seat and foolishly began to lower your guard a little, your sullen seatmate was likely to suddenly push off from the bus wall with his feet and launch you and your books into a heap onto the floor of the aisle, at which point the seat had to be fought for all over again. One particularly nasty time an older kid in the seat behind me tapped me on the shoulder and when I turned to see what he wanted, he punched me in the side of the face with his hand wrapped in a chain bracelet. I couldn't chew for a week and I had bloody cut marks from the links embedded in my cheek for a long time after.

So when the town of Newfane ended the bus from the Texaco station after my freshman year, it was no loss to skip the Dover bus altogether and start hitching rides all the way to Brattleboro. In some ways it was easier because there were no bus schedules to coordinate. But more on that later.

It wasn't only the Dover school bus environment that could create altercations. But one would think that on Easter Sunday differences might be set aside. Not so. On years when the family finances were good, the week before Easter Mama would take us into Brattleboro and get us outfitted with a suit and tie so we'd look our best at the service, and we'd subsequently wear it to church the rest of the year.

One Easter when I was ten or so we stopped at the store in Newfane on the way home from church so Mama could pick up some things she needed for our holiday dinner. I stood outside the store looking ridiculous with my cow licked hair standing on end and wearing my ill-fitting suit, sized to actually hang right sometime during the middle of the next twelve months of growth but way too big on this day. One of the local kids made what was probably a completely accurate remark about how foolish I looked, and after a few moments of verbal escalation we were locked in a wrestling match on the commons in front of the jail, rolling around on the grass and destroying my suit in the process.

I sometimes think that international diplomacy among nations is modeled on the behavior of children. Both follow patterns something like this:

"He tore my suit up!"

"He grabbed me and tried to knock me down so I was just holding on to him to protect myself!"

"I grabbed him because he was hitting me and I had to stop him!"

"He hit me so I had to hit him back."

"He hit me first."

"He called me a bad name that my dad says no one should say so I had to hit him."

"He said this suit made me look like a dork, so I just told him he looked ugly without even wearing a suit."

...and so on. It really is a wonder that any sensible adult can be persuaded to have kids.

6   SWIMMING POOLS AND ARCHERY

One of the rituals of every summer was making a swimming hole on Smith Brook. Each spring the brook would flood from melting snow in the surrounding hills. The placid clear trickle of summer would become a roaring current of brown water and white foam five feet deep or more and filling the banks from side to side, ripping every trace of last year's swimming hole away and filling its pool with new rocks and gravel. When the floods receded, much of the brook was beyond recognition. Only the biggest rocks weighing several tons could be counted on to remain in place from year to year, and to this day when I walk down to the brook I see the signature boulders I remember from my childhood, while everything else has changed.

When summer came we would be desperate for a place to get cool, and we needed a good pool that we could stretch out in for a proper soaking and a little swim. So when the water receded we'd survey the stretch of brook alongside our field for the deepest spots and we'd set to work making the best place bigger and deeper still. We'd use shovels and buckets to carry away the smaller gravel and we'd use long iron pry-bars to break big rocks loose and roll them out of the hole. On the downstream end of the pool we'd build a dam from the rocks and gravel. The dam was porous since the gravel was very coarse grained, so it couldn't hold back a head of more than a foot or so. But if you started with a place where the water was eighteen inches deep, dug out two feet from the bottom, and built a dam that raised the water level a foot, you'd have a pool between four and five feet deep, and that was enough to get relief from the heat. Making a pool deeper than that was nearly impossible since you had to work with your head underwater with a diving mask, and raising rocks weighing a couple hundred pounds from such a depth was more than two boys could do.

We spent hours of every summer day in those pools, either working on improvements, or playing, fighting and relaxing in the cool water. I learned that I could float indefinitely on my back if I put my heels on a rock at the shoreline, and I could almost go to sleep like that. The pleasure of lying in that cool water after spending the afternoon in the hot sun mowing grass was unforgettable.

There were three different places that typically provided the best pools. The first spot was far downstream past the barns. We used it for a few years but it was two shady and had too many mosquitoes. We then moved well upstream to a spot with a big bolder on the upstream side of the pool. The bolder was nice since you could lie on the warm rock if you got cold from too much time in the water, but the space between the rock and the best dam site was too short and the resulting pool wasn't as big as we wanted. So after a couple years there, we moved to another spot a little further downstream. This place allowed us to make a pool that was about fifty feet long, and you could actually swim a few strokes in it. On the side of the brook closest to the house we used the few flat stones we could find to make an imitation of a patio. On the other side there was a steep embankment including a tree stump that fish would sometimes hide under.

When I was about fourteen, I went to the Newfane flea market with Papa and came back with a spear gun. A few words should be said about this flea market. These days flea markets tend to be filled with people selling off-brand, salvaged, stolen, or new merchandise that's deeply discounted, but when the man who ran the Newfane store launched a local flea market in the mid 1960's it was more of a community garage sale where everyone showed up with whatever stuff they had that was ultimately destined for the dump, but which they might sucker someone into buying for their spare change. I think it has been fairly well established that my father collected and saved everything he could acquire. The flea market presented a golden opportunity for Papa to expand his operation by collecting and saving everyone else's stuff, too.

Being a crafty sort, Papa used to have his own stall at the flea market as a way to justify his going with Mama. He'd load up the car with rubbish from the barn and make tags with outrageous prices on it. A dirty old Sunoco oil can with a screw top might demand five dollars – after all, they don't make cans like that anymore! He'd set up his wares and then ask me to watch the stall while he roamed around and looked at the gear on offer from the other sellers. Invariably the car returned home more heavily loaded than it had been in the morning.

I suspect my father was far from unique in this behavior. Our town was loaded with people who would hang a sign proclaiming "Antiques" outside their houses. Sometimes the merchandise would really be the furniture they used day in and day out. But if you stopped by and you wanted it, they'd happily sell it to you.

Flatlanders and out-of-staters were regarded as an incredibly peculiar, astonishingly wealthy, and surprisingly gullible lot, meant to be taken advantage of whenever possible. They drove expensive cars that could be taken more than thirty miles from their mechanic without excessive worry, and they drove them terribly. Massachusetts drivers were widely regarded as the worst, although Connecticut drivers were reputed to be the fastest. None of them were believed to have an ounce of sense when it came to driving in snow. And they had no idea of the value of money. So if they wanted to buy the old rotting wagon wheels or blown glass bottles that we Vermonters found in our barns, it was our obligation to ensure that they paid the maximum possible amount. Maybe the oil can price wasn't such a bad idea – who knew what they did with this stuff when they got back home to their cities?

It was this philosophy that drove the whole antique store thing. Fortunately, we lived off the main road or I expect that Papa would have tried a retail career as well.

But I digress – this was intended as a conversation about spear fishing. You could only imagine the delight of a boy who'd been raised on episodes of the old Lloyd Bridges TV show *Sea Hunt*, where Bridges would regularly stave off certain death in the slobbering maw of a shark with a well timed shot through its eye. To have my own spear gun! Now I could safely swim the treacherous four foot deep waters behind our dam on Smith Brook. I'd pop on my swim mask, spring load the spear gun, and go swimming around the pool looking for prey. Sadly it was an off year for sharks in Vermont waters, but there were many small fish, and in sufficient quantities one might imagine that they could present a threat. I should say here that the single spear that I had was missing its tip, so it terminated in the blunt end of its shaft, which was some three eights of an inch in diameter. The successful deployment of such a spear at a fish whose length was five or six inches tended to put a rather serious hole in it and pretty much terminated its existence without further discussion. Given the fact that the firing range was often so close that the tip of the spear passed through the fish and embedded itself in the brook bed behind it before the back of the shaft had completely exited the barrel of the gun, Smith Brook spear fishing was rather less sportsmanlike than Mr. Bridges would have preferred.

Terrestrial archery was more satisfying, and in another flea market acquisition I managed to obtain a nifty small game bow and arrow set. It wasn't enough to bring down any major animal, and in my hands it wasn't much of a threat to any other intended target, either, but it was no toy. To try it out, I carried the bow out to the far end of the field in front of the house, at the opposite end from the barn, some two hundred fifty feet distant. The barn seemed like a worthy target – despite the range and my lack of experience it was big enough that it should be easy to hit and it was a relatively indestructible structure so damage wouldn't be an issue. I strung the bow and fit one of my three arrows to the string, drawing it back to my cheek. I knew enough to aim above my target, since Newton had declared that an arrow's flight would be impacted by the pull of gravity, so I chose a spot up near the roofline as my mark. I let the string go with a twang, and watched with awe as a third of my ordinance went sailing off, seemingly impervious to the earth's tug, way over the barn roof and off into the woods beyond. Half an hour's searching for it convinced me that there was no chance I'd ever see that arrow again, but I consoled myself with the fact that I had two arrows left and a bow that could shoot them with more power than I had ever imagined possible.

So back I went to my spot in the field for a second try. This time I aimed lower, preferring to undershoot since that would give me a fighting chance of finding the arrow, and also not drawing the string back quite so far as to limit the flight range. After a number of shots landing in front of the barn, I finally, and triumphantly, hit the barn dead center. But this was a short lived victory as well, since the impact of arrow and barn board had shattered the shaft completely. I was down to one arrow.

Now I was truly poised on the horns of a dilemma. I had one arrow left and nothing I could trust to shoot it at, but I had become completely addicted to the feeling of the string's release and spectacle of the ensuing flight of the arrow. I wanted to shoot more, but I really didn't want to lose that last arrow. Being a thinking type, I quickly came on a solution. If I fired the arrow straight up, I could shoot as hard as I wanted too, and when the arrow came down it would just embed itself in the dirt, which being far softer than barn board wouldn't cause any harm.

Brighter readers will no doubt recognize the flaw in this plan, but it wasn't apparent to me until I had fired the arrow nearly into low earth orbit, where owing to the glare of the mid day sun it disappeared completely from my sight. I am here to testify that it is an unsettling feeling standing in the middle of an open field knowing that a lethal but invisible projectile will be landing somewhere in your immediate vicinity in the next four seconds, a feeling that tends to make the four seconds seem more like a week. But in a moment the arrow plunged into the ground about fifty feet away from me, burying itself eight inches into the soil. I had cheated death again.

These same brighter readers will also assume that at this point I might have decided that there had been sufficient danger for one day and retreated to the house for some Kool Aid. But I was looking for improvement, and the answer seemed obvious. Knights in the middle ages used shields to protect themselves from arrows, and a shield could protect me in the same way. So after some poking around in the barn for a suitable piece of defense, I found the lid from a metal garbage can and went back out in the field. I put the lid on the ground next to me, fired the arrow skywards, and then quickly grabbed the lid and held it over my head. Again the arrow landed thirty or forty feet away, but with my shield in hand I felt no danger at all. Thus defended, I proceeded to fire arrows for the next hour or so. Fortunately, an arrow never hit the lid, because in retrospect there was probably a good chance that it would have pierced right through it. But from a psychological perspective, it made me invincible and that was what mattered.

A few days later I learned another lesson about archery: do not leave your fiberglass bow strung in the hot afternoon sun throughout the afternoon. I did this with mine and it twisted into an unusable pretzel. I suspect that had my archery career not ended so quickly, my life would have done so instead, so this outcome was probably all for the best.

But let us return to that recurring dream of finding the elusive fishing hole where nobody ever went and where some grandfather of a trout had been growing for twenty years until it reached Hemingway proportions. The search for that locale sent us into some pretty obscure places. On one occasion, Paul David and I walked the mile up Grout's Road to Kenny Pond, which we all knew as Grout's Pond since the Grouts lived at the far end of it, even if they didn't own it, whereas there was nobody whatsoever bearing the name Kenny in any of the admittedly constrained circles we moved in. This pond was formed by a man made dam that must have been built a hundred years previously. It looked like it was intended to create a mill race, but the volume of water flowing out of the exit was far too small to have done much of anything constructive. The pond itself was a couple hundred feet across and possibly a third of a mile in length. Unlike the brooks in our area, it had no trout, but it did have perch and what we called rock bass – a small mouth bass with hard, spiny fins and thick, heavy scales. I don't recall ever eating these, but we would catch them and throw them back.

The pond was located in a sort of saddle between the hills, and its outflow ran away from the valley that our house was in. To our young imaginations that far side of the pond was pretty wild. If you chose the right direction you could go twenty-five miles before you hit a paved road, with only a couple of dirt tracks in between. At the time of this story, Paul David might have been thirteen and I would've been about eleven, and we had no idea where the brook running out of Grout's Pond went. But we thought it was just the kind of place that might lead to a previously undiscovered fishing hole swarming with monster trout, so after some discussion of pros and cons ("we'll get lost, be eaten by bears and never be seen again", "no, there will be a fish big enough that we can't carry it", "ok, let's go") we decided to see where it went.

The original plan was that we were just going to go a little way down it and then we'd turn around and head home. But every time we began to think we ought to return we'd convince ourselves that around the next bend we'd find just what we wanted, that deep shaded pool with overhanging rocks to provide the perfect hiding place for our catch.

So we kept on going, aided by the fact that we were walking downstream and thus downhill, which made going forward far preferable to going back. Other brooks and springs joined the little stream from Grout's Pond, making it grow bigger and wider and making the pools broader and deeper and hence more alluring. But the afternoon was heading toward evening, and now it was a very long way back home, long enough that making it back before dark seemed unlikely.

I don't think my brother and I were unique at that age in having a remarkable capacity for being unable to accept reality. We knew if we turned back we would barely get home before dark if we made it at all. But despite the fact that going forward only made the situation worse, what was ahead was unknown and hence potentially miraculous, whereas what was behind was a known and certainly not miraculous hard hike back. So we kept going.

We saw the first house along the way because its lights were visible through the trees. This woke us up to how late it was and made us really worried about the possibility of being stuck out in the woods at night. People who have never lived in rural areas often have little idea what darkness really is. In most urban or suburban settings, it is perfectly feasible to go outdoors for a four or five mile walk at night without a light, even when there is no streetlight nearby. The night sky in the city or in the suburbs shows a smattering of dim stars but any moisture in the air reflects thousands of street lights so that the color of the sky is a glowing deep purple that is positively ablaze compared to the black of night in the country. On a moonless night in the back country of Vermont the sky is filled with a quantity of stars that seems simply staggering to an urban denizen, but as many as there are, they provide almost no usable light because the space between the stars is black as, well, as black as night.

Walking along a dirt road at night a person can tell when they are on the road by how it feels under foot. The hard packed portion where car tires spend most of their time is smooth and quiet underfoot, but straying either into the center of the road or to the side one encounters loose stones that crunch when walked on. If there are openings in the tree canopy overhead, it's possible to walk along and stay on the road even on a moonless, cloudy night. If you wave a hand in front of your face, or if there are branches overhead, there is some slight sensation of a change in the light that yields a sense of depth. But it is a spooky feeling.

Under the trees in the woods it's a totally different story, especially during the summer when the trees are covered with leaves and there's no snow to provide a light background. Here the black is inky and thick, and there is no more hint of light than there is in a deep, dark cave. Unlike being on the road surface, there is no tactile sensation to guide where to walk. It is easy to walk straight into a tree trunk, or get a branch in the eye, or smack your shins on a fallen log. And walking in a brook bed filled with rocks and boulders is a good way to break your leg. Your best bet is to stop and wait until morning, which we most certainly did not want to do.

Fortunately, where there's a house, there is usually a road, and scrambling up the embankment from the brook we found a dirt road running parallel to the watercourse. So we abandoned our pursuit of the perfect fishing hole and focused on walking until we got somewhere where we could phone home. At the least we were confident that we would come to a village somewhere along the way. It is a truism of the Vermont backwoods that if you think you are lost, the way to get unlost is to walk downhill until you hit running water and then walk downstream. All waterways eventually lead to habitations. Even at ten years of age, we were well aware of this.

As we walked, dusk turned to complete darkness and

although we were hungry we were becoming more concerned about the consequences (more specifically, consequences with respect to our posteriors) of calling to be rescued from wherever it was we were going to emerge. Our current scenario was without precedence in our household, and it was thus unknown what punishment would be required to balance the scales of justice.

Ultimately we ended up at the general store in Williamsville, where there was a phone we could use to call home. There was much admonishment about how worried we had made our parents. I must confess that it took a while for it to occur to me that they were actually worried that we might NOT come back and not the reverse.

7   UNSAFE AT ANY SPEED

There is a joke about a Vermont farmer whose Texas cousin comes to visit him. It hits a little close to home for me. It begins with the Vermonter proudly showing off his farm to his cousin. "Ayup, our farm starts where that stonewall hits the road over they-uh, then it goes up the hill to that maple tree you see off they-uh, then down to where the two brooks join over they-uh, and then back down along the other stone wall to the road.".

The Texan replies: "That's it? Shoot, it takes all day for me to drive across mah ranch!"

And the Vermonter goes: "Ayup, I had a car like that once, too".

Well, we had a *lot* of cars like that. Cars were as big a part of the American dream for us as for anyone, but our dreams probably were a little more on the nightmarish side than what normal people have in mind. Like a radioactive element, Papa's cars could be described by a half life whose span varied from two weeks to a couple months. After that, chances were pretty good that the car would break down, often in spectacular fashion, usually on some remote dirt road that Papa took because its route more closely approximated the straight line that a theoretician would tell you is the shortest distance between two points but that anyone experienced in Vermont roads would consider only in the most dire of emergencies, and even then only when accompanied by at least a partial departure from sanity.

Our cars were invariably no less than ten years old (a very long time in those days of far less reliable designs) and usually consumed nearly as much oil as they did gasoline. Amongst its many necessities, the trunk of any of our cars always had a case of 10W30 at the ready and acrid blue smoke marked our passage down every back road. Even in those pre-catalytic converter days, our family's individual contribution to lowering global air quality was noteworthy.

On one memorable occasion it was decided that the fifteen year old 1950 Chrysler New Yorker that Mama had been driving needed to be retired. In our local classified ad paper, the Town Crier, a local was offering a 1955 Chevy Bel Air for a hundred dollars, and my parents decided this might be a candidate despite its almost unheard of three figure price tag. So on a frigid January night, the family went to see it in a place south of Brattleboro. My memory is vague, but I do recall the typical Vermont scenario of two dozen derelict cars parked in disarray outside an old farm house.

After a test drive and much conversation and chin-stroking, it was determined that the Chevy from the advertisement met our exacting standards, and moreover, the seller also had a 1956 model, and that was only fifty bucks. Perhaps Papa rationalized that the bonus car made the deal two cars for an average of seventy-five dollars, and this allowed the transaction to fit his economic model, if only by technicality.

Paul David and Johanna bundled in with Mama in the '55 and I got in the '56 with Papa. As we headed up Route 30 the weather thickened and by the time we got to Newfane it was snowing hard. Route 30 was well cleared as usual, but the plows hadn't been down Wardsboro Road yet and it had a pretty thick snow covering with only a couple tracks from other cars making their way up the hill. Mama had been ahead of us and from her tire tracks it was apparent she'd done OK getting up the hill.

Leaving the village the road rounded a gentle curve to the left and then presented a hundred and fifty yards of straight, flat surface before beginning a mile long hill. At the start of the hill was a concrete and iron bridge over the Smith Brook that had been built in the late 1950s to replace an old wooden covered bridge that was too expensive to maintain and too far off the beaten path to have any tourism value. The new bridge had all the functional and aesthetic charm of a storm drain on the Mass Pike. In the construction process the town road crew had disassembled the covered bridge and heaped its timbers and boards by the roadside. Never being one to miss a chance for a unique purchase, Papa had bought the bridge from the town and moved it to our field where he piled it in a heap, and it promptly began the usual rapid decomposition to topsoil that happens to just about anything left on the ground in those parts. Six or seven years later, Mama had sent Paul David and me out to the pile with hatchets to convert what little was still above ground into kindling. Denial of the opportunity for Papa to erect his own personal covered bridge somewhere on our property created the predictable intra-marital row, but it also extracted what would probably be the only real value that would ever be recovered from it, as its splinters stoked the black iron stove in our kitchen for a couple of winters.

But back to the tale at hand. After the bridge, the road bent slightly to the right, past the neatly Germanic home of the Mannerhopfs. Then came the tricky part as the hill steepened and the road bent sharply to the left and then back again to the right. After this treacherous *S* curve came the steepest part of the hill, a four hundred yard stretch to the crest. On slippery days, if you wanted to make it over the top, you had to attack the hill at the highest speed you dared and come around the S curve like a world cup slalom champion. First you'd take the left-curving portion with the back end of the car fishtailing behind you on the right. Then as the road bent to the right you'd cut the wheel hard that way and goose the accelerator, which brought the back end around to line up with the front. Skillfully timed, you'd end up with the car facing straight up the hill right at the end of the S, and you'd have enough speed to get over the steep part.

But things could go wrong, and in my experience, things that can go wrong usually do. And so it did a few years later with Paul David driving Papa's powder-blue and faux wood-paneled 1961 Ford Country Squire station wagon, a car so rusted along the rocker panels that it looked like some unique form of metal eating vermin had been gnawing on it and left it to turn gangrenous. It was a rare thing for either of us to be driving unaccompanied by my father, and hearing what was about to happen might give you some sympathy for his position. Because Paul David came sailing just right around the first, left-bending part of the curve, but he gave the car just a little too much gas going into the second, right-bending section so that the back of the car swung out to the left, where it was in the lane used by oncoming traffic. Now oncoming traffic has never been all that significant an issue on Wardsboro Road. In fact there were many times that I walked the two miles from the village all the way home and never saw another car. But on this particular day, and at this particularly critical time, the problem of oncoming traffic chose to achieve its full potential. Avoiding the unwanted oncoming car required turning the wheel to the left and hitting the gas again to make the back end come in, and Paul David executed the maneuver perfectly, allowing the other car to slip past unscathed. We, however, were not so fortunate, since the Ford executed a perfect three hundred sixty degree spin and buried itself nose first into the snowbank.

It's an interesting sensation, running off the road into a truly big snowbank. I recommend it, but the snowbank must be judiciously selected to avoid inconvenient impurities such as guardrails, tree stumps, bridge abutments, boulders, or parked cars. Assuming that such an example is available, the experience is unforgettable. There is the sudden surge of adrenalin as the brain prepares for what seems likely to be a huge smash. Then the front bumper contacts the snowbank and a shower of snow flies over the roof of the car. This is followed by a *whoomp!* sound as the snow lands on the car's hood and roof. Immediately all is quiet and muffled, like being in an anechoic chamber. A soft blue light filters through the snow into the car. The feeling is uncomfortably close to what entering heaven might feel like. But Saint Peter is sadly (or gladly, depending on your perspective) absent, and in the real world, if you are a teenage boy entrusted with your dad's car, there will be hell to pay.

At night it's most spectacular, since the snow flying over the car is momentarily illuminated by the headlights and looks for all the world like the explosion of a tanker truck in a Hollywood chase scene. Then the snow collapses onto the car and everything goes black. The eyes adjust in a few seconds to reveal a gentle yellow glow filtering from the headlights through the snow heaped on the hood and windshield. One of my high school friends treated me to this experience once. Not intentionally.

But in either case the next step is the same – developing a strategy for getting out of the car. If the snowbank isn't too big or the car wasn't moving too fast, then this could be as simple as climbing into the back seat, rolling down the window, and heaving yourself out. But if the car is buried deep enough to cover the back windows, there is a problem, because the only way to get out is to roll down the windows and dig a path out by shoveling snow *into* the car. Parents tend to frown on this exit strategy, since drying out a wet car interior in winter time is not a simple matter.

This part of the problem is where the 1961 Country Squire station wagon shows its finest strengths, because it includes a dashboard switch that allows the driver to lower the tailgate window, providing an escape route by which Paul David and I were able to climb out the back onto the road. Released from our frozen tomb, we admired his handiwork. The car was neatly buried so that only the portion behind the rear tires stuck out into the road.

There was nothing we were going to do with the car at this point, so we walked the mile and half home, contemplating the medieval tortures that Papa was likely to inflict on us in punishment for our transgressions. But since we were needed to provide manpower for extraction we were spared corporal punishment, and after being subjected to the usual discussion about the appallingly minute level of intelligence we both possessed were trundled into Mama's car along with tire chains, tow chains, shovels, brooms, planks, jacks, old rugs and the usual paraphernalia required for getting stuck vehicles unstuck. An hour of shoveling cleared the car, a few minutes with the jacks got planks under its wheels, and tire chains were fitted to Mama's car to prepare it for its task of pulling the station wagon out.

A word about tire chains is in order. Where I live in California today, people know about tire chains primarily because when an Alaskan storm front comes through and dumps snow in the mountains, the local news men come on the TV and sternly admonish people not to leave the beach and drive into the mountains without chains. It doesn't seem to occur to these talking heads that most people with enough sense to bring chains would never leave the beach to go where it's snowing anyway, and true enough, most people don't. But those who do go usually have a nice brand new shiny set of chains that snap on fairly easily, although they do make the fingers cold.

Let me assure you that these elegantly Californianized chains are not remotely similar to the chains Papa had. His chains were probably acquired second hand at a flea market in the nineteen thirties and had first seen service in the Franco Prussian war. They were rusted and inflexible, had missing links that were replaced with pieces of wire coat hanger wrapped around multiple times, were meant for a smaller tire than our current vehicle was fitted with, and

108

usually had at least one broken segment that came around and slapped the underside of the wheel well with every revolution of the tire so that the car went down the road going *whap! whap! whap!* at a level that frightened children and wildlife as far away as western New Hampshire. The clasps that locked the chains to the wheel would have been nearly impossible to close on a workbench in a garage that was heated to room temperature and outfitted with a full complement of lubricants, pliers, hammers, vice grips and screwdrivers. Out in the snow, with darkness coming on and temperatures in the low twenties, putting chains on became a torturous ordeal that left fingers numbed, frozen and cut to pieces. I hated putting on chains with a passion – it was the single worst part of winter as far as I was concerned.

As always happened with these events, the sun was down and full darkness was nearly on us when we finally towed the station wagon onto the road. Aside from having its grill stuffed full of snow and some pieces of rusty rocker panel knocked off a few weeks sooner than would have otherwise been the case, it was none the worse for the wear. So chilled to the bone we all drove home for a late dinner.

I suppose this must bring us back to finishing the story of the '56 Chevy. As Papa rounded the upper part of the S curve, it was clear that things were not going right. There was no fishtailing. There was no sense of extreme speed. In fact, there was an appalling shortfall of any sort of sense of danger. The car's engine was struggling to summon the energy needed to make it up the hill at all. And sure enough, when we got onto the steep part of the hill after the S curve, we continued to lose speed until we came to a halt about five hundred feet from the crest, with the wheels slowly and helplessly spinning, and blue, oily smoke puffing from the exhaust.

So we backed down to the nearest driveway, turned around and drove back to the village for another run. Same result. Three times Papa tried coaxing the car over the hill, and every time he fell short of the crest. Beaten, he drove to the Texaco station in Newfane and called home on the payphone for Mama to come get us. The car sat in town for two days until the pavement cleared enough to make it possible to get it up the hill.

I remember this car lasting for only a couple months before it made way for a nice new Chevy – a 1957. Although this model is regarded as *the* classic fifties Chevrolet today, I can assure you that it was no big deal in those times. It seemed like everyone had one. But Papa's was one of the better cars I remember him getting, and it really had little problem until the next fall, when he sent me out on a late Sunday afternoon to change the summer tires to snow tires. Tire changing was a semi-annual event for us (sometimes more than semi-annual if there was a surprise late snowstorm in the spring). Like a lot of boys, I was anxious to demonstrate my mechanical aptitude and was happy to do anything I could that involved working on the car, especially if I could do it unsupervised. So I gladly accepted my assignment, despite the fact that it was late and getting cold and dark.

My father had taught me his time honored process for tire changing, learned by him in those romantic days when cars were named for dashing explorers like DeSoto, LaSalle or Hudson, all of whom had roamed the earth and met their demise centuries before the tire iron and scissors jack had even been dreamed of. The first step, assuming it worked, was to set the handbrake. If, as usual, it didn't work, you'd put the three speed, column shift manual transmission in reverse as the best substitute. If the car had hubcaps (no more a given than the functionality of the handbrake), you took them off. Then you loosened the five bolts that hold the tire on by about a half turn each. There were two types of wrenches used to remove the bolts. The tire jack handle had a wrench at the end of it that was good for loosening the bolts because the handle's length gave the leverage needed when the bolts were tight. But it was cumbersome to use it to remove loosened bolts because its end was so long that it would hit the ground with each turn so you had to keep repositioning it on the nut. But there was another wrench shaped like a cross with shorter arms that you could use to spin the bolts free very quickly.

With the bolts slightly loosened, you raised the car up with the bumper jack until the tire was off the ground. Snow tires required more clearance than summer tires, so you had to get some good air between the ground and the summer tires you planned to remove. With the tire airborne you'd check the car to be sure the jack was solidly in place by trying to rock it a little. If it fell off the jack, you started over. If it didn't, you'd spin the bolts off one at a time, placing them each in the upturned hubcap so that you didn't lose them in the grass.

Once all the nuts were off, you'd slip the summer tire off and put the winter tire in its place. This could be difficult depending on the style of bolts. On older cars, there was an actual bolt that threaded into a hole in the wheel drum. These were a nuisance to put on because it was tricky to line up the holes in the rim with the holes in the drum. Newer cars had threaded studs sticking out of the drum and these served to guide the rim into proper place. Then nuts were screwed onto the studs.

The '57 Chevy was the new type with nuts on studs, but when I tried to loosen the nuts on the left rear tire I couldn't do it. I was only thirteen or fourteen at this point, but I was reasonably strong, so this result surprised me. The nuts must really be rusted on there, I thought. What a job like this needs is leverage. So I went down to the barn and rummaged around in the near darkness until I found a nice piece of cast iron pipe about four feet in length. I slid this over the jack handle and put the wrench end onto the nut in a way that the pipe tilted upwards at about thirty degrees from horizontal. I pushed down on it with my hand until the pipe made the wrench handle flex quite a bit but the nut still didn't pop loose. So I played my last card – I stood on the end of the pipe. This got the result I was looking for as the pipe quickly lowered to the ground, but the wrench popped off the rim.

When I went to put it back on, I found to my dismay that the torque of the wrench and pipe had twisted the stud right off the wheel drum. In the end of the wrench was the nut with the broken-off half of the stud still inside it.

I knew this was not good, but I had a job to do and I might as well try to loosen the other nuts. So I moved my pipe and wrench combination to a second stud and tried again. This unfortunately produced the same result as my first effort – another twisted off stud.

Now one would think that someone with an ounce of common sense would switch tactics at this point. Maybe put some penetrating oil on the studs, or tap on them with a hammer while trying to turn the wrench. Or at the least, ask a higher authority for advice. But to me the answer was not so obvious. After all, I'd never even heard of anyone twisting a tire stud off a car before, and here I'd done two of them in five minutes. The chance of it happening again must be equivalent to being struck by lightning three times. Couldn't possibly happen. But of course it did, and now I was confronted by a car whose left rear tire was only held on by two bolts. I now could see that this matter perhaps did merit consultation with Papa, so I went in to explain the situation.

Once again I was informed of the relatively insignificant level of intellect that my maker had bestowed upon me. And to my memory that was the end of the '57 Chevy's road career, since it was replaced by a ten year old Rambler and left to rust through the winter.

This pattern of cars meeting their fate at the end of summer happened fairly often. Take the Dodge van Papa came home with sometime around 1971 or 1972. It was dark blue in color and had the engine sitting between and a little behind the two front seats, so a third passenger with short legs and a strong back could sit between the driver and the passenger on its metal housing. More usefully, in what I'd like to imagine was incredible American engineering ingenuity but more likely was nothing more than ordinary happenstance, you could lift open the engine housing and add oil without getting out of the car – a very welcomed feature indeed in the midst of a freezing rain storm.

The van had a three speed column shift, and the back was totally empty, no seats and nothing on the walls. From an auditory perspective riding in this vehicle was very much like putting one's head inside a metal snare drum as it echoed and amplified every road noise to a deafening roar.

Fall in New England always means leaves dropping from trees by the cubic yard, and at our house it also meant apples without number since right outside the kitchen there were about a dozen apple trees with all different types – not that we knew what these types were, but we knew they were different from each other. Around midsummer the first apples started to ripen and from then on we ate apples and apple by-products until we couldn't stand them. Mama made apple sauce in huge containers and froze it for the winter and she made jelly that she poured into jars and sealed up with paraffin. From July until October, apples were everywhere.

But in late October the trees began to go dormant, and the remaining fruit dropped from their branches by the hundreds and then by the thousands. The lawn was covered with decaying soggy rotting apples, and if we didn't rake them up and take them away they'd ruin the grass for the next year.

The juice in the apples turned to a fine hard cider as they rotted, and this brings to mind the story of Oscar the pig. The reader may remember that Mama was Norwegian, and any Scandinavian worthy of the name who lived in a rural area raised pigs. Pigs were easy to keep. They ate practically anything organic and could be penned in a fairly small area, which I will grant was transformed into a foul smelling sewer in short order, but still, that was a small price to pay for an animal that would grow from a little piglet into a couple hundred pounds of pork chops, pork loin, bacon and ham in the span of a summer.

Oh, and how could I forget to mention the trays of liverwurst and pans of blood pudding? These are the little known dark secrets of pig farming as practiced by northern

Europeans – gut wrenching, gag inducing delicacies that perhaps appealed to a palate deadened by years of eating canned *fiskebolle* four times a week but were never meant to be consumed by God fearing Americans. In the year of Oscar's demise I concluded several fine autumn evenings sitting at the kitchen table and staring with clenched jaws at an untouched plate of blood pudding while waiting for bedtime to relieve me of my sentence. But liverwurst was inescapable. Almost every school lunch bag I ever carried featured one liverwurst sandwich paired with a second peanut butter and jelly combo. Somehow I did get used to that.

But that's jumping to the end. The point was that Mama felt we needed a pig, so we got one. She named it Oscar, which turned out to be a joke whose punchline would become evident to me nearly thirty years later, but in the near term created something of a neighborhood diplomatic crisis.

Down Wardsboro Road around the corner was a little house that squeezed in the tight valley cut by Smith Brook, and the family who lived there was the Wilkinsons. Not that this name was very distinguishing in Newfane where forty percent of the people seemed to be Wilkinsons, but anyway, they were THE Wilkinsons to us, just like the bridge below their house (the one where I sent my trout into the trees) was Wilkinson's bridge. We didn't have that much to do with them since their kids were all a good deal younger than us, but now and then we'd be down there talking about goings on. So I remember shortly after we got our pig I was sitting on the Wilkinson's porch telling Mr. Wilkinson how we'd got this pig. "So what'd you call him?" drawled Mr. Wilkinson in that classic laconic Vermont accent that has always made me suspect that the natives are really escaped Alabamans. "Oscar", I replied brightly. "My mother named him." At this, Mr. Wilkinson fell quiet for a while, and then shortly got up and went in the house without saying any more. Only later did it dawn on me that Mr. Wilkinson's first name was also Oscar. For lesser sins did the Hatfields and McCoys launch their relationship.

This made me wonder what my mother had against Mister Wilkinson that she would name our pig after him. But a few years ago I was reading a biography of the famed Norwegian explorer and scientist Fridtjof Nansen that among other things described how in his later life he had been instrumental in promoting Norway's independence from Sweden. And the Swedish king at the time? No less than Oscar the Third! When it's about Swedes, the Norwegians never forget. And it's quite a thing to have a mother construct a joke that sends her son into spasms of laughter decades after her own funeral. But unfortunately Mister Wilkinson knew less about Swedish kings than I, and I doubt he ever did see the humor.

One fine fall Saturday we went to Brattleboro for our weekly shopping. When we came home, we found that Oscar had determined that the fence around his pen didn't present the same impediment to his current multi-hundred pound physique that it had to his little piglet self back in June, and by the time we arrived he'd been gorging himself on boozy dropped apples long enough to have gone three sheets to the wind. He was staggering around like a Bowery drunk, and if he was unwilling to return to his pen, he also wasn't very capable of putting up substantial resistance. The biggest problem was that he kept falling down, and once down he displayed little inclination to get up unless we gave him a good thrashing with a springy branch that stung his hide. This made him whine and snort in the most ridiculous manner, but we finally got him herded back into the pen, whose walls we stoutly re-enforced in the interest of swine temperance.

We had to do something with all these alcoholic apples, so the usual ritual was that one weekend when most of them had dropped, the whole family would get out and rake them into big piles. We'd then shovel them into our wheelbarrow and cart them to the compost heap. People in cities today know of compost because the Brookstone catalog sells composting units for about the price of eight of Papa's cars, and these composters are capable of reducing the lawn clippings from a thirty square foot yard into mulch that can be put into their window flower boxes. I suppose that on the highest of conceptual levels this is something like our compost heap, but ours was behind the barn and basically we threw everything into it that could be counted on to rot and decay in less than a couple years. This included grass clippings, leaves, all our organic household garbage, cow pies gathered from our field, and especially rotten apples off the lawn. The theory was that eventually it would produce fine, rich soil that could be mixed into the garden. The reality was that the heap grew into a foul smelling mountain that because it was behind the barn was of no concern to us whatever. I don't remember any of it ever being transferred to the garden, and I know I would have rebelled in the strongest terms had I been asked to try to do it.

Those wheelbarrows full of apples were heavy and it was quite a long way to the compost heap, and this led Papa to a bright idea. We'd use his Dodge van to move the apples instead of the wheelbarrow. This concept had the advantage that we could move the equivalent of ten wheelbarrows full of apples in one van load. The efficiency and progress of our modern mechanized world would be demonstrated and the wisdom of his purchase of the Dodge van would be proven as well.

So he drove out across the lawn to where we'd raked up all the apples, about two hundred feet from the driveway. Wanting to maximize the load he could carry, he laid a plank across the back of the van to hold the apples so that they couldn't roll out the door until they were at least a foot deep at the back, and we set to shoveling apples into the van with a will. Soon we had a pile that was probably two feet deep at the center and tapering down to the height of the plank in the back, and we were ready to go unload at the compost heap.

Why it was that so many of our family disasters seemed to end with winter coming on at about quarter to six on a Sunday evening in late October or early November is anyone's guess, but this night was no different. My father got behind the driver's seat and began to execute a three point turn to head to the compost heap. His first move brought the front of the van right up within a couple feet of the trunk of one of the apple trees. The lawn was inclined toward the tree at that point, and the van had mashed a lot of apples into the very wet grass as he moved that way. The van was outfitted with Papa's usual junkyard special tires that cost a dollar fifty and had less value of remaining tread on them. So when he tried to back up, the wheels just spun on slick apples and the van hardly moved, except a little sideways. He tried pulling forward a little more to get a different purchase, but still there was no traction. One more try and the van was almost bumper to trunk with the tree, and the wheels still spun. Paul David and I tried pushing, but our sneakers got no purchase on the wet grass and our efforts were fruitless.

Papa got out and assessed the situation. He was rightly concerned that he was going to spin the back wheels down through the turf and bury them in the soft soil below. By comparison to many other stuck car situations we'd had to deal with over the years, this one was pretty simple. Jack up the car, put a plank under each tire, and we could be out of there in twenty minutes.

But Mama was calling us for dinner, and there wasn't any more we could do today anyway even if we did free up the van, so Papa decided he'd leave it there until tomorrow. In the morning the top few inches of the ground would probably be frozen hard and it wouldn't be so slick anymore, so he could probably just drive the van away like it was on pavement. And even if there wasn't a freeze, he could put planks under the tires in the morning just as well. So we went in and had our dinner, watched a little TV and went to sleep.

The next morning we got up to find that it had unexpectedly snowed about eighteen inches. Everything was buried deep. This meant we weren't going to move the van for a few days, but these November snows never lasted, so we were confident that there'd be a few warm days and by next weekend the van would be free.

But of course this was no ordinary winter, so in a few days we got another snow and the van was even deeper in. And then more snow. And it became apparent that the van wasn't going anywhere until spring.

My father could always resuscitate one of his other disabled vehicles with jumper cables, Hot Start carburetor spray, and the appropriately encouraging language necessary to coax it into an operational state adequate to allow driving to the garage in town where the local mechanics could bandage it to last for a few months, so he wasn't too perturbed by this. Besides, as we had just convincingly demonstrated, the van wasn't the best winter vehicle anyway since it was so light in the back that it could get stuck almost anywhere. So there the van sat for the winter, growing a fine high white hat of snow on its roof and with drifts four feet deep piled against its sidewalls and doors.

Spring came and with it the melt. The reality in Vermont is that there are six seasons, and what the calendar calls spring is really not Vermont spring. Vermont spring is May to June when the air is cool but not humid, and other than small dirty piles under the eaves on the shady north sides of buildings the snow is all gone (except for the oddball fluke storm like the one on June 3 that I remember dropping four inches of snow on us – it was all melted by afternoon, but still, that was uncalled for...), and everything has turned green. After that is summer, when the plants grow like a jungle and the lawn has to be cut every five days or you can't get the mower through it without a superhuman effort and it's hot and humid with thunderstorms in the evening. That's July and August. Then there's early fall. When Labor Day rolls by it's like someone throws a switch. Suddenly it's not humid and the crisp air of the morning lasts all day. It's too cold to even consider swimming, where just last week all you wanted to do was lie soaking in the brook. But it's still green, and the garden is providing all the vegetables that just make it to ripeness in the short Vermont growing season. That's September and maybe the first couple weeks of October.

Next comes the true autumn, where once every five years or so we'd get the right combination of cold, frosty mornings and warm, sunny, and windless days that produce those glorious foliage pictures that lure all the city dwellers up to look around, but usually is abruptly terminated in a howling rain storm at thirty-eight degrees that blows every leaf off the trees and renders the entire state a sullen grey until spring comes around again. That's second week of October through the first week of November.

Then there's hunting season, which goes from the end of true fall until about Christmas time. The leaves are well and truly off the trees, the woods are full of hunters, and only a damn idiot or a person from Stamford, Connecticut would go walking on the dirt roads or in the woods without dressing in brilliant red from head to toe in hopes of avoiding getting a 30-06 shell shot through the back of his head by some drunken hunter from New Jersey who can't tell the difference between a buck and a Buick. The trees are grey, the sky is grey, the weather is cold and damp. You won't see hunting season pictures in the state's travel brochures.

We're not done with the seasons, but this is probably a good time to talk about the place of guns in the Vermont culture of those days. As far as I could tell, the rites of passage dictated that all boys got an air rifle at age six. Once they had demonstrated that they could use it to kill anything that moved and weighed less than six ounces, or when they reached eight years of age, whichever came first, they got a .22 rifle, handy for obliterating any trespassing gray squirrels. At ten they got an over and under shotgun, which had two barrels one above the other. On top was a .22 rifle and below was a twenty gauge shotgun. Ostensibly a weapon for hunting small game like rabbits, this also enabled enterprising boys to clear away most of the birds within a quarter mile of their house. At twelve they got a twelve gauge shotgun – good for potshots at migrating Canadian geese, and at sixteen they got a 30-06 rifle and ascended into the ranks of the deer hunters. I suspect that by thirty they were graduating to tactical nuclear weapons mounted on cruise missiles, but by then I had long left the state, so I can't speak with authority on this point.

I never got into the whole gun thing. In fact, I never even got the air rifle, although Paul David did, and he also got the over and under. I shot them now and then, usually (and wisely) closely supervised. Papa had guns of his own, and while he was not a hunter, he did use them and from what I could see he was a pretty decent shot. I remember early one morning him seeing a woodchuck out in the vegetable garden gorging itself on the hard earned produce, and although Papa never once worked in the garden that I can recall, his blood boiled with righteous indignation at the sight of this vermin eating vegetables intended for *his* dinner. So while I was sitting there eating my bowl of Rice Chex, immersed in reading the back panel of the cereal box and blissfully unaware of my father's murderous intent, he got out his .22 rifle, lowered the kitchen window, took aim, and shot that woodchuck dead to rights. It was another case of two deaths with one bullet, since he simultaneously killed my appetite for the rest of the morning.

One day a long, thin box from Sears Roebuck arrived in the mail. Papa grabbed Paul David and me to watch him open it up, and out came the biggest bolt action rifle I'd ever seen. It was an Army surplus Mauser, a vintage German rifle from the first World War that had been sitting in mothballs in some government warehouse or store-room since the Harding administration. After spending half an hour cleaning and oiling the gun, Papa carried it down behind the barn, fitted a bullet big enough to sink an aircraft carrier into the chamber and slid the bolt into place. He raised its barrel and pointed it at the woods midway up Newfane Hill (where hopefully there was no one hunting at the moment), and squeezed the trigger. This produced, in rapid sequence, a blaze of flame out the barrel, a deafening explosion, and then the most frightful string of foul language from my father. He was routinely capable of truly artistic flights of curses when prompted by fairly benign causes like, say, a tangled extension cord, and he could really raise his game for a more significant event like this one, where he was convinced that his collarbone had been shattered by the recoil of what he now recognized to be a shoulder-mounted cannon.

His injury, overstated though it turned out to be, officially ended any possibility of further use of the Mauser and the rifle was retired to the attic, never to my knowledge to be fired again.

On another occasion, I was asleep early on a Saturday morning, but my slumbers were being disturbed by a woodpecker on the roof. Woodpeckers dig into wood to try to get out beetles and bugs to eat, and this woodpecker somehow got the idea that he could extract his breakfast from the ridgepole of our metal roof. A woodpecker has the ability to drill its target with an incredibly rapid succession of pecks, almost like someone discharging a clip from a Tommy gun in an old mafia movie. This woodpecker fired off five or six bursts in succession, bringing me out of deep sleep into a state of semi consciousness. Down the hall I could hear Papa get up out of his own bed, cursing and swearing at the woodpecker. Then he went clumping downstairs and for a while I didn't hear him anymore.

I should say here that Paul David and I slept in a bedroom tucked up under the pitched roof of our house. The ridgepole where the woodpecker was doing his work was about eight feet above my head – very close. So I could hear him very clearly. Du-du-du-du-du-du-duh! Then a pause. Then another Du-du-du-du-du-du-duh! Pause again. Then Du-du-du-*KA-BLAM!* Silence.

Papa had gone down to the kitchen, grabbed his rifle, headed outside the house and shot the woodpecker stone dead right over my head. A couple minutes later he came back up the stairs, closed his door, and went back to sleep. For myself, I didn't shut my eyes once in the next eighteen hours and it was a week before my bowels began to move again.

The fact that I didn't develop my own private arsenal between the ages of six and sixteen set me apart from most of the other kids in our town. Other kids slaughtered everything that moved and their parents would proudly drive down Wardsboro Road with a dozen squirrel tails streaming out horizontally in the wind from the car aerial to which they were tied. I'd have been happy to bring down something a little bigger and more noble, but the chances of even seeing a bear or a buck were really low and I had no interest in sitting in the cold and damp waiting for such a miracle to happen. To me the most practical use of guns was when the neighbor's cow got loose and was eating vegetables in our garden. Not many things would divert a cow from such a treat, but a few well aimed air rifle pellets in the tender parts right around the base of the tail seemed to be one of them. In such a circumstance a cow can betray a blend of speed and athleticism that the species is rarely given credit for possessing.

But I have digressed. We were discussing Vermont's seasons, and we had just described hunting season. After that there's winter, January to March, which not surprisingly consists of lots of snow and cold – especially the third week of January when the jet stream routinely sends air from the mountains of Ellesmere Island southwards so that in the morning the thermometer often reads twenty below zero or colder. This is not that urban-hardship synthetic twenty below zero wind chill factor stuff the newscasters are always complaining about from their comfortably heated studio news desks, but a real on-the-thermometer twenty below zero. I'll grant that it gets even colder in other parts of the country, but that's for someone else's story.

I always had the theory that once it's less than about ten or fifteen degrees below freezing, the only difference lower temperature causes is that you get cold to the bone faster. The air feels the same – it's dead dry. And there's never any clouds. It won't snow when it's that cold because there's no moisture. Above plus twenty things change and it can snow.

I always liked it best when it was around plus twenty-four because there wasn't much damp in the air, but it wasn't that terribly cold.

That's not to say it couldn't get above freezing in winter in Vermont. It often does and there can be freezing rain or just plain wet rain. But after the front causing the storm passes through the temperature usually plummets below freezing and then everything becomes a mess of frozen ruts and ice crusted snow.

April brings mud season. The snow begins to melt and the first place the resulting water goes is down into the dirt roads in between the snowbanks, with the water often running in steady streams. Cars churn the roadbed into thick mud, and if there has been a heavy melt it can get so deep that the car sits on its chassis with the tires spinning. Getting stuck in mud is a hundred times worse than being stuck in snow or ice. Emancipating a car from mud invariably results in getting completely filthy since at some point the driver is going to hit the throttle while you are behind the car, showering you with mud and dirty water. Often the only way to escape the morass is to jack the car up out of the mud and lay planks down to drive on. Even this can be difficult as attempting to raise the car is just as likely to bury the base of the jack three feet underground while the car sits unmoved with its floorboards sitting on the mud.

It's even worse off the roads maintained by the town. At least the roads have beds that are mostly gravel. Driveways through fields like ours are often formed simply by driving cars repeatedly across the grass, mashing the topsoil into a pair of hard packed tracks for the tires. But with the addition of water the tracks turn into a slurry that could swallow a mastodon. I can recall trying to walk out to the road one day in high rubber boots that came to just below the knee. At each step I'd sink so deep that the mud was within an inch of going over the top of the boot, and the mud held the boots so fast that my stocking foot sometimes pulled out when I tried to take a step, leaving me standing like a stork on one booted foot as I tried to maintain the balance needed to get my other foot back into its boot. When this time of year came around we generally parked our cars right by the road and walked the hundred yards between them and the house, but even then we'd get disastrously stuck at times and might take hours to just get the car to go ten feet from the driveway onto the road.

The point of all this discussion of seasons is to explain why we made no attempt to move the van until mud season ended. By this time it had been sitting with frozen apples on its all-metal floor for four months of fall and winter and then with thawed apples for another six weeks of mud season. Apples are acidic, and when melted, they dissolve metal pretty effectively. So perhaps we should not have been as surprised as we were to find that the floor of the van had a hole eaten through it big enough that a sofa could have fallen through.

I had fond memories of that van. Once Papa took Paul David and me on a rare camping trip to the northern part of the state. The plan for accommodations was that Papa would sleep on a mattress on the floor of the van while my brother and I pitched the allegedly waterproof canvas tent that served as our bedroom on most hot summer nights at home to avoid the stifling heat of the uninsulated second floor of our house. As any seasoned pessimist could have predicted, on our first night out the heavens opened and rain poured in fine biblical style. The tent, made in times prior to today's exotic space age fabrics that weigh less than an aspirin tablet and can be nearly submerged before any moisture appears in the interior, leaked like a sieve and our sleeping bags, made with heavy batten-style insulation wrapped in a cotton outer material, absorbed what seemed like forty gallons of water each. Battering on the doors of the van awoke our father but not his sympathy, and he allowed us to sit upright in the front seats the rest of the night while he continued to doze peacefully on its floor.

I still recall driving down the New Hampshire side of the Connecticut River a little later on that trip and getting pulled over by the state police, not because of anything I had done, but because the van had a temporary cardboard license plate reflective of the fact that Papa had just purchased it from a used car dealer and the metal plates had not yet arrived in the mail. I was fifteen at the time and driving on a learner's permit with Papa in the passenger's seat. I loved driving that van. I liked the three speed column shift for one thing, and I thought I was pretty good with a clutch. Plus it was cool to sit up ahead of the front tires with a steering wheel whose orientation was nearly flat, just like a big bus. But I didn't care for having the cop shine his flashlight in my face, and later when I found that I shouldn't have been driving in New Hampshire on a Vermont learner's permit, I was pretty relieved that he didn't ask to see my license.

But that was last year, and now the van was in trouble. Papa laid a sheet of plywood over the hole to allow continued service in dry weather, but later in the year the engine developed a head gasket problem. Always the mechanic, Papa took the head off with the intent of having it ground flat and replacing the gasket, but that never happened. Instead the top of the block quickly rusted over and the van never ran again. It did provide a handy storage place for some of the more abysmal specimens in Papa's ever expanding rubbish collection.

My current car is a twelve year old vehicle with 135,000 miles on it. Despite its years, the California environment has left the exterior paint and body almost like new. There is a slight patina of corrosion on some of the metal parts resulting from spending time near the ocean. Inside the floor mats are clean enough for a baby to play on, the seat leather is clearly not new but is very nice. The trunk usually has nothing in it, but its floor is clean enough to use as a surface to prepare food.

It would have been difficult to comprehend that, when new, our Vermont cars might have ever been in a state remotely approximating my car of today. The paint was usually so chalky that if you brushed against the car while walking alongside it, there would be a big mark on your clothes where the paint had transferred over. The chrome on bumpers peeled off in big sheets like the bark from a birch tree. The salt that the road crews poured out by the truckload at each storm attacked every bit of metal like a cancer. If a fender had a dime-sized bubble just visible under the paint in September, by April there'd be a hole big enough to stick your head through. You had to be sure your tetanus shots were always up to date if you planned to be around our cars.

Every exposed bolt became coated with rust so thick that just getting a wrench onto its head was a major struggle, and turning it was almost impossible. We used penetrating oil by the quart. Mufflers rusted through and made cars sound like bulldozers, and the only remedy was often to cut the pipes leading in and out of it with a hacksaw and splice new pipes into place, since there was no removing the bolts that attached them to the muffler.

To combat this decay some Vermonters had their car sprayed with oil in the fall. It was a matter for debate whether this actually improved anything. Oil sprayed cars did rust less, but the price was a horribly messy surface of oil and grit that made everything filthy when touched.

Inside the car was as bad. Getting in and out with boots covered in snow, salt and mud made the floor a sandy wet mess that destroyed floor carpets, so everyone had plastic floor mats bought at discount department stores. Through a complete lack of engineering foresight, cars of that era had a switch mounted on the floor where a tap from the left foot toggled between high and low beam lights at night. The switch inevitably corroded into one position.

The trunk was the worst. It was the storage place for all the implements needed to free a stuck car, and when these things were returned after use they inevitably filled the trunk with dirt. Not that the dirt only came from the outside. In the trunk we typically carried buckets full of sand or ash from the coal furnace to provide some friction when on ice, and this was augmented by planks for mud, multiple jacks, tire chains, rugs to lie on while putting on chains or to put under tires for traction, cases of oil, jumper cables, rags, shovels, brooms, scrapers, and anything else that might be needed in a pinch. The trunk was not a place for the fastidious.

There are many other great car traumas to be told, like the short lived '59 Cadillac. In the mid sixties Papa worked a variety of consulting jobs as a draftsman, technical writer, mechanical engineer, or machinist. These were usually in places in Connecticut or New York that were far enough that he would rent a small apartment at which to stay for a week or sometimes a month at a time, and he would only return home on weekends. It wasn't unusual for him to come home really late Friday night, and when we got up in the morning, we'd find a new car in the driveway.

Well, not a *new* car, a *different* car. They were *never* new. They were never even what the marketing departments of used car dealers like to call *gently used. Pre-owned* would have been a most optimistic euphemism. My father's cars had mostly been intercepted just before the paperwork to have them crushed into scrap was completed and press-ganged into one last partial year of service before their automotive death was well and truly certified.

But back to the Cadillac. One Saturday morning Paul David and I woke up to find a three tone green 1959 Cadillac in the yard. This is the one that the Batmobile was based on, with tail fins like a great white shark, each having a pair of red tail lights seemingly designed for intergalactic space travel. Even thirteen years after its manufacture, this car was *cool*. The body was mostly a lime color, but it had trim of forest green and white. It even had detachable covers for the rear wheel wells so that with the covers in place you could only see the bottom third of the back tires.

As usual when another car showed up, we were drafted into the process of wiping it down with rags from Papa's collection. It's hard to convey the level of degradation to which a textile had to sink before my father would relegate it to rag status, qualifying it for use in wiping up paint, grease and oil. Towels in our house were used until they were completely threadbare with gaping holes in them, and since our well water had more minerals in it than any vitamin supplement available without a prescription and we always line dried them, they were typically as soft to the touch as a sheet of exterior grade plywood. Towels on the verge of complete disintegration could join the rag pile. In addition, there were old pairs of underwear and once-white T shirts that each looked like they'd been attacked by flocks of rabid moths. At the upper end of rag quality hierarchy would be pieces cut from worn out sheets. Below that came pieces of towel, with demoted underwear at the bottom. We'd dutifully dig into the rag pile for a sheet piece and wipe down the interior first, then we'd use towels for the exterior, and finally we'd attack the engine with underwear. Invariably, this was the only cleaning the car would ever get while in our possession, but it was a rite of passage that indicated a momentary pride of ownership. The cursing would begin later, although usually not all that much later.

Papa was really proud of this Cadillac. At a price of a hundred and fifty dollars it was truly a machine of luxury. Its styling and class were inarguable, and it had features we'd never dreamed could be within reach of our family. There were power windows, for one thing, and power seats. My heavens, what an invention! Once we had wiped down the car, Papa had to demonstrate these wonders. Up and down went the windows. Just amazing. Next the seats. He ran the front seat all the way forward to where a four foot six woman of eighty-five pounds weight could comfortably reach the accelerator and grasp the steering wheel. Then he pushed the lever to the back position. Nothing. *Nothing!* The seat stayed right where it was, six inches from seat back to steering wheel. It didn't move.

I think I have said that my family has the sort of DNA that produces height. Mama was within a couple sheets of paper of six feet. Johanna reached the same height as an adult. Paul David hit about 6'4", and I topped out at 6'8" by the time I was halfway through college. Papa was 6'6", and he was big, too – weighing over two hundred and fifty pounds at the time of the Cadillac seat incident. With the seat all the way up he had as much chance of getting behind the wheel as he did of getting into the glove box. After some perfunctory hammering and banging on the seat motor accompanied by appropriately colorful language, he disconsolately trudged into the house and called the village garage, whose minions shortly arrived with a tow truck to remove the offending vehicle. Within a few days they had the seat in the maximally extended position, from whence it was never again moved. It was unnecessary for Papa to counsel Paul David and me that touching that seat lever would result in capital punishment. But the bloom was off the rose for the Cadillac. It had betrayed a faith and was never regarded with the same fondness again. When it began losing power because its rings were so worn that the engine compression was inadequate for it to generate any torque, it was relegated to the permanent collection alongside the barn.

So it went for one car after another. There was the 1952 Hudson where an over-weight friend of Papa's had ridden as a passenger and broken the mechanism that held up the seat back. Papa solved that by removing the back seat cushion and propping the passenger seat up with a length of two-by-four. There were a series of Ramblers, which often had the curious design feature of a transmission that was shifted by push buttons on the dashboard – an innovation that the marketing people should have known eliminated the sexy appeal of shifting with a big, powerful lever. The last of our Ramblers also had that new unibody construction, which meant that when the body ultimately and inevitably rusted through, it was able to tear along the passenger floor like a sheet of wet newspaper. As the car went over uneven surfaces, the body flexed and the tear would open a couple inches so you could see through to the pavement. Sometimes when it hit a pothole full of water the splash would come right up into the car.

Then there were the Volkswagens. I swear to god, I'll never drive a Volkswagen for the rest of my life after all the VW disasters we had. This car was very popular with Vermonters in the late sixties and early seventies, partly because they were more fuel efficient than American made cars, but also because with the engine providing weight for better traction above the drive wheels they were not bad in snow. Other Vermonters used to talk about how easy they were to work on, that the engine could be removed by taking out just four bolts. Over time I learned a valuable life lesson from this: never buy a car where part of the sales pitch is how many bolts it takes to remove the engine. This simply is something you never want to need to know.

Our first Volkswagen was one of the old vans, an early sixties model. This is the classic hippy bus with the V-necked front trim and the little oblong windows around the roof line. It was a cool car, no questioning it. But it did its best work when parked, and in motion it had several critical deficiencies. For one thing, it used the same engine as the much smaller Beetle, so it was chronically underpowered; not a good thing for driving in a place where hills are the norm. Moreover, its flat front meant that simple air resistance wouldn't let you exceed about fifty miles an hour even when on the level. Then the engine was air cooled, and the cooling air entered the engine compartment through tiny little slits on the sides of the body. In the summer it would regularly overheat on hills, something that no doubt contributed to shortening the life spans of the engines. Volkswagen engines could be counted on to seize up or throw a rod at the most inconvenient time. When I was in college I remember driving the Beetle then serving as Mama's car to a friend's house outside Boston on a Christmas Eve trip and having it throw a rod on I495 just south of Route 2. First there was a horrible grinding noise that sounded like a big block of ice had broken loose from under the rear wheel well, then all the warning lights on the dashboard came on at once, and the car began to slow down. Pushing the gas pedal down did nothing, and the car rolled to a halt on the shoulder. I turned the key to try to start it again, and the engine spun madly without any sign of spark. This event demonstrated the utility of the four bolt engine mount design, since the local garage could remove the engine and replace it with a re-manufactured one it in relatively short order. But it would have been better engineering to make a car that didn't feel compelled to implode in the first place.

Papa's van threw a rod, too, out on some back road in the middle of Vermont. At the time, he was working for a place in Vergennes that made parts used in the Apollo program. Now my feeling is that if NASA's top management had any idea that parts needed to send man to the moon had been contracted for design and manufacture in Vergennes, Vermont, they would have cancelled the entire space program rather than run the risk. But we used to watch all the Apollo launches on television and take pride in the fact that Papa was in some way a key contributor to the success of each launch.

Or not. The primary thing I remember about those launches is that they rarely took off on time. There was always a countdown for many hours before the launch, and the newscasters would come on with solemn pronouncements like "It's T minus three hours twenty-two minutes and seventeen seconds, and we have just received word from Space Flight Mission Control at Cape Kennedy that NASA engineers have determined that there may be a problem in a valve controlling the secondary lateral thruster fuel mixture. Countdown will be halted while engineers study the problem." Tension would rise until you could cut it with a knife. The Soviets were gaining on us, and this infernal valve was going to make the launch late. Third World peasants would seize on this valve issue as clear evidence of the superiority of the communist way of government, and if something wasn't done immediately then tomorrow morning there'd likely be a framed color photograph of Leonid Brezhnev hanging in our dining room. The situation was obviously critical.

Sometimes the delays lasted days, but more often a few minutes passed and the announcer came back to say that they'd solved the problem. Now that I'm an engineer myself, I realize that I'd rather be damned in hell before they tried to launch me into space on a rocket that had a problem that some budding genius decided had been solved and adequately tested in just a few minutes, but back then it seemed a tribute to American efficiency and know-how.

And of course, on one occasion it turned out that this valve was the piece that Papa's company had provided. It was quite exciting and gratifying to feel that one's own father had the stuff to impede the progress of an entire nation, even if only for half an hour. The whole story reminds me of a quote from Neil Armstrong that I read much later. Apparently a reporter asked him what he thought about as he lifted off into space and Armstrong mused about the sense of awe that struck him when he considered that he was sitting on top of a mechanical wonder costing many hundreds of millions of dollars, assembled from hundreds of thousands of parts, made by hundreds of contractors, and every one of them the low bidder.

Had it been me, I'd have been thanking my stars that Volkswagen wasn't one of those contractors. Which brings us back to my father's van, broken down on a lonely dirt road somewhere between Rutland and Grafton. Or more to the point, it brings us back to my father, who showed up at our house around two in the morning having hitchhiked and walked the rest of the way home.

Upon arriving home after such an ordeal, you or I would collapse in bed and sleep until nine-thirty in the morning when we would awake, have a breakfast of three scrambled eggs and toast accompanied by a sixteen ounce mug of hot cocoa and maybe some pancakes or French toast, read the article in Brattleboro Reformer about the riots in Detroit, and after everything had settled for three hours, start thinking about who we could call to deal with the marooned vehicle while we sat comfortably at home watching re-runs of The Fugitive on afternoon TV. But neither you nor I would ever have owned that Volkswagen van, and you or I surely would not have driven it over that road at that time of night. So in that context, maybe it made sense that my father woke my brother and me from a dead sleep, bundled us into my mother's American made Chevy, a Chevy that required the disconnecting of fifty-three wires and twenty-nine rubber hoses in addition to the removal of forty-seven bolts, eighteen Phillips head screws, twelve slotted screws, and seven compression-fit rivets to extract its engine, and drove us fifty miles back over those same dirt roads at three AM to recover his stricken automobile.

I should interject here that this business of doing things in the coldest, darkest part of the morning seemed to be a favorite past time of Papa's, and it clashed with my own personal bio-rhythms in the worst possible way. When I was young, I woke up slowly and it always seemed like my body couldn't generate any warmth until I'd eaten breakfast. But it wasn't unusual in the winter to be woken in the dark by Papa, who would solemnly inform us that it had snowed two feet and if we didn't start shoveling in the next three minutes, the snow would become so deep that we would never be able to deal with it and we would be trapped in the house until spring, or maybe later. So up we'd get, bundling into our winter gear with Papa grumbling about how slow we were moving and how bad the snow was going to be as a result. Breakfast first was out of the question; the house might be fully buried by the time we were done. So out we'd go, into the dark and cold, shoveling snow with teeth chattering and noses and ears freezing. Usually it would be Paul David and me manning the shovels while Papa swept snow off the cars with his favorite winter implement, a broom. Shoveling a two hundred foot long driveway after a foot and half snowfall is no fun under any circumstances, and under those conditions it was something only a Solzhenitsyn could appreciate. Except we didn't have the benefit of a bowl of cold kashi to start our morning.

Such was my condition when we arrived at the derelict Volkswagen sitting pulled off the road and partly covered by snow. We chained up the Chevy tires, hooked a tow chain to the undercarriage of the VW, and then pulled it all the way home at about fifteen miles an hour, arriving in the morning light. A few months later, with the four bolts exercised to good effect, the van was equipped with a re-built engine and was roadworthy once again. At least to the extent that any of our cars had ever been roadworthy. For in a subsequent episode on the same commute the gearshift lever fell off and my father was reduced to driving home at under ten miles an hour using a screwdriver to shift between neutral and first gear, the only two choices he could make. Shortly after that the van was sent to pasture.

The other joy of Volkswagen ownership was the heating system. Most cars of that vintage provided heat by running the hot engine coolant to a small radiator in the passenger compartment and blowing air over the radiator to transfer the heat. Being air-cooled, Volkswagen needed a different approach, so their engineers made a vent system where the passenger compartment air would circulate close to the engine and pick up its heat. The only problem with this is that after a couple winters in the salty Vermont roads the vents rusted through. By itself, this meant that warm air no longer circulated into the passenger compartment. This wasn't all that good, but it was fairly pleasant in comparison to what subsequently happened when in another year the muffler also rusted through and leaked exhaust into the vents. At twenty years old when I first heard Bruce Springsteen singing about riding through mansions of glory in suicide machines, I couldn't say much about the mansions but I had a good idea exactly the sort of machines he had in mind.

All these cars were a significant bone of contention between Mama and Papa. In those days, many Vermonters appeared to measure their status by the number of Cadillacs they had sitting on concrete blocks out behind the barn.

You'd drive by what had been a thriving farm a half century earlier and there'd be fifty or sixty derelict cars sitting out there. Often the hood would be up, or the trunk lid would be up, and they'd be rusting and sinking into the soil. Papa had pride, and would never have left a door, hood or lid open, but at his peak, he only got us up to nine cars, so he was really of little consequence in the overall scheme of things. Even so, it hit hard at Mama's Norwegian sensibilities for neatness.

The winner of most battles is he that makes most skillful use of allies, and my father hit on a diabolical plan to enlist my brother and me on his side by transferring ownership of one of his cars to each of us. This gave us a stake in keeping the cars, so we'd argue on his side. At fifteen years of age I thus got the 1961 Ford Country Squire station wagon signed over to me, the same one that Paul David had buried in the snowbank during its brief tenure as a road-worthy vehicle. This car had imitation wood paneling on its sides that was applied with something not too dissimilar from wallpaper paste and which was now peeling like sunburnt skin. Complementing the luxurious wood grain was a powder blue paint job whose rakish look was somewhat compromised by having the lower eight inches of the body entirely consumed by orange rust. But it was the most reliable car we had for starting in the cold.

I should say at this point that my father always felt he should hang on to any car that had at least one truly superlative attribute, which they typically all did. The '54 Hudson was the fastest car he ever had. The '64 Ford Falcon was the best looking. The Dodge van carried the most cargo. The '48 Plymouth had the biggest trunk. The '59 Cadillac gave the most comfortable ride. And on and on. When you get a car that's the best at something, you don't let it go easily.

So I had the Country Squire, which was the most reliable cold weather car of all time, and I would proudly start it up on those twenty below zero mornings and use it to jump start the cars that were actually qualified to go out on the road. And around the house I used it to drag big flat rocks up from the brook to build a patio in front of the kitchen, stonework which is still there to this very day, I might add with some (but limited) pride. I'd find a rock in the brook that looked like it might work – preferably something three feet on a side and eight inches thick or so. We had several heavy chains with hooks on either end that were meant for work like hauling logs in the woods. I'd wrap one around the rock and hook it to a string of three other chains so it would reach up the bank of the brook, and then I'd get in the car and drag the rock up out of the brook and across the field. A lot of the times the chain would come off the rock and I'd have to go hook it up again, but eventually I'd get it up the embankment. Once it was in the field it was usually pretty easy to go the rest of the way if you weren't too concerned about tearing the sod up really badly. But given that grass grew back faster than you could ever cut it nobody really cared much about this.

Once I'd unchained a rock in front of the kitchen I'd use one of our iron stakes to pry it into place. It wasn't the flattest patio you've ever seen, but it was good enough that nobody has ever felt it necessary to remove it, either. Not bad for a fifteen year old.

Having finished this project, I concluded that I really needed a vehicle with more utility, like a pickup truck. Now seen in dim light and at sufficient distance, a station wagon does appear to have some of the properties of a pickup truck, except for the annoying roof over the back part of it. I thought about this for a while and then I hit on a solution, which was of course to remove the roof. So one summer morning I got out my hacksaw and some other tools, and went to work. The interior trim for most cars of that era was held in place by zillions of Phillips head screws, so I spent about two hours removing screws until my hands were all blistered, but eventually I had popped out all the glass and had the interior behind the driver's seat down to bare metal. I then used the hacksaw to cut the roof supports off at the level of the sidewalls. Next I used an electric skill saw fitted with a metal cutting blade to cut across the roof right behind the driver's seat. Voila! Instant pick-up truck!

Next I decided that I needed to spiff up the paint job. The only paint available was the red paint we used on the house, so, not bothering even to wash down the existing surface, I got a gallon of this and painted the car with a four inch paint brush. This didn't achieve quite the level of gloss I was looking for, but the rust didn't show so badly anymore and overall I thought it was an improvement.

When Papa came home that weekend I think he must have recognized that what I had done was inevitable collateral damage from his particular form of familial warfare since he didn't thrash me as I might have expected. Perhaps he even felt a little pride in the resourcefulness I'd demonstrated. I don't know. But I do know that I was required to park the car well out of sight behind the barn thereafter.

I might add that in Vermont in those days registration didn't stay with a car. You could register a car and if you bought another one, you could transfer the registration to the new one on payment of a fee of ten dollars or so. Since it took a while to get the registration papers from the Motor Vehicle department, they had a provision giving a grace period when you decided to use a previously unregistered car on the road. So my father would often have one registration for all his cars but he'd have the transfer papers for all the unregistered cars all written out and ready to go. If he got pulled over driving a car that wasn't actually registered, he'd pop the papers and his ten dollars in the mail right away and transfer the registration legitimately. But if he didn't get caught, and he almost never did, he saw no need to waste the money needed to have multiple cars properly registered.

Papa was always on the edge of the motor vehicle laws. I'll never forget going for my driver's license test using my father's Ford Falcon on my sixteenth birthday. I passed the written test and then went out for the driving part of the exam, where I was accompanied by one of Brattleboro's police officers doing extra duty as the test proctor in a moment of boredom. I was a conservative driver and I did well on the whole test until we got to the end, where I was asked to parallel park facing upwards on a steep hill. I backed the car neatly into the space, cramped the wheels against the curb, put the car in first gear and shut it off, feeling confident that I had nailed the test.

But the officer wasn't finished with me. "Start it up and straighten the wheels", he said. "And leave the car in neutral and set the parking brake". Well, there was a reason I hadn't set the parking brake, which was that we had never in my memory had a car where the parking brake actually worked. The road salt always rusted the brake cable up, so that for one thing the brake could never be set enough to hold the car, and secondly, it often couldn't be released if you did manage to set it. We were under strict orders never to use the parking brake as a result.

But this was an officer of the law telling me to do it, so I did, holding my foot firmly on the footbrake during the operation. "Take your foot off the brake", said the officer. I explained to the officer that if I did this, the car would roll down the hill, and the officer then explained to me that state law required a working handbrake, wrote me a ticket for defective equipment, and informed me that I had failed the test.

When I told Papa what had happened, his reaction was that this was typical of what happened when he tried to do something nice for someone, that now he was going to have to spend seventy-five dollars to get his hand brake fixed, and that this would be the last time he'd let anyone use his car to try to get a driver's license. I ultimately passed the test using the Benson's Volkswagen a month or so later.

Papa seemed to take an almost perverse enjoyment in being able to manage his derelict fleet through the meteorological vagaries of winter. Extreme cold was his special forte. Whenever the weather map showed a high pressure system coming towards us from Canada, he'd be outside wiring up strings of extension cords across the snowbanks to power an assortment of accessories. Heated dipsticks would be heating the oil, battery chargers would be charging the batteries, and jumper cables would be, well, not jumping, but at the ready in case they needed to. He'd even stick a lit hundred watt light bulb next to the engine block if it was going to be really cold. To slow the dissipation of engine heat he'd fetch a stack of Coolidge-era quilts from the barn and spread them across the hood, and he'd put a sheet of cardboard in front of the radiator behind the grill. Anything to keep the heat in. Then he'd set an alarm to wake himself up every three hours throughout the night, and he'd go clumping down the stairs and out the door to start each car and let it run for five minutes, allowing the engine to warm up enough that in the next three hour interval it wouldn't get as cold as the air around it.

But there was a lot more to winter than getting a car to start. At times it seemed like most of what happened in everyday life in Vermont was either preparation for winter, dealing with it as it happened, or getting over it once it was done. Winter was the very essence of life in Vermont.

8 THE WEATHER OUTSIDE IS FRIGHTFUL

Winter almost always arrived in fits and starts. The first snow might come in late September or it might come in early January. Through November a given day could be warm enough for shirt sleeves, or we might have a raw damp cold that found its way through every piece of clothing and gnawed at our bones, or we might get a dry Arctic spell of cold that stung our ears and nose and made our toes ache.

Blue skies were not the norm by any means. Even without precipitation there was usually a leaden gray canopy overhead. A November day might begin the morning warm and blue, but around two o'clock wispy streaks of white would begin to appear high in the sky and they'd get thicker and thicker until the once comforting sun was nothing more than a pallid white disc behind the clouds. As the sky thickened and turned purple, temperatures would slide towards freezing, and in the night a wet snow would fall.

Many of these fall storms started with powdery snow flakes that gradually fell thicker and heavier, becoming wetter as the storm intensified. Wet snow is sticky and it would cling to every branch of every plant. When morning came the weather might turn to freezing rain, and then the snow already on the trees would act like a sponge and hold every droplet that touched it. The cover of frosting gave the scene out of our windows the appearance of a fairytale world, but the weight of the supersaturated snow would crush garden plants to the ground, and pines would sag like tired old men under the load. Softer trees like birches would bend in big parabolas, and the trunks of some would splinter under the load. On bigger trees with harder, less flexible wood, big branches would shear off and fall.

Trees were everywhere, and the power company had no choice but to thread electric lines through a maze of branches. When limbs fell or sagged they tore wires from poles and sent houses into darkness and cold. If this happened in the middle of the night, the first hint of a problem might be that you'd wake from a deep sleep because you were colder than normal. A few minutes of groggy contemplation about the contradiction that it was cold but there was no sound from the furnace blower running would bring understanding. Then, if he was home, eventually you'd hear Papa get up and make his way downstairs. A couple minutes later an ungodly racket would penetrate upwards as he shook down the ashes from nine months back when the coal furnace had last seen service, and you'd hear the scraping of a shovel on the stone floor and the rattle of coal being heaved into the firebox. It was comforting, but it would be at least an hour before the slightest warmth from that source would penetrate upstairs. In the meantime, you'd have to curl into a smaller ball, pull the quilt tighter over your head until you were nearly suffocating from re-breathing your own air, and hope you could fall back to sleep quickly.

In the summer the bedroom I shared with Paul David was oven-hot while in the winter it was like an igloo. I suppose you could say that the average temperature was quite comfortable, though we would not have appreciated this application of mathematics. Situated on the northeast side of the house, our room stopped getting any sun after noon and had plenty of time to cool off by nightfall. It had a single four paned window that faced north, and as elsewhere in our house, this was augmented by a removable storm window that we put up in the fall and removed in the spring. Having the storm window meant that there were two panes of glass between us and the elements, but even so, the room was often cold enough that the condensation from our breathing turned to thick frost on the glass of the inside panes. We dealt with this by wearing flannel pajamas and sleeping under eider down Norwegian quilts that weighed enough to make it a struggle just to roll over.

The first year we were in Vermont, whenever it snowed we'd clear the driveway by shoveling as has been described earlier. There was no possibility of plowing the old roadbed because trees and vegetation grew too close on either side, and if there isn't a lot of room to push the snow for the first snowfalls, the snowbanks get too high and too close to plow later in the year. But shoveling was a lot of work, since the driveway was not short. The worst was when you finally got up to Grout Road, since the passage of the town snowplow would push a pile of hard packed snow four feet deep into the mouth of our driveway and it could take almost as much work to clear that away as was needed for all the rest of the job.

After that first winter my parents realized that we had to do something different so they began to drive down the middle of the field on the other side of the house to create a new driveway. This approach left lots of room for a plow to pile snow. Clearing driveways was one of the many kinds of seasonal jobs that people would do in Vermont, and it was no trouble finding a local fellow with a truck and plow to do our driveway. It was a learning experience for both parties. You didn't just show up with a plow, drive down the driveway a couple times, and then go home to celebrate. You had to have a plan that took into account where you were going to leave the snow when you came to the end of each pass, and you had to think about what that meant you could do in the next storm, and the storm after that. If you hesitated and

142

gave up momentum with a big pile of snow ahead of the plow, you probably couldn't get it moving again so it would be left right where the doubt hit you.

Usually when the first storm came the driveway through the field would be plowed so wide that three cars could pass side by side. And at the end of the driveway the snow would be pushed up onto the lawn almost into the apple trees. You'd think they were plowing out a Walmart parking lot. But by late February Mama and Papa would be fretting that if we got another snow storm it wouldn't be possible to plow because the driveway had narrowed so much. Sometimes in heavy winters we'd have to hire someone with a bulldozer to push the snowbanks further back into the field, an expensive operation that we wanted to avoid if at all possible.

At the end of the driveway there would be snowbanks six feet high and sometimes they'd extend thirty feet back from the plowed area. As kids we'd tunnel into these like a pack of moles and make a warren of igloo-like caves and interconnecting passages, burrowing away until the melted snow seeping into our clothing turned us nearly purple from cold and we had to go back to the house to avoid hypothermia. Along with the heaps of snow that accumulated at the base of north-facing roofs, these snowbanks would almost always help us remember winter until they were the last snow to melt well into May. The melting process inevitably revealed six months accumulation of dirt, leaves, lost mittens, and reconstituted frozen dog poop, which upon thawing instantly provided the same gratifying odor it had exuded on the day of its conception.

There weren't very many times when the first storm of the year didn't leave Papa fuming over the plowing contractor's lack of foresight. If the first snow came before the ground was frozen, the plow would scrape the sod up in big curls like the peel of a navel orange and deposit it in the snowbank, and Papa would rant that they were setting the plow's blade too low. Or they'd plow the snow right up to the barn door, making it impossible to get in or out without a major trenching operation. They wouldn't plow the driveway wide enough, so that we'd have to pay a fortune for a bulldozer later in the year. Or they plowed too wide and ruined all the grass. Getting it right wasn't easy. Might not have even been possible.

Despite contracting out the driveway plowing there was still plenty of shovel work for us to do. There were paths to the barns and to all the various doors to clear away, and a lot of these were in places where the plow dumped big piles of snow that we had to dig through. Both barns had doors that were under the eaves and when the snow inevitably fell off the roof it would bury the path in a crunchy mass of broken icicles and hard packed snow that took hard work to clear away.

But the big shoveling event was clearing off the roofs of the house and the barn. In years when snowfall was light, or if there were warm spells that melted a lot of it down, we might not have to do this. But most years we had to clear the roofs at least once and in extreme cases it might take two times. Having some snow on the house roof wasn't bad since it served as an insulator on cold nights and helped keep the house warmer. But Vermont's back roads were littered with old barns and houses whose roofs had collapsed from the weight of snow. Because it broke into a mass of interconnected splinters of beams, rafters and roof boards, a collapsed roof was a nightmare to try to repair, and when a barn fell in the owner often couldn't afford to do anything about it. Once the insides of the barn were exposed to the elements, it didn't take much more than a decade or two for it to decay into a pile of rotting wood overgrown with small trees weaving their roots among the wreckage. Our property had already experienced that on a small scale with both our henhouse and our icehouse.

The flat roof of our kitchen was an invitation to disaster. The snow from two sides of the second story would slide off the steeply pitched and slick surfaced metal roofs onto the tar papered kitchen roof and sit there. On days where the

144

temperature was in the twenties, the roof was warm enough over the kitchen to start to melt the snow there, but the last four feet of the roof was over a porch with no heat under it, so any water would often re-freeze there, forming a dam of ice. Water backing up from that dam could get under the overlapped pieces of tar paper and leak into the kitchen. So the kitchen roof always got a lot of shoveling every year to keep it clear. Often there'd be a ladder leaning against the roof all winter long so we could get up and shovel at a moment's notice.

The snow from any roof formed a big pile under the eaves below, and in more than one year there was so much snow in front of the kitchen that the height of the pile reached to within a foot or two of the roof. On those occasions we'd take an aluminum flying saucer sled and go up to the ridgepole at the very peak of the house. Teetering at the pinnacle, the death defying rider would quickly pull his legs onto the flying saucer, grip the canvas handles for all he was worth and go ripping down the steeply pitched second floor roof, out across the kitchen, and, flying through the air across the gap above the snow pile, terminate by crashing face first into the embankment left by the snowplow on the other side of the driveway. The entire journey took less than three seconds, but it was as exhilarating as any amusement park ride and as soon as we cleaned the snow out of our ears and nose we'd scramble back up the ladder to do it again.

When it came to shoveling off roofs, the gray barn separated the men from the boys. Its metal roofing had a rusted surface textured like sandpaper and it really held the snow. Its eaves were a full two stories above the ground, and its ridgepole was three stories high. On its west side, the foundation was nearly four feet above the ground, so sitting on the ridgepole at that end of the barn was an experience that would awaken any latent tendencies to acrophobia.

To clear a roof like this, you'd start at a side of the barn that ran at right angles to the ridgepole. You'd lean a ladder against the wall at the lowest part of the roof and climb up carrying a broad bladed snow shovel. The snow might be three or four feet deep, and you'd use the flat blade of the shovel to make two vertical cuts in it, one parallel to the ridgepole and one at right angles, in much the way you'd use a flat spatula to cut a piece of lasagna in a baking pan. Then you'd slide the shovel underneath the cube of snow you'd just marked off and pry up. This would typically break its contact with the roof and it would then roll off and crash in ruins below the eaves. Then you'd climb down, move the ladder three feet towards the ridgepole, climb up and cut another serving loose, and keep repeating the process until you reached the ridgepole.

At this point you would have cleared a section of roof about three feet wide running from the eaves to the ridgepole. Next comes a tricky part. You'd move the ladder you had just been working with around to the same side as the eaves and just below the cleared section, and you'd lean a second ladder against the wall right next to you. This second ladder had a hook at the top of it designed to grab onto the ridgepole. You'd climb up the first ladder until your belt was even with the roof. Then you'd lift the second ladder, which in the particular case we are discussing was a very old single-piece ladder made of heavy wood, and slide it up the cleared section of roof until you got the hook over the ridgepole where it now formed a sort of staircase to the peak of the roof. You'd shake it a bit to be confident that it had a good hold on the ridgepole, and thus assured, you'd step off the first ladder onto the second.

Now you'd resume cutting lasagna, two cuts with the shovel, pry the block loose from the roof, and let it roll off. Move up a rung, two cuts, pry, roll off. When you reached the ridgepole and finished the row, you'd work your way back down to the eaves, scraping loose any snow that had stayed behind to make a smooth place to put the ladder for the next row. Then you'd go back to the ridgepole where, standing with one foot on the north side of the roof and the other on the south side, you'd move the ladder over to the area you'd just cleared, go back down to the bottom, and resume work on another row. This would repcat until you'd gone all the way across the roof and cleared everything, at which point you'd drag the ladder back to the side where you started, climb down to the eaves, and scramble onto the first ladder that was still leaning against the wall. You'd lift the second ladder off the ridgepole, slide it down the roof and lean it against the wall next to you, climb down to the ground, put everything away, and go in the house to have hot chocolate, congratulating yourself on a job well done.

That was the process viewed from a purely academic perspective. But the particular day we are discussing included a deviation from the ideal. I was sixteen at the time, and about half way through the job. Since I was away from the scary end of the barn, where a fall would be a significant event, I was relaxing a little. There was a *lot* of snow on the roof, and the pile of cleared snow under the eaves that my effort was creating was truly impressive. I finished cutting the sixth or seventh row, cleaned it up, and moved the ladder along the ridgepole. I went down to the bottom, cut loose a couple blocks, and rolled them off. I moved up, and all of a sudden I heard a loud rushing sound and could see the heaps of snow in front of me racing past. The rest of the snow was sliding off the roof! Half my job was going to be done for me and I'd be indoors warming up in no time. Life was *good*.

It's funny how when something really bad is happening everything seems to slow down and you have time to notice all sorts of trivial details that you'd have thought would have been just a distraction. I distinctly remember that feeling of satisfaction that the job was complete. But just as clearly, I remember the annoyance that came with the recognition that the snow was sliding up the roof, and not down. That certainly wasn't expected, nor was it right. And then suddenly it dawned on me that the snow wasn't moving at all. It was me and the ladder I was standing on, and we were sliding down the roof together, and if I didn't do something *right now*, I was going to land on the ground two stories below entangled in the rungs of this damned ladder and likely would break both my legs.

At the last moment where there was any chance to have a surface to push on I stepped off the moving ladder onto the very lip of the roof and was able to get just enough purchase to jump away from the ladder towards the huge pile I'd been forming. Down from the two story height I plummeted feet first, embedding myself all the way up to my armpits in close packed snow.

With muscles slack in the aftermath of the adrenalin rush, I struggled to escape from the grip of the snow and finally worked my way free. I was plastered with snow from head to foot, so I stood aside and brushed myself off while my nerves settled a bit.

The ladder I'd been standing on a moment earlier was lying in the snow a few feet away. I looked at it to see what had happened. At first I expected that the ridgepole hook had come detached from the ladder and let it go, but the hook was still tightly fastened in place as it should be. What had actually happened was that I hadn't cleared the surface properly before I'd moved the ladder over the last time, and there had been a block of ice under the ladder about halfway down its length. When I stood on the lower part of the ladder, this ice had acted as a fulcrum so that after a little jiggling from my walking, the hook had finally popped off the ridgepole and let us both go.

And so with rubbery legs I dragged the ladder back into place and completed the job, applying an attention to detail rarely witnessed in the barn roof clearing business.

Although sledding had been a big deal before I'd become a teenager, by the time I'd graduated to clearing the barn roof I'd long outgrown it. But sledding was an art in itself, and you had to have the right sled for the snow conditions. These varied hugely depending on recent weather and the choice of sledding run. So we had an accumulation of toboggans, flying saucers and Flexible Flyer-styled runner sleds to suit the circumstances.

Right after a storm when the plow had been down Grout Road but the salt and sand truck hadn't, the conditions were great for a run from Grout Pond down to the house on a runner sled. This entailed walking the better part of a mile to the crest of the hill, but the rush of the long run that you got in return could be well worth it. You'd lie on the sled on your belly facing down the hill with legs dangling behind. To slow down you'd drag the toes of your boots behind you, but usually you'd ride with legs bent up to avoid this – after all, the whole object was speed. You'd grip the steering handle, which allowed you to flex the runners a little to the left or right and provided something approximating steering. Most of the job was up to gravity.

The downhill run from the pond began with a really steep stretch of about seventy-five yards. You'd lose a little speed as the road flattened where a small stream ran down from the right and through a culvert under the road. The road bent left, and a hundred feet past the culvert there was another steep section followed by a longer flattening and another curve. Then came the main event, a really long steep run down to the Fifty Cent Bridge where you got some serious speed and the cold wind in your face would burn your cheeks like fire. After the bridge was a flat stretch and a short uphill. If the snow was good, your runners didn't have much rust on them, and you had dared to not to drag your feet at all even when reaching top speeds so that the sled could go for all it was worth, you might make it over this uphill part with enough momentum to continue the rest of the way, but more usually you had to get off and walk a hundred feet or so. From there on the slope was enough to keep you moving but not to give you the rush of the upper part of the road.

Grout Road is narrow at the best of times, and if you meet a car while driving, each car has to make a good effort to get far to the side in order to get by. In the winter it was far worse since the snowbanks at the sides covered a good deal of the road surface. There were a few wide spots where meeting cars could still squeeze past each other, but in a year with heavy snow there were long stretches where only one car and maybe a pedestrian or two could fit between the banks. Fortunately there wasn't a huge amount of traffic, but there was no guarantee of not meeting a car on one of these sled runs. When that happened, the strategy, such as it was, was simply to crash into the snowbank on the side of the road. To execute this maneuver you'd steer at the bank and then just before impact you'd stick your hands out in front of you so that your face didn't have to take the full crash impact. Usually the sled would stop first and you'd go sliding off it and bury the upper part of your body in the snow. The impact would push your sleeves up past your elbows and the icy compacted snow in the bank would scrape your forearms raw. If the snowfall hadn't been heavy you'd penetrate into older snow that was really crusted and loaded with road salt, and then all the cuts would sting like mad.

And if you were really flying, you'd come off the sled enough that your pants would act as a big scoop and snow would end up packing itself down inside your underwear. That would wake you up!

You had to be ready to go to catch that window between plowing and salting. Newfane's road crews were incredible at clearing the roads. If snow was falling they'd be out all night, and no matter how hard it came down it was a rare thing for any road in the township to have more than a few inches of snow accumulate before the plow came through. I can only remember one time when we couldn't get down to the village, and that was a huge snowstorm accompanied by a howling wind that made the snow drift so deep across Wardsboro Road that it took bucket loaders to clear it away and we missed a day of school. Although they'd cancel classes for a bad ice storm at times, the plowing was so thorough that missing school for snow was almost unheard of. But the normal pattern was to see a plow go by every hour or so, and when we'd go off to school in the morning we might have to wade through two feet of unplowed snow in our driveway to get to the road, but once there everything was clear.

A toboggan was the best choice when the snow was fresh and powdery and you couldn't sled in the road, but you needed a steep hill to make the first few runs in uncompressed snow possible. The best place for this was McPherson's hill behind the Benson's house. This hill was in the bottom third of a very long field that stretched nearly a quarter mile up to where the McPherson's horse barn sat overlooking our valley. The upper part of this field was also on a slope, but it was nothing like the precipitous drop of the lower hill. The horses had apparently learned that coming up the lower hill was hard work, so they spent most of their time up above. The McPherson's themselves were near-mythical beings, heard of but never actually seen in the flesh. But we made good use of their hill.

Wading through deep, loose snow to the top of a steep hill while dragging a wooden two man toboggan is hard work, and even on a bitter cold day you'd arrive at the top panting and overheated. Paul David and I would sometimes try to share the load and drag it together, and other times we'd take turns hauling it singlehandedly. Much of the time I tried to con him into taking my turn, and although I'm sure he saw right through it, he'd usually oblige. The first run was always a disappointment, since the toboggan would be plowing and compacting the snow and didn't pick up the kind of speed you'd expect in return for the effort of climbing the hill.

On the way back up it was tempting to walk where we'd just sledded down since the footing was better, but the point was to make a good trail for the toboggan and putting big boot holes in it was counterproductive. So instead we'd work on mashing down a walking path for climbing up, and we'd keep taking the toboggan down the same run, widening it and extending it.

After a few runs the speed was starting to get exhilarating and now it was time to begin thinking about constructing jumps so we could get some air. Getting a good jump going was an invariable objective of any off road sledding venture and we'd usually deliberately choose the run to go over the top of a woodchuck hole to facilitate this. In the winter the woodchucks were hibernating, but in the summer they dug into the hillside and kicked all the dirt out of their house onto the downhill side of its entry. The resulting mound was a good start for a jump, and when enough snow was piled on it we could eventually get airborne.

Of course having taken our first taste of air we wanted more, and pretty soon we'd have built a massive mound and we'd go hurtling over it and soar for many feet before landing. Steering control isn't a major feature of a toboggan, and sooner or later we'd hit the jump a little off to the side, and the toboggan would land partly off the trail, tipping over, smashing us together in a heap, and dumping us into the loose snow, which penetrated every seam in our clothing, going up our sleeves, down our necks, into our waistlines, and down our boots. While it was well designed for pushing through soft snow, the curved front of the toboggan wasn't the greatest thing for a crash, and the poor passenger in the front usually gave his folded up legs a good bruising upon impact.

Sometimes we'd get freezing rain that made a layer of crust on the snow so hard that you could walk on it. In these cases McPherson's hill was usually nearly impossible to climb – imagine walking uphill on a hockey rink tilted at thirty degrees and you have some idea – and instead we'd go to the Muller's fields on the other side of Grout Road from our own place. The Muller's field had a gentler slope, but at the bottom was a small stream with a number of trees growing next to it. The stream had little enough water so that in places the snow went right across it, but there were also openings into the water. This meant that directional control was an important element of sledding here if you planned to stay dry.

If the surface was really hard you could use a runner sled, but you had to be careful. The crust might be quite solid out in the open, but under overhanging tree branches or in places where the tips of hay below might protrude above the level of the snow, the surface could be much weaker. If you came flying down a crusted hill on a runner sled and hit one of these soft areas, the runners would cut through and the sled would stop almost instantly. But you the rider would not: you'd shoot right off the sled and continue careening along on your stomach with no control whatever until your progress was halted by, depending on your fortune, (a) crashing into a tree, (b) sliding into the stream and getting a good soaking, or, in the best of circumstances, (c) gradually losing your speed and coming to a halt on the flat part at the bottom of the hill.

Usually we were smart enough to sled in the fields where the opportunities for collision were more limited, but I remember one time going up into the woods on Newfane Hill with Paul David on the idea that we'd sled down the logging road. At one point my sled got away from me and went crashing away out of sight among the trees down below us. After a little discussion, we decided to leave the trail and try to follow my sled's trajectory on the crust between the trees. Since we now had just the one sled for the two of us, Paul David lay down on it and I lay on top of him. My weight was enough that he could barely move his arms to steer, and he was grunting and snorting just to draw a breath, while I was laughing so hard at all the sounds he was emitting that I could hardly stay balanced on top. The hill was pretty steep, so he dragged his feet for all he was worth to keep us from gaining too much speed.

And for the most part he was successful, but when you hit a pine tree trunk square on, limited speed is still too much speed, and we went sliding headfirst into the trunk, cutting up our faces and smacking our heads. As much as it was painful it was also so ludicrous that we sat for a while simultaneously moaning in pain and laughing while trying to rub the pine pitch off our skin.

More often when the snow had a layer of crust we'd use flying saucers. These were completely lacking in steering other than what could be obtained by leaning left or right, but they distributed weight enough that puncturing the crust was much less of a hazard. The biggest irritant with a flying saucer was associated with jumps. You'd go soaring through the air and lose hold of one of the handles, and the saucer would come out from under you. Then you'd land on the crust with your backside. If the crust didn't break this was no big deal, but if it did, the effect was like falling posterior first through a pane of glass while moving parallel with the plane. It felt like your entire sitting faculties had just been sliced off. To add insult to injury, on impact you'd almost always lose hold of the flying saucer and it would continue the rest of the way down the hill, coming to a stop much further away than it would have gone had your weight been on it. You'd then have to trudge haltingly down to retrieve it, moaning in agony and rubbing your damaged rear end at each step to ease the pain. But of course, none of this changed your approach on the next run, except maybe you held the hand grip just a little tighter as you took to the air.

Not everything in the snow was about thrill seeking. Building snow forts was another major activity. It was best when the snow was standing several feet deep in the field and there had been a mixture of snowfalls and freezing rain. With these conditions we could use a flat snow shovel to cut blocks out of the snow and use them to build walls almost like a mason working with cinder blocks. A room could be made by cutting blocks down to the level of the turf and piling them up. A wall that stood four feet high outside the room became a seven foot wall on the inside, where the floor was the bare ground. At times we'd make large multi-room structures with a maze of interconnected rooms. Then we'd hunker down inside and imagine that we were defending the Alamo against Santa Ana.

Although our town had no ski areas itself, Newfane wasn't far from two of the more prominent Southern Vermont resorts in Mount Snow and Stratton. Despite their geographic proximity, with their luxury lodging and fancy restaurants these places were a world away from where we lived and the rare times we visited them were almost always in the summer. During my childhood I only once skied at a commercial ski area, and that was on a school sponsored ski day where for something like a quarter we got to go to the rickety Maple Valley in Dummerston. The non-subsidized price of lift tickets was simply out of reach for most Vermont residents.

That's not to say we didn't ski. After all, Mama was Norwegian, and Norwegians begin cross country skiing practically before the doctor cuts the umbilical cord. Even today if you board almost any T-bane train in central Oslo on a winter weekend you'll feel that you are the only person without skis. Everyone else is going to the end of the line where they'll strap on their bindings and disappear out into the countryside.

Such spontaneous ski outings were more difficult in Newfane, but that didn't mean they didn't happen. We just had to wait for the right circumstances; good snow, a nice day, and a small enough slate of guests to care for that there was a little time to be away from the house.

Our equipment was never great. It made no sense for our parents to buy anything expensive when they knew that next year we'd be grown out of it. So we'd have the cheapest boots, and some years we wouldn't have proper ski boots at all so we'd have to jury rig the bindings to hold a regular pair of boots in place. When we got older and skied for greater distances we started having somewhat better gear, but there wasn't ever a significant ski outing where I didn't spend the last half of it in an agony of frozen toes that were clamped too tightly or with blistered heels from boots that were too loose. And our skis were heavy hardwood affairs from an earlier time, so you got a serious workout from them.

But that still didn't stop us from getting out after a good snow. Everything we did with sleds when we were younger we did with skis later. Especially jumping on McPherson's hill. Skis gave us much better control than toboggans, and we'd side step up the hill after each run down to pack down larger and larger areas. We'd make a slalom course from the few trees on the hill and use our poles to fill out the gaps, swerving down the course with empty hands. At the bottom we'd use a stone wall at the side of the hill for the best jump we'd had yet. Jumping in cross country skis with the heel unattached isn't the smartest thing a kid could do, and there were many times when a jump ended in a high speed face first crash into the snow that left us feeling our limbs to make sure nothing was broken, or rubbing our heads where the back of our own ski had managed to give us a good whack.

By the time we were in high school cross country skiing was beginning to gain popularity in Southern Vermont. One winter Mama entered us all in a cross country ski race that turned out to be a total fiasco. Several hundred racers, most of them from elsewhere, lined up at the top of a broad sloping pasture in Putney. The starting horn blew and everyone tore off madly down the hill for the other side, where the course passed from the field through a wagon-width opening in a stone wall and onto a forest logging road wide enough for two skiers. Thirty seconds after the starting horn the entire race roster was packed around the opening in the wall like pigs at feeding time, where we waited for about fifteen minutes for our turn to pass onto the trail.

Under the trees the chaos continued unrelenting. The trail had two parallel tracks packed by the previous skiers. A racer could go outside the tracks, but he'd find himself in a thicket of uncleared brush or deep powder snow that cut his speed by two thirds. Novice skiers fell left and right off to the side of the trail, and there were few gaps in the oncoming skiers to allow the casualties to get back in line. So they'd do what they'd have done in their cars in Boston and just jump out into traffic. Sometimes this worked, but often it resulted in a chain reaction collision with five or ten skiers going down in a heap of bodies, skies and poles. Sorting that situation out was, of course, even worse than getting one downed skier to step into line. The skiers behind the crash would have to come to a stop and wait until the carnage was back on its feet before they could go again. And like traffic on a freeway, the stoppage would ripple back up the line, forcing other skiers to stop for no reason that was apparent to them.

I had the bad luck to be at the forefront of one of these collisions. At one point the course passed down a steep hill, and with a trail of two deep tracks heading straight ahead it wasn't possible to control speed by turning. Skiers nervous from the velocity would panic and fall, and then they'd be faced with getting back into the fast moving line. The smart ones stayed off the track and worked their way to the bottom of the hill, but not everyone had that patience. Up ahead I could see a woman casualty on the left side finish up with brushing snow off herself and glance over her shoulder up the hill. I was flying towards her at about twenty miles an hour thinking *there's no way she's really going to step onto the track, is there?* And sure enough, there was a way and she did. I tried to dodge around her but ended up having my left ski go right between her legs. Fortunately the heavily quilted ski clothing from that era made marvelous padding and the collision wasn't too bad, but having the guy behind me ski over both of us and collapse onto the heap didn't help. After that I lost count of the number of additional participants in our pile of wreckage and focused on getting myself out of the way and collecting up my poles, skis, mittens and hat.

So my one experience in organized ski racing was about as enjoyable as driving in Los Angeles rush hour traffic, and as far as one could possibly get from the relaxing feeling of solitude that we were used to getting when we went skiing on our own. Never after that did I have the least desire to participate in anything even so simple as a 10k run.

Most of our property was on the north facing slope of Newfane Hill, and it contained a section that we called the Six Acre Lot. This part of the hill wasn't so steep as the rest of it and it had been open pasture as late as the 1930s. At the top of the lot were two gigantic pine trees, by far the biggest trees on the hill and easily recognized as landmarks from the valley below. Seedlings dispersed from these two trees over the years had populated the entire Six Acre Lot below, and during our childhood it was a uniform thicket of dense pine, unlike the rest of the forest which was a mix of oaks, maples, birches, and alders. These pines grew so closely that the lower branches eventually died from lack of light. Walking through these trees was like passing a gauntlet as the dead branches would whip your face and claw at your arms, cutting you into a pulp of scratches.

One winter Mama decided that what was missing in the Six Acre Lot was order, and that Paul David and me were just the two to provide it. So we had to climb up the hill from the house every day after school and saw dead branches off the trees. The old road to the abandoned town on the hilltop went through the lot, and its course left a small gap where the pines didn't grow as well. We dragged all the branches we cut to this gap and made giant heaps of them. Whenever it would rain we'd have a burning day and make huge fires among the trees. We'd start them up with a little newspaper and once that got going we'd throw a few cups of kerosene on the flame. Pretty soon there'd be a roaring fire so hot that the rain made no impact on it, and we'd drag more and more dead branches to keep it going.

By keeping at this for several weeks we managed to clean up the trees over a significant part of the lot. But in the spring when the snow melted we discovered a shortcoming in the plans. The snow had been standing about three feet deep during the time we did all this work, and when it melted away in the spring the trees stood with a thicket of dead branches from the ground to an adult's waistline. Above that was nice and clear up to ten feet off the ground, but this only meant that the branches didn't whip you in the face as you passed. It was still a mess. The logical solution would have been to cut the rest of the branches after the snow was gone, but in spring and summer other tasks always had higher priorities, and to my knowledge it was never done.

The Six Acre Lot was the source of most of our Christmas trees. It would never have crossed our minds to pay money for a tree. The usual scenario was that a couple weeks before

Christmas, Mama would ask Paul David and me to go up in the woods and cut one. After protracted groaning about the unfairness of this demand, we'd grab a saw and a hatchet and go plunging through the snow up the hill in search of a suitable candidate. We weren't all that particular in our selection, and some years when we couldn't find a small tree that met even our lowest of standards we'd cut down something twenty feet tall, saw off the top six feet of it, and leave the rest behind. Environmental consciousness would come later in life, but in the meantime we'd drag our tree down the hill to the house, where we'd knock the snow and ice off it to the best of our abilities and haul it into the living room to set up. Rarely were these trees the symmetrical, well groomed wonders that people have come to expect at Christmas, but they worked for us.

I suppose we enjoyed Christmas as much as everyone else does. Although I didn't appreciate it at the time, our mother was really incredible at cooking and baking for the holidays. She made all kinds of traditional Norwegian cakes, cookies and candies and there were huge multi-course meals. We celebrated Christmas in two phases. In Norway presents are opened on Christmas Eve, because Christmas morning was reserved for attending church. We'd honor the first half of this tradition by opening all the gifts that came from Mama's family the night before. All our aunts and cousins were fabulous knitters and we'd have package after package of handmade woolen sweaters, hats, scarves, mittens and socks all made with artistic and intricate Scandinavian graphic designs. As might be expected from kids at our age, despite the fact that they would become critical to our outdoor comfort the rest of the winter, these fine presents interested us about as much as oatmeal for breakfast. But then there'd be Norwegian chocolates, and that would perk us up a good deal.

Christmas morning was American style, with the focus on toys and sports gear. When we'd finished tearing everything apart, we'd have breakfast and if it was nice out Mama would always try to get us to go skiing if there was good snow or for a walk if not. We of course reacted as though this demand was an act of supreme cruelty. Now if I go back for Christmas I know exactly how she felt, and I always want to get out on Christmas and walk up to Grout Pond or beyond.

Spring would eventually come, but winter let go as it had arrived, in fits and starts. The first signs would be in late March. The dirt began to show through the hard packed snow on Grout Road. The sump pump in the basement started running, trying in vain to keep the floor from flooding. Mud season came, and in the flower beds daffodils would start to bloom. Water ran down the road in big rivulets looking for an opening in the snowbank where it could escape. We'd build dams out of snow on the road that backed up lakes many inches deep behind them, and eventually a car would come along and burst the dam, causing a minor flood below.

Winter's last foothold was always in the mounds of snow on the north sides of the house and barn where the snow from the roofs had formed big piles during January and February, and the shade from the buildings would slow the melting process so that it wasn't unusual for there to still be a heap of dirty, icy snow in those places well into May. Then the apple trees would begin to bloom, the grass would start to grow, and before you knew it, summer was upon us.

And summer meant it was time for baseball.

9 THE HITCHHIKER'S GUIDE TO BASEBALL

Given that eighteen players are supposedly needed to fill out two teams, one might think it unlikely that baseball would be the game of choice for Paul David and me. But it was. We were fanatical about it from even before the days when the Boston Red Sox first captured our attention. As soon as we were old enough to muster the coordination needed to make a bat contact a ball we were out playing hardball in the field every evening we could.

The routine started in the spring as soon as it became warm enough to hold a bat bare handed. We'd be out on Grout Road playing a game called Five Hundred. The way this worked was that one of us (us being Paul David and me and the two Benson boys) would take a bat, toss the ball up and hit a fungo to the others, who were all lined up in the road a hundred or so feet away. The first kid to shout "I got it" got to field it and throw it back into the hitter. If he caught it in the air, he got a hundred points, a catch on one bounce was seventy-five, two bounces fifty, and anything else that was still moving was twenty-five. If you muffed the chance you got nothing. The first to five hundred points became the new hitter, which was what everyone wanted to do.

Of course, hitting fungos with the intent that they will land a hundred plus feet away in between two snowbanks separated by only fifteen feet of roadbed requires a degree of skill, and there were many balls that landed well out in the snow. A ball covered with the icy, crystallized snow of spring was a painful thing to throw with a bare hand, tending to tear away at your fingertips. A dose of sandy mud picked up from the road surface and added to the ice didn't improve this. And even when the ball landed where there was no snow, it might very well come down with a splash in a big muddy puddle and shower the would-be fielder with dirty water.

Then there was the hitting part. Hitting a baseball when the temperature is about thirty-five degrees is murder on the hands, stinging like an attack of bees on fingers. We had never even heard of batting gloves, and if we had been told about them we would have laughed hysterically at the idea that anyone could be such a sissy as to want to wear them. We swung the bat until our hands were as leathery as the pads on a dog's foot, and if the bat stung a little, well, that was March baseball in Vermont.

Three or four weeks after the road cleared enough to play five hundred, the field in front of our house would open up to the point where we could shift our games there. At the start of spring, the grass would be matted flat and slippery as the devil from the wetness. Because the ground a foot down was still frozen solid, snow melt that couldn't find a way to run off was unable to seep into the water table, so it tended to just pool on the surface. This was a hellish mess on which to play a game of real baseball, and we usually continued our games of five hundred until things got a little drier and we could play actual games.

With apologies to those who don't know the rules of real baseball that were the starting point for our games, the way it worked was as follows. The team in the field had two players; a pitcher and a fielder. With all of fair territory to cover single-handedly the fielder only rarely got to actually catch anything. Most of his job was to chase down the ball as fast as he could and get it back into the infield.

A batter couldn't draw a walk and couldn't even reach first by being hit by a pitch, and he could decline to swing at an infinite number of pitches with no consequences. If he swung and missed at three pitches before putting the ball in play, he was out on strikes. Alternatively he might reach base by a hit or an error, or be out by a fielding play. Stolen bases were not allowed, and the runner couldn't leave the base until the ball was hit.

A key rule was that when a runner was on base, there was a force situation in effect at any base ahead of the runner. This meant that when the second batter hit the ball, if the fielder could get it back to the pitcher to touch home before the runner could get there, the runner would be out with no tag required.

These rules made a catcher unnecessary. We built a backstop made of chicken wire behind the hitter to stop pitches that weren't hit, and the hitter threw any pitch that went past him back to the pitcher

This method of playing produced surprisingly balanced games until we reached our teens, and then the field became too small for us. We used to hit from the road towards our house, but as we became older, we started knocking out windows now and then. The parentally imposed penalty for breaking a window was that we had to measure the opening for the broken pane, buy the glass at the hardware store in Brattleboro out of our own money, and replace and re-glaze the broken pane ourselves.

So we reversed the field and hit from a point alongside our house towards the road. The difficulty with this orientation was that the right field line reached the embankment for the brook about forty feet past first base. If all of us had hit right handed, this probably wouldn't have mattered too much, but I turned out to be the odd duck in this.

When I first began playing baseball, I grabbed the bat and held it in a way that seemed natural to me and hit from the right side of the plate, but as it happened I had my hand grip upside down from what right handed hitters normally do. When I reached seventh grade and began to play for our school team, the coach (who was also our teacher) told me that either I had to switch my hands around, or I should hit left handed since that would make my current grip be the right way to hold the bat. Hitting left handed proved the more comfortable option, and also different from what everybody else did, which was appealing, so I went that way. But this was a nuisance for our games at home since it meant the most natural direction for me to hit put the ball into the brook or lost it in the underbrush lining the shores.

This is not to say that right handers wouldn't put the odd ball in the brook now and then as well. It's just that a lefty would be inclined to do it most of the time. And this was a big problem in spring with the brook at full flood filling its bed from side to side with a roaring current. When the ball went in the water a breakneck race along the shore line ensued, with all four of us thrashing through branches and thorns trying to keep the ball within eyesight while finding a stick that could reach it and pull it close to shore at a place where we could get our hand on it without falling in and getting soaked with icy cold water. Sometimes we'd run two or three hundred yards along the side of the brook before retrieving the ball. Only rarely did it ever completely escape us.

A baseball was of incredible value to us and risking drowning was a perfectly acceptable option if we were likely to retrieve the ball as a byproduct of the effort. The life of our baseballs was a full and complete one. At the start, they were beautiful white objects with bright red stitching. But in the first day of use the ball would be marred by a number of green grass stains and as time passed the accumulation of these stains caused its color to mature to dark brown with a greenish tint. Then the stitching would begin to fray and eventually a seam would start to split open. A bit of the leather cover would start to flap loose and as the piece of partially detached leather got bigger, the ball would go flying off the bat making a strange flapping noise like a Canadian goose winging south for the winter. When the loose cover began making the ball difficult to throw, we'd peel it off completely. Inside was a tightly wound ball of string surrounding a little rubberized core. Each new hit caused the ball to go off the bat like a comet trailing an unraveling strand, and in the process making the ball a little smaller each time. To slow down this process we'd wrap the ball with black electrician's tape, but this didn't last long and persistent string loss was inevitable. Eventually only the golfball-sized core was left. Although it was too small to use for a baseball game, this core was amazingly springy and sooner or later one of us would be unable to resist the temptation to hit a fungo that carried it out of sight over the barns or into the trees and that would be its end.

If a batted ball didn't go into the water, it could still be incredibly hard to find. The bushes around the brook were thick and dense, and later in the year when the water was lower and the brook bed exposed, the ball could easily hit a rock and carom in a random direction without our having a chance to see it happen. We learned from early on that when the ball was hit towards a place where it could be lost that we had to follow its flight intently and remember exactly where it penetrated the undergrowth, since this would greatly decrease the time needed to find it. Many times we'd search for fifteen or twenty minutes before we found the ball, but we were relentless about it and it would take extraordinary circumstances for us to give a ball up for lost.

On hot summer days we'd finish the washing up after dinner and go out to play baseball in the relative cool of the evening. We'd play until the sun went down and then on until it was so dark that every fly ball was a menace to the safety of the outfielder. As the evening air cooled, the black flies would come out and drive us to distraction. You might be just ready to throw a pitch or to swing the bat, and a black fly would go right up your nose. They'd be in clouds swarming around your head and they'd crawl behind your ears and bite the sensitive skin there. If you had outfield duty you'd inevitably be out there waving your glove around like a signal corps officer with a semaphore flag to try to ward off these pests. As dusk came, barn swallows would come out and begin diving and darting all around us, getting their fill of bugs, but still never taking enough to help us out. And just before it got so dark that we had to quit, bats (the flying mammals, that is) would join in the fray.

Bats were fun to watch in flight. They were incredibly maneuverable, using their sonar to track flying bugs. At times we'd have the house windows open with no screens, and a bat would fly through the opening chasing a bug attracted by the light. The bat would then be in our living room, darting around with Mama and Johanna shrieking in terror and Paul David and me trying to catch it. The first time this happened we tried knocking it out of the air by swinging towels at it, but the bat easily dodged these. Then Papa got the bright idea of using a fly swatter under the theory that the sonar wouldn't reflect off the wire mesh very well. He was right, and in just a couple swings he swatted the bat onto the floor where it lay momentarily stunned. We then swept it into a cleaned out mayonnaise jar so we could look at it for a while before letting it go outside. Close up these things were pretty scary, and you can see how their faces must have been inspiration for the satanic gargoyles on the facade of Notre Dame Cathedral in Paris.

When we got to high school age, we stopped our two on two games with the Bensons, but Paul David and I still hit batting practice for hours on end. We built a good, sturdy backstop of heavy fence wire that caught all but the wildest of wild pitches and foulest of foul tips, and we'd follow a routine where the hitter batted until he had a combination of ten hits and strikeouts, with all strikeouts being on swings. The pitcher was motivated to go hard on the hitter because he had to chase down any ball that was hit, so strikeouts were strongly preferred, and failing that, poorly hit dribblers on the ground that wouldn't leave the infield were the second choice.

It can be imagined that our field was not Fenway Park. Until the whole field got incorporated into the lawn system, we generally would mow the infield. But the grass was still long by the standards of most baseball fields, and the outfield was usually hay that was a foot to eighteen inches tall and very thick. A ball hit into the outfield would typically bounce once and then come to rest in some tussock of grass, and it usually took a little looking around to find it.

We didn't have a true pitchers mound, but we did have a section of two by four pine spiked into the ground for a rubber. Home plate was another piece of wood cut into the traditional shape.

I'm not sure if this was true for Paul David, but I always harbored dreams that one day a Red Sox scout was going to drive by our house while on vacation and on seeing me hurling bullets passed my opponent would issue me a contract on the spot. As a result, I threw every pitch with extra meaning. Neither of us had any idea how to throw a curve ball, but we had read about how pitchers were supposed to snap their wrist or use some unusual grip to get motion on the ball, and so of course I threw the ball every crazy way I could imagine in the hope of coming up with something that would send Harmon Killebrew back to the bench shaking his head and muttering curses to himself once I got called up to the bigs. As might be expected, all these different deliveries and grips did very little for my control, and my poor brother was the recipient of a huge number of welts and bruises from the assortment of wild pitches I hurled either behind him or at his head.

As we got older, we got better and began to hit the ball farther. In 1971, Ted Williams became manager of the Washington Senators and wrote a book called *The Science Of Hitting* whose allure was so great that it actually convinced me to spend my hard earned lawn mowing money for a copy. I studied this artifact like it was the Dead Sea Scrolls. I was convinced that if I could only master the principles in this book that I'd be hitting them out of Fenway in a couple years.

And it did make me better. For one thing, it taught me how to hit the ball up the middle, so there was more time spent hitting and less spent looking for the ball down by the brook. But the book nearly caused a death in the family, so maybe it wasn't such a good thing.

It happened like this. I was probably sixteen by this point, a senior in high school. Like a lot of sixteen year olds, I was having trouble relating to my parents and they clearly were having every bit as much difficulty figuring out what sort of animal they had fostered, too. One day my father and I had one of those rare arguments that instead of ending with us both walking away fuming, led to him trying to understand why I thought my situation was so much more onerous than what my friends went through. My line of argument went something like: "My friends' parents are interested in what they want to do and they do things with them. They play baseball with them." This of course was completely forgetting that most kids of the time were born when their parents were in their twenties, whereas Papa was fifty when I was born and was now over sixty-five. If he had ever had an interest in baseball, he'd presumably lost it when Cy Young retired. But I shamed him into agreeing to go out and pitch batting practice to me. His one condition was that we had to use a softball instead of the hardball we always used. Fortunately I agreed.

So out to the mound went my dad. I should say that at this point I was well over six feet tall and although I was skinny as a rail, I was pretty strong, and I hit baseballs like a machine. I stepped up to the plate with a closed stance, bat held completely vertical, hands at what would have been the letters if I had been wearing a shirt at all, and concentrating on hitting line drives as Ted Williams would have wanted. Papa threw the first pitch – underhand – and I brought the bat around with all my strength, hitting the ball squarely out on the fat part of the bat. It was just like the Splendid

Splinter planned it, head down, eye on the ball, legs, hips, shoulders and wrists each contributing their share of the force needed to maximize bat speed at the moment of impact, perfect follow-through, all combining to produce a screaming line drive that would have gone three hundred feet into dead centerfield without every getting more than six feet off the ground if it hadn't hit my father square in the middle of his forehead.

Instantly he collapsed in a heap as though an assassin had shot him. I still remember thinking, "Oh, damn, I've killed my father. This is going to be inconvenient." I ran out to the mound and found him still breathing, so I helped him to a sitting position. His forehead had a huge red welt, and I could see the imprint of the seams of the ball embedded in his skin. He sat dazed for a minute, and then I helped him to his feet. He walked slowly and silently back to the house while I gathered up the bat, ball, and gloves. He never did pitch batting practice again.

Of course, Papa wasn't the only one in the family to suffer for our baseball. Johanna used to come out, and being envious of the fun Paul David and I were having with our hitting, she'd want to take a few swings. Being eight years younger than Paul David, she was less accepting of being hit by my wild pitches, and she failed to see the humor when the ball hit the part of the backstop that was right above a wasps nest and made bees swarm out around the hitter.

Then there was the time we almost gave Mama a heart attack. In one of the rare opportunities she had to take a break from the bed and breakfast work between tourist seasons, she would sometimes sit out on the lawn behind the house on a folding lounge chair, and she'd set out a tray table to have a glass of iced tea or cold water. Meanwhile we were on the other side of the house hammering pitches to the far corners of the field. I took a particularly big swing at one of Paul David's nastier offerings and hit a towering foul ball that went up over the roof of the house and landed right on the tray table, making a sound like a baking tin being hit by a hammer and spilling tea everywhere, frightening Mama half to death. She came roaring around the house and forbade us to play baseball until further notice. I still remember thinking how unreasonable she was.

Mostly we used baseballs that we bought at the discount department store in Brattleboro for ninety-nine cents. These were meant for American Legion or Little League games and they were considerably below the standards of Major League baseballs. After a little use they'd get knocked out of shape, and some of them would get quite oblong after several weeks use. But we'd keep hitting them,

At the department store we used to stare longingly at the official Major League balls. We wondered what it would be like to hit such a ball. But these cost $4.95, about five times what our normal ball cost. It was nearly a fortune. We couldn't imagine that anyone could afford such a thing.

But then came the day that our desire got the better of us and we bought one. Held in the hand it didn't feel that much different, but it was an artifact of immense religious and cultural significance to us. We were hesitant to even play catch with it, since one of us might miss it and let the ball get a grass stain on its virgin white surface. But over a span of a few weeks, we did play catch with it, and then inevitably it did get a little dirty. Now the bloom was off the rose, and it was only a matter of time until we would subject it to the ultimate indignity and hit it with a bat.

From the batting cage to Grout Road was probably between two hundred and two hundred fifty feet, with the shortest distance being to what in a real ball park would be the power alley in left-center field. Across the road was the Benson's house, which was set back another seventy-five feet or so. It was a rare thing for us to hit one of those dead ninety-nine cent balls to the road, even after a few bounces. Of course the length of the grass kept the ball from going very much beyond where it first landed. I can't recall which of us had the first swings at our new major league ball, but I definitely remember the result. The ball hit the clapboards of the Benson's house right between its two second story windows, well over three hundred feet away. We were completely stunned. It was an Alamagordo-like moment: "I have become the destroyer of worlds!" We had found the key that unlocked the door to Ruth-like power. But it was a power to great for us to wield. Use it and we would send everything on the Benson's property to ruins. Windows, cars, gardens - nothing would be spared destruction.

So with a wisdom that our previous history had never hinted we might possess we put our Major League baseball away and went back to our ninety-nine cent projectiles.

When we reached high school age our baseball related activities only intensified. Neither Paul David or I played much in the way of organized high school sports. Mama and Papa had no interest in it and didn't encourage us to pursue it.

We'd have liked to play sports with our high school teams, and I did play soccer for a couple of seasons, but the transportation situation for baseball was prohibitive. There never had been a late bus for students who participated in after-hours activities, but after my freshman year taking that Dover bus, getting to and from school required hitch-hiking at all times. Paul David and I would get up on our own at six AM, eat a bowl of oatmeal or some scrambled eggs and toast, grab our books and the liverwurst and ketchup sandwiches we'd made for lunch the previous night and left in the refrigerator, and we'd get out on Wardsboro Road by six-thirty to catch a ride with Mr. Swenson or whoever else would be driving down the road to work. If we were lucky we caught a ride with someone going to Brattleboro, but if not we'd be dropped in a place like the covered bridge in Dummerston where we had to find a second ride the rest of the way. And if we were too late getting out on the road, we'd have to walk the two miles to Route 30 in Newfane before getting a chance for a ride.

The high school was on the south side of Brattleboro and Route 30 came in from the north. Most often our ride would drop us somewhere in the middle of Brattleboro, a pretty much un-hitchable mile from the high school, so we'd have to walk that stretch almost every day. And this all happened whether it was raining or snowing or twenty below zero.

Getting home was better in some ways since it usually wasn't as cold going home as it was getting to school in the morning. On the other hand, we usually knew the people who picked us up in the morning and had their schedules figured out, but the afternoon was the luck of the draw. Very often we'd be in the open bed in the back of someone's pickup truck. Usually we'd sit on the side wall of the bed and get blasted by the wind, which was nice on hot days but bitter cold in the winter. Now and then there'd be a dog in the back, and if it was a German Shepherd he'd look at us with deeply psychotic eyes as if considering which of us to tear apart first. On such occasions we'd try to seem as inanimate as possible to avoid attracting attention. Other times it would be riding in the cab with a construction worker who was already into the fourth can of the six pack of Budweiser he'd bought after leaving his job, and with a rifle rack right behind us featuring a .22, a shotgun and a 30-06 deer rifle so he'd be prepared for whatever was in season that happened to come near the road. And when we got dropped off in the village of Newfane, having to walk the two miles out our road to home was pretty common.

Of course, it wasn't always wonderful for the driver who picked us up either. If it was raining, they'd get a soaking wet mess of teenager dripping all over their interior. One particularly memorable hitch home happened after a trip to the orthodontist. My teeth weren't the most well organized when I was a kid, and Mama decided I needed a bit of cosmetic dentistry. The initial assessment was that I had too many teeth for the size of my mouth and some would have to come out. So one day after school I walked to the orthodontist office in the middle of Brattleboro and had all four of my second bicuspids pulled out. Having completed his handiwork, the dentist stuck a cotton roll into each of the gaps and sent me on my way. I then staggered down to my usual spot at the start of Route 30 and stuck out my thumb, my face slack from Novocain, puffed up from a mouth full of cotton rolls, and a crust of blood around my lips. Of course, the woman stopping to give me a ride couldn't notice any of this until it was too late and I was in the seat next to her.

"Where are you heading?", she asked.

"Vewfaf", I replied brightly.

"What?"

"Vewfaf!"

"Are you OK? What's the matter?"

"I haff fuf teef puff"

That terminated the conversation and we completed the trip in silence.

The funny thing is, people tell similar stories about this sort of experience now and it seems like a pathetically horrible situation for an unfortunate but persevering child. But it never felt like that to us at the time. It was just how things were and there was no more point in being unhappy about it than worrying about the sun setting in the evening. Expectations change with the times, I suppose.

As I became older hitch hiking gave a great sense of freedom. I couldn't afford a car and had someone given me one, I couldn't pay for the gas to go anywhere, but I could hitch hike anywhere I wanted to go. In my later high school years and into college, I thumbed rides all over Vermont and the more rural parts of New England, and when in college I hitched to places as far away as Philadelphia. One year I went to spend winter break with Paul David, who was going to the University of Vermont in Burlington while I was at the University of Massachusetts in Amherst. On the morning I was due to return I got up to be on the road at sunrise to allow the maximum possible daylight to cover the two hundred mile trip. It was thirty below zero and the wind was screaming across Lake Champlain and blasting through campus – the coldest weather I've ever experienced. Since most people had the sense to stay indoors there was almost no traffic, and I was shivering so hard I couldn't stay standing in one place on the side of the road. But the drivers were really sympathetic and would go out of their way to take me further than they actually intended to go.

Most of the rides were mundane, but a few stood out. On one really cold day a Honda N600 with four people already in it pulled over to give me a lift. This was the first automobile from Honda imported into the US around 1972, and it was so small that you could just about put one in the glove box of today's Mini-Cooper. Folding 80 inches of me into that vehicle was quite challenging even without the other passengers. As it was three of them crushed themselves into the back and I sat in the front passenger seat which was slid forward as far as I could let it. The car was designed so that the gear shift lever came out of the center of the dashboard, and in high gear the end of it wanted to be roughly where the ball of my left hip needed to be. Perhaps feeling a bit uncomfortable at how far into my personal space he needed to go to move the lever, the driver asked me to do the shifting, and being out on I91 in this death trap while struggling to get it into fourth gear so we could attain as much as half the speed of the surrounding trucks helped focus the mind to a much greater degree than the clouds of marijuana smoke swirling around us all would have normally allowed.

In my last year of high school the math department got a teletype connection to a time sharing computer at Dartmouth College. I would bet that this computer had less processing power than my electric toothbrush has today (and it shared it among the entire student body of the college), but I was quickly addicted to programming. I found that I could get much more done if I did my work in Dartmouth's computing facility where I wasn't constrained by the 75 bit per second connection speed we had from the high school, so sometimes on weekends I'd hitch the seventy odd miles along the Connecticut River to Hanover and park myself behind a terminal for the day.

I was hitching back home after one of these sessions when a big stretched Ford van pulled over to give me a lift. It was stuffed with a class of college students returning from a field trip in parts north to their campus in western Massachusetts. The van had four rows of seats behind the professor, who was driving, but each row was crammed tight with four students across. The only place I could sit was in the middle on the metal engine cowling. This is a miserably uncomfortable place to be in most circumstances, but today it turned out to be the best seat in the cabin.

It was the last week of August and the day was sweltering like sub-Saharan Africa. Each side of the van had a row of square windows that could be popped out at the bottom and all were pushed as far out as possible so that the air roared through and among everyone. Even so the guys all had shirts off and the women were down to tank tops.

On the floor behind the driver's seat was one emptied case of beer and another that was half way gone, and everyone was partaking freely. After a few miles, the guy sitting against the left side of the van in the row of seats directly facing me began asking the professor to pull over so he could heed the call of nature. The good educator was having none of it – he just wanted to get the trip over, so he instead drove faster. The student rocked back and forth in his seat, fighting for mastery. Suddenly he brightened, reached for an empty bottle, and in one continuous motion unzipped his jeans and began to fill it.

His short-lived pleasure at this solution soon turned to an even blacker despair when he realized two truths. The first is that the bladder of a young adult male has a carrying capacity substantially in excess of an empty twelve fluid ounce beer bottle. The second is that this emptying business is a process that is substantially harder to stop than it is to not start in the first place. For those with an unsympathetic sense of humor, the young man's look of anguish was now almost comical. But this fellow wasn't in college without the requisite intellectual qualifications, and in no time flat he recognized

175

that he needed to empty his container. Reaching his arm out the pop-out window he held the bottle as far below the opening as he could and began to pour it out. But his care was in vain, as the contents merely blew upwards and right into the window behind him, simultaneously drenching all his shrieking fellow students and winning him his school's *Least Likely To Get A Date* award without opposition for the next four years running. I thought I was going to tear a muscle in my rib cage holding back the howls of laughter that were trying in every way possible to escape my mouth. Had I not succeeded the other passengers would have been fully justified in dismembering me and leaving the pieces in a garbage bag among the trees by the southbound off ramp at Weathersfield. It really is a good thing that it's no longer legal to have open alcoholic beverages in a vehicle.

Despite the freedom it gave, having to hitch rides did make after school activities really difficult. With the unpredictability of ride timing we needed something like an hour and a half from leaving school to be sure to make it home before dark, and in the short days of winter and early spring, this precluded sports. So high school baseball was out, but that didn't stop us from playing some pretty good games in the summertime. I suppose if there is something called "organized baseball", what we played was the opposite: "disorganized baseball". We'd get on the phone (I say "we" but this was more due to Paul David than me) and call around to all the other kids in Newfane who we knew had an interest in playing, and then we'd find someone over in Dummerston who could get together a team from their town. We'd rope the local minister into being the umpire, since no one was going to get too out of hand in front of a man of the cloth, and we'd choose one of the local grade school fields to play on. We'd drag some lawnmowers down to the field and cut the grass (all of this without getting permission from anybody), and Saturday afternoon it was *Play Ball!* These games were terrific fun for us – games where you played by the real rules. You could steal bases, there were called balls

176

and strikes, and people playing all the defensive positions so that there was a real challenge to hitting. When we started this I played third base, and I like to think I was a decent enough fielder, but by the time I was a senior I had grown to 6'6" and was too tall to get down for hot grounders if I had to dive. So I tried pitching, but I was pretty one dimensional. I threw reasonably hard, but still couldn't throw a curve. The one breaking pitch I did learn was a spitball, which I got away with mainly because the minister probably couldn't believe that a kid in our town would try such a thing.

When I wasn't pitching I'd play some first base and some outfield. I tried catching one game when our usual catcher couldn't come. I always thought the catcher's gear was really cool – especially the mitt. So I was really excited about the chance to give it a try. Within one batter excitement had turned to a mixture of humiliation and stark fear. First, I couldn't scrunch myself up behind the plate enough to deal with low pitches unless I knelt on the ground. Second, every time the batter swung, I simply could not resist closing my eyes, and this had a predictable effect on the number of pitches that went sailing past me to the backstop. Since I was kneeling it took me twice as long to get the ball after a miss as it should have, so any runner on first base could pretty well expect to get to third on the next pitch and score on the subsequent one. I yielded the position to a teammate after one inning and never caught again.

The local supermarket used to give out S&H Green Stamps, which Mama had collected for a few years, but lost interest in. When I found out that the redemption catalog had baseball gear, I started collecting the stamps she was going to throw out and I used them to get two really nice thirty-five inch ash bats made by Adirondack. I still have them, but they've absorbed enough moisture to nearly double their weight and they'd be impossible to use today (at least this is what I tell myself to avoid accepting the alternative explanation – that from my years of sitting behind a desk I now only have half the strength today that I did as a teenager). I loved those bats and I felt like I was already all-star material when I hit with them. Bats and gloves were a big deal to us. Early on we mostly had Hillerich and Bradley bats, but I got to like Adirondack best. There were no aluminum bats in those days, so when we hit you'd hear that nice satisfying *crack!* of wood on horsehide, not the cheesy *ding* of aluminum that everyone knows today.

If an inordinate amount of our time was spent playing baseball, we might have consumed even more listening to broadcasts of the Boston Red Sox games on the radio. Outside of New England everyone who follows sports hears about how the Red Sox are religion to their fans, and that was certainly true for us. I first became aware of them in 1967 when they had their miracle year and went to the World Series after being the last place team the year before. But the year we became truly addicted was 1969, and the reason for our habit really stems from the fact that Mama upgraded her little green bakelite Motorola kitchen radio with a nicer one that also received FM and had a built in clock. She gave the green radio to us, and it opened whole new worlds. We'd lie up in our bedroom and listen to Kasey Kasem's American Top Forty radio from WNEW in New York as it faded in and out, or we'd tune in to the Red Sox games in the summer and the Bruins hockey in the winter. Ken Coleman and Ned Martin were the two announcers for the Red Sox, and we were so familiar with them that they seemed like uncles who lived too far away to visit but whom we talked to on the phone all the time.

Home games were easy, since they came on at seven o'clock and were usually done at nine-thirty, but the real test was when the game was played on the west coast at Anaheim, Oakland, or against the new Seattle Mariners team, which had just started that year. These games began as late as ten-thirty at night, and it was not unusual to be woken out of a sound sleep at one AM by Ned Martin, who was letting us know in an excited voice that Reggie Jackson or Joe Rudi had just ended the game with a home run off whatever useless retread of a relief pitcher our team had found itself depending on to protect a tie or a slim lead at the end of the game.

The long experience Paul David and I have in following our team since those days has made us both realize the importance of pitching, but at the time we couldn't understand how our heroes could possibly be twenty-three games behind the Baltimore Orioles. Our hitting was the equal of anybody's. We had Carl Yastrzemski, who'd won the Triple Crown in 1967 and the batting title in 1968 and was on his way to forty homers in 1969, even with half the city of Boston raining boos on him every time he came up for reasons we couldn't comprehend. We had Rico Petrocelli, also on his way to forty home runs, a ridiculous amount for a shortstop of that era. We had Reggie Smith, fast as lightning and one of the best young center fielders of the day. We had Tony Conigliaro, returning from a whole season away after his horrible beaning by Jack Hamilton in 1967 and hitting thirty-five homers. Slick fielding George Scott played third base and added more power. How could such a team be beat?

Of course, when your one-two pitching punch is Ray Culp and Sonny Seibert, life is likely to be difficult, and it was for our Sox. But it didn't matter that they needed a radio telescope to see first place, they were still our heroes and we listened to every minute of every game, sitting through two hour rain delays and hanging on every word as Martin and Coleman told us stories of the old days when giants like Williams, Mantle and DiMaggio roamed the earth.

Baseball on television was a different experience for us. When the Boston stations could be received at all, we could get NBC, which carried the baseball game of the week with Curt Gowdy announcing. Gowdy was an authoritative figure who seemed part of the very fabric of baseball and his voice always made us feel we were closer to the heart of the game. Since they never played the Red Sox, it was something to see the National League teams like the amazing Mets of 1969 with Seaver and Koosman, or the Cincinnati Reds with

Johnny Bench.

But it should be understood that TV for us was not the television of urban life. In Newfane there was no cable distribution. Consumer satellite TV had yet to be invented. The nearest broadcast television stations were in Manchester, New Hampshire, and Schenectady, New York, or in Boston. All of these were at a distance that strained against the very limits of what a television set of the day could receive. Now that I'm a communication engineer I know that broadcast TV signals are designed for line of sight transmission – meaning that it is expected that a straight line unobstructed by hills or buildings can be drawn from the receiving antenna to the transmission tower. In practice some minor blockage is acceptable, but when there are many hills in the way, as there are anywhere in Vermont, reception becomes very dicey since the signal arrives by reflecting off one hill, then another, then another, losing much of its remaining strength with each bounce and becoming distorted by the arrival of reflections from multiple paths.

You received the television signal with an antenna mounted on the roof of the house and placed as high above the ground as you could possibly get it without fear that a howling winter gale would blow it over and take the chimney it was strapped to with it. A flat cable ran from the antenna through a hole drilled into the house to where the television sat and its two wires were screwed onto the back of the set. When it stormed at night the cable would smack against the supporting pole and make a ringing sound like a bell that kept us awake all night. And the longer the cable had to be the more signal quality was lost before it reached the television, so the set had to be positioned for minimum cable length.

By the time the signals had propagated across the hundred or so miles needed to reach our house, they had been so attenuated that it made a big difference whether it was summer, when there were leaves on trees, or winter, when the ground was covered with snow that reflects signals in a different way. The net result was that for part of the year we could get stations from Boston and Manchester, and then at other times we could only get Schenectady.

In this era of digital seventy-five inch diagonal ultra-high definition curved-screen three-D televisions with Dolby 5:1 surround sound speaker systems it may be difficult to appreciate some of the deeper implications of a simple statement like "we could get stations". In no way should this be taken to imply an experience that was even remotely equivalent to "just like being there". In the evolutionary scale of communications technology, we were much closer to "Mr. Watson, come here, I want you" than we were to internet streaming. We considered reception to be good if the audio was mostly intelligible over interference like hiss, buzz and crackle, and the seventeen inch black and white picture had sufficiently little snow and ghosting that you could identify that the shapes moving around on the screen were people and not armadillos. A TV picture was acceptable if the vertical hold mostly kept the picture steady in front of us, although it was not uncommon for it to roll so that the top half was on the bottom and the bottom half on the top with the thick black synchronization bar through the middle. The idea that there were places on earth where one might watch a televised baseball game and actually see the ball was about as imaginable as envisioning seeing a planet orbiting a star in another galaxy through a pair of opera glasses. There just was no expectation that this was possible.

One of my earliest memories of watching Vermont television was the funeral of John F. Kennedy a few days after his assassination in 1963. It was a rare sunny and warm day in late November and because the country was still in shock we were given the day off from school. Paul David and I were outside getting in a last chance at playing baseball before the snow came, and Papa insisted that we should come in and watch. I burst in to tears at being required to sit still in front of the screen watching the seemingly interminable proceedings. My father then told me: "Years from now you will remember that on the day of John

Kennedy's funeral you cried. Not because your President had died for our country, but because you wanted to play baseball." And as you can see, he was right.

The story of broadcast media in mid century is one in which people gradually abandoned radio for television, but for Paul David and me the reverse was true. Prior to getting the green radio, once it was too dark to be outside our typical evening had been spent trying to decipher the meaning of the fuzzy images on the television, but with advent of the radio we would go to our shared bedroom and listen to sports or music while reading books or doing homework.

Our room had two built-in bunks placed end to end so that they filled the length of the room. These were tucked under the sloping roof which came to within about a foot of the bed on the side where both bed and roof met the wall. A combined head and foot board kept Paul David from kicking my brains in as we slept and was topped by a narrow shelf with a lamp on it. Under each bunk there were three big drawers that held most of our clothing. From the side of the bed to the opposite wall might have been five feet. That wall had two cabinets with fold-down desk tops designed so that we could each sit on our bed and write or study on the folded-down desk. When folded up, the desks acted as the door for a cabinet filled with the usual kid's collection of books, games, rocks, squirrels tails, old copies of sports magazines, lizards in jars, coins, marbles, glass insulators from electric lines, and whatever else we came across that seemed to have investment potential.

I'd lie on the bunk with the radio going and read adventure books I'd found in the barn. One favorite was James Oliver Curwood's *Kazan*, an obvious Jack London knockoff to someone with broader knowledge, but for a less judgmental twelve year old a gripping thriller filled with tales of a loyal Alaskan sled dog protecting his wounded master from wolves and thieves. Another was *Man-Eaters of Kumaon*, a series of tales about an impossibly courageous hunter who tracked down tigers that were killing and eating unfortunate villagers in Bengal. When I was twelve or thirteen our school had a truck that came with paperbacks that you could look at and order to buy – you'd pay something like twenty-five cents a book and six weeks later they'd arrive at the school and you'd carry them home at the end of the day. I got all of Tolkien's books this way and became a complete addict.

We were late to the party, but Paul David and I discovered rock and roll in 1969 while listening to American Top Forty radio from New York in what were probably the last couple years when it was worth listening to. Overnight I became a big fan of bubblegum pop and soul, into the Beach Boys, Hollies, Foundations, Simon and Garfunkle, Supremes and all those kinds of bands. I still love that music. Any night in the winter when there wasn't a Bruins hockey game or a local high school basketball game on, we'd listen to music and read from the end of dinner until it was time to go to sleep.

The year after Mama upgraded her radio she also upgraded her record player and gave us the old one, so we began to buy singles and then later lps. In today's era of downloadable music it's hard to remember how commonplace vinyl records were then. Sleepy little Brattleboro with its 12,000 inhabitants probably had eight different places where you could buy records, and even the little store in Newfane had a bin with the top forty singles and a hundred or so albums. A chart single was seventy-nine cents, but in Woolworth's in Brattleboro for a dollar and a half you could buy a shrink-wrapped pack of five singles that had fallen off the charts before they could be sold at full price. The catch was that you could only see the label of the record on the top of the five, so you'd search through the packs to find one where you really liked the single you could see and if you got lucky with one of the other four, it was still a better deal than buying one single at a time.

But buying records was expensive, so one had to learn how to make one's way in the world. For me, that effort began with the roar of a lawn mower.

10 THE GREEN, GREEN GRASS OF HOME

Mama believed strongly that children should have responsibilities and chores. The fact that this wasn't a belief system that I shared with her was, unfortunately for me, irrelevant. So Paul David and I both spent lots of time working around our place. In general, Paul David was assigned tasks that suited him; jobs like tending the vegetable garden that required intellect, judgment, thoughtfulness and care. On the other hand I seemed to be assigned the tasks that required brute force and ignorance, which in retrospect were well matched to my own ample abilities in these categories. So among other things, I mowed the lawn.

It sounds so simple: *I mowed the lawn*. But mowing our lawn was like going into battle with a Grendel-like monster from the middle ages. It was impossible to vanquish. Every time I had one part of it under control, another part was getting so thick that I would barely be able to get the mower through it. And the size of the lawn was always expanding as well, as Mama's never ending Scandinavian thirst for order demanded that more and more of what had been pasture needed to join the lawn. By the time I was twelve I was spending an hour behind the mower every day just to keep up.

After numerous arguments with Mama and Papa about

how I was always behind, a summit meeting was held after which, like some back country Winston Churchill dividing up the Middle East in 1919, I made a map of the lawn defining five sections, each needing about an hour and a half to mow, and the plan was to mow one section every day. When section five was done, the next day it would be time to cut section one again.

On a purely abstract and theoretical basis this plan didn't seem especially unrealistic. Two of the sections were mostly lawn that was open field under the sun and in sandy soil. In these areas the grass wasn't thick and it didn't grow that fast, so cutting it once a week was reasonable. But in other places reality displaced theory in a significant way. The ground under apple trees stayed moist even on hot days and the grass grew fast here. Even worse was the section that covered our septic leach field. Here the soil was rich in nutrients, there was shade from trees, and there was plenty of moisture. If you paid a little attention you could almost see the grass grow. In a week it would get so thick that I could only push the mower into it slowly or the engine would stall. Then I'd have to drag the mower to a place where the grass was thin and I'd already cut it so that I could pull the cranking rope and get it running again.

But as bad as these thick sections were on a five day schedule, rain made the situation worse. Rain caused two major problems. For one thing, it made me miss a day of mowing so I'd get to each section a day late. That was bad, but of course rain also made the grass grow better, which was worse. It was almost impossible to get through any week without at least a couple days of rain, so I was always falling behind, and could only recover by doing two sections in one day, which meant two hours of mowing, not one.

A word about our mower is in order. At times we used to see commercials on TV in which a smiling homeowner with every hair perfectly in place and dressed in clothing suitable for a golf outing in the Hamptons mounted a shiny behemoth of a tractor and took it for a spin around his half

185

acre green for five minutes, producing a neatly manicured slice of paradise that was camera-ready for the cover of the annual *Your Perfect Lawn* issue of Better Homes and Gardens, completing the job faster than his wife could prepare him a mint julep. These tractors could mow a swath two yards wide with one pass. They had electric starters that required nothing more than a turn of a key. I suppose some of them had eight track tape players, self-sharpening blades, and even air conditioning. I fantasized about being that man. My fantasy never came true.

Having heard about our cars, I suspect the reader might hazard a reasonably accurate guess about what our mowers were like, and perhaps there isn't much need to elaborate. But please indulge me.

From the operator's perspective, there are several attributes of a mower that impact job satisfaction. First, it must be possible to start it. This seems fundamental, but it's remarkable in my experience how often this key element has been overlooked.

Second, the mower should be wide. The amount of time it takes to finish a mowing job is directly proportional to the width of the mower. If mowing a section of lawn takes an hour with an eighteen inch mower, it can be done in forty-five minutes with a twenty-four inch mower, thirty minutes with a thirty-six inch mower, and twenty minutes with a fifty-four inch mower. Our math courses in school weren't that good, but I still knew that wider mowers meant more time to play baseball.

Third, the engine should be as powerful as possible. A powerful engine can cut thick grass fast, and that means the time to complete the job is limited by how fast you can push the mower, not by how fast the mower can cut the grass.

I suppose the reader will not be terribly surprised at receiving the information that our mowers typically were grossly deficient with respect to all of these critical attributes.

Our first mower was made by a company called Clinton, which might help a reader understand the conflicted emotions I faced a quarter of a century later when this very name appeared on a presidential ballot. Our Clinton mower was eighteen inches wide. I believe the next standard width down on the scale is mostly used for shearing sheep.

The Clinton was made before small engine starters had a spring-loaded rope cord mechanism that could automatically rewind the rope. It had a starting cord that was stored by winding it around the mower's handle. If you misplaced it, you couldn't start the mower until you either found it or made another one. The cord had a wooden T shaped grip with a hole drilled through it. The starting rope passed through this hole and had a knot at either end. One knot kept the rope from slipping through the T handle when it was pulled. The other knot fit into a slot in the starting spindle on the mower. To try to start it (note the key word "try"), I'd fit the knot in the slot and manually wind the cord around the spindle until the T handle was right up against it. I'd then grip the handle with the cord passing between my index and middle fingers, put my foot on the base of the mower as a brace, and give it a hard pull. This would make the engine spin perhaps ten revolutions. If the stars aligned, the carburetor was clean and hadn't yet flooded, the spark plug gap was set right, and I pulled the cord hard enough, the mower might actually start. More frequently it sputtered once or twice and then came to a halt. Then I'd rewind the cord around the spindle and try again. On most days seven or eight tries resulted in success.

The Clinton was unusual in using a two stroke engine that required mixing oil into the gas. Burning this combination produced a thick blue exhaust that, when mixed with the dust, pollen and fragments of cut straw ejected from under the mower, was quite delightful to inhale for an hour at a time. Getting the fuel mixture right was critical to maximizing the power the engine could produce, which, given that it had almost none in the best of circumstances, meant that careful measurement of oil and gasoline was mandatory.

The Clinton engine was so pathetic that in thick grass I developed a technique in which I'd press the handle down close to the ground to make the mower tilt onto its back wheels, then push the mower forward a foot and a half, lower it down onto the erect blades of grass gradually enough that the mower could cut them without stalling, and then repeat. It took forever to mow like this.

One hot summer day there was a loud crunching sound and the engine quit. When I tried to start it again there was no resistance to pulling the cord. The connecting rod from the piston to the drive shaft had shattered, and the Clinton was well and truly dead. I couldn't have been happier.

After this we turned to more conventional mowers with four stroke Briggs and Stratton engines. These didn't require mixing oil with the gasoline and as a result the cancer risk associated with mowing dropped substantially. But these next generation mowers typically either were found at the dump or bought at the flea market for a song. Papa would find a mower with the handle broken off or a missing wheel, and we'd take the engine from it to put on a mower where the body was fine but the engine was dead. That might produce something serviceable for a summer. But it was always a struggle. The carburetor would get clogged with pollen and would have to be taken apart and cleaned. Or the cord retractor spring would break, and getting one of those back together was always a nightmare. At times it seemed like I spent as much time taking lawn mowers apart and re-assembling them as I did mowing.

Even when everything was working fine there were always hazards. The soil under the grass was full of big rocks, and in the winter the frost would randomly reposition them in the soil – meaning that for every rock that sunk in deeper, another would push up out of the ground. A rock that the mower fit over nicely last year would contact the blade the next year, killing the engine and putting a big dull dent in the cutting surface that had to be sharpened again. So the first couple of mowings each spring would be a learning experience as I figured out the new rock configuration.

Now and then I'd hit a garter snake, and inch long snake segments would go flying out of the discharge chute and across the grass. Under the apple trees I sent slices of dropped apples flying everywhere. I was always watching ahead of the mower for anything I might be about to hit, but when the grass was thick it could hide a lot and anything I missed was likely to be cut to pieces.

I usually mowed without shoes, and after the day's mowing my bare feet would be colored a thick dull green half way to the ankle from walking through the sap-covered ends of cut grass. Before I'd go to sleep at night I'd have to go down to the brook with a bar of Lava soap and a hard bristled brush to bring my feet to a sort of olive-tinted skin tone again. The soap would turn to a bright green lather as I scrubbed.

Poison ivy was another big problem. I generally knew where it grew and would wear shoes to mow those places, but newly incorporated lawn might have unknown patches in it, and I'd learn about them the hard way. Some people aren't bothered by poison ivy, but I'm not one of them. The rash from it would start with a little itching between the toes, but this would soon turn into big oozing blisters, and it would gradually spread up to my knees. The itching was an unrelenting torture. It was as hard to keep from scratching the poison ivy rash as it is for a junkie to skip his next fix. I couldn't keep my hands off it, and I'd get the rash in between my fingers and thence up my forearms as a result. It was horrible stuff, and the only relief was to soak it in cold water. Many weeks had to elapse before it would heal up on its own.

Previously we have considered three important attributes of a lawn mower. There is a fourth, and less obvious one, which is that when the job is completed it must also be possible to shut the mower off. Usually this was easily achieved by turning the throttle off. But one day I was using a newly jury-rigged mower and when I'd finished my mowing I found that the throttle on this particular engine couldn't be turned far enough to make the mower stop. One solution was to let the mower idle until it burned away all its fuel, but that could take hours. I decided instead to detach the spark plug wire. I knew the connector at the tip of the plug would be so hot it would burn me if I tried to grab it with my fingers, so I went down by the brook and found a stick to use to pop it off.

Unfortunately, I hadn't thought carefully about the implications of the electricity carried by this wire. The stick I had chosen was wet, and I was standing with bare feet in wet grass cuttings. When I knocked the spark wire free with the stick the resulting shock felt like it broke my elbow and it took several minutes for my arm to get any feeling back. They never warn you about these things in advance.

The job wasn't just pushing the mower, either. There was plenty of trimming to do where grass grew around obstacles like apple trees, flower beds, stone terraces, buildings and wells and the mower couldn't reach it. This was well before the invention of weed whackers, and I mostly used a sickle to do the trimming. This required good accuracy since to cut well a sickle relies on the speed with which it is swung, and often the grass I was trimming came to within a quarter inch of some valuable object. Embedding the tip of the sickle in the bark of an apple tree wasn't good for either the tree or the sickle. Keeping the sickle sharp was also important, so I'd carry a whetstone in my pocket and use it regularly with a technique a neighbor showed me in which I'd rapidly sweep the stone back and forth on alternate sides of the blade. It took some practice to develop the coordination needed to do this in a way that made the blade sharper yet left one in possession of all ten fingers.

As if mowing our own yard wasn't enough, when I got to be about twelve years old I found that mowing grass for neighbors was a good way to put spending money in my pocket. When I first started the typical rate was a dollar an hour, but as I got older and more productive I'd get a dollar and a half. Somewhere along the way I figured out that if I charged by the job and then worked really fast I could do much better. I told one man down the road from us that I'd mow his lawn, do all the trimming, rake the mulch, and take it away to his compost heap, all for five dollars. When I finished in just over an hour he was very unhappy to be paying so much, but he'd thought it was reasonable when I first gave him the price, so I didn't see what the problem was. He grumbled a lot but kept me on for several years after that.

Some of the places where I mowed had their own mower, and these mowers were invariably much better than ours. It was almost a pleasure to mow with a good machine. But some of the places I worked needed me to bring a mower. If the job was within a mile of our house, I'd just push it down the road while walking behind it, but I got jobs at places as much as four miles up Wardsboro Road. For these I'd tie the mower behind my bicycle with a length of rope and tow it. This was better than walking, but not much. The small wheels of the mower couldn't turn over all the rocks on the side of the road, so I had to ride in the center part where the dirt was hard packed. Even there it was slow going, and if a car came I had to dismount and haul bike and mower to the side until the car passed. In places there were steep hills, and on one occasion I got too much downhill speed and the mower flipped upside down, nearly jerking my bike out from under me and spilling most of its gas all over the road before I could get it upright.

Despite all its undesirable characteristics I think I preferred cutting grass to working in the vegetable garden. There was something satisfying about watching the mowed portion grow with each pass of the mower. By contrast the vegetable garden was a never ending fight against weeds. I detested pulling weeds. You had to get down on your knees and crawl around among the plants, struggling to get a hold of the weed low enough that the roots would come out when you pulled. It was back breaking work. Picking the vegetables was more rewarding, at least if they were big. Digging potatoes wasn't bad. Turning over a good shovel full of dirt under the potato plant could bring up half a bucketful of potatoes, which felt like real progress. Tomatoes were good that way as well. Peas and beans were a little slower, and raspberries were no fun at all.

In July we'd typically go to a local strawberry farm and pick strawberries until we didn't want to see them again, which maybe isn't saying that much since in all honesty I didn't want to see them while we were in the car on the way there. You'd pay the farmer some small amount for the berries and put in the labor of harvesting yourself. We'd pick so many quarts of strawberries that they'd completely fill the back of our station wagon. Mama would then make different kinds of preserves from them; jelly, jam and a simple mash of berries with sugar that she froze and used to make cakes later in the year. I hated picking strawberries. The sun was blistering hot, the baskets took forever to fill, you'd be crawling around in the dirt on your knees, and if you wore jeans the knees would get all red from kneeling on berries. Somehow Paul David seemed to enjoy it, but I'd whine like an underfed dog the whole time.

Much of the country has hotter summers than Vermont, but we would have felt no better knowing that the heat and humidity we suffered in July and August was even more oppressive elsewhere. The upstairs of our uninsulated house baked all day under its tin roof. It was often so hot in our bedroom that sweat would bead up on our skin and roll off in big drops even if we lay uncovered and motionless on the bed with nothing on but a pair of gym shorts.

The solution to this was to sleep outdoors. Paul David and I would pitch our two man canvas tent out on the lawn and go out to sleep sometime after dark. Even in the tent it would be pretty hot when we first lay down, but in the deep of the night it would get very comfortable, and some nights if a front went through it could even get cold. It could be eerie out in the tent at night. We'd hear animals snuffling around outside – raccoons or porcupines or skunks. Further off on the hillside a bear might moan. They never came close to the house, and in fact I never actually saw a bear growing up, but that didn't make us any less afraid when we heard them.

Some nights there'd be thickets of fireflies outside and we'd get a jar and try to catch them. This was pretty tricky, since their light would flash on for a brief instant and then go out for a couple of seconds. During this time they were completely invisible, and since they were also flying on a trajectory best modeled as Brownian motion, anticipating where they might appear next was as much guesswork as skill. On firefly nights not much sleeping took place.

The best remedy for heat was getting in the water. We used our pool in the brook constantly, but the real treat was going down to the West River at the Brookline bridge, an iron truss structure built after the flood from the 1928 hurricane destroyed the previous bridge. A couple hundred yards upstream from the bridge a length of fast moving water made a hard left turn and settled into a calm, deep pool nearly a quarter mile long. The east bank of the pool had as much of a sandy beach as anyone had a right to expect in Vermont, and it sloped gently into the river so that poor swimmers could get wet safely.

Better swimmers could strike out across the river, where in the middle the depth might have been ten or twelve feet in summer. There were some big underwater rocks that came close enough to the surface that they could give a resting place on the way across if you knew where to find them. The biggest of these was called Red Rock for obvious reasons, and a boy standing on it would find the water's surface at his thigh where in one step the depth would be three times his height.

We learned to swim in this place. Swimming lessons were held early in the morning in June so that no one else would be wanting to use the beach, but that meant the water was so heart-stoppingly cold that it completely took our minds off the fear of drowning. I suppose this was the right thing for building confidence.

Striking out for Red Rock was a rite of passage. The

bigger kids would always talk about it and we could see them out there standing on it and playing in the water around it. It only took about 10 yards of swimming across a section where it was too deep to stand, but for a novice it seemed a long, long way. For several weeks I'd paddle a little way into the deep water and then turn back to the beach. Then I decided to go for it.

I'd learned to have my eyes open underwater from an early age, since we needed to do it to work on our pools in the brook. You'd only get a blurry, ghostly perspective of what was down there, but it was better than nothing. Swimming to Red Rock the water became deep enough that I couldn't see the river bottom, and I was close to panic when suddenly a large orange shape loomed up in front of me. I felt like I could barely make it, but before I knew it I was over it and felt its solid surface under my feet. I stood up in triumph like it was now my rock.

Each trip to the river required loading the car with an assortment of black rubber inner tubes, towels, diving masks, fins, fishing poles, bait and anything else we might decide we'd need. If we wanted to fish we'd walk from the beach side down to the bridge and cross to the other side. Here the river had cut into granite ledges that sloped into the water much more steeply than on the beach side, and a simple cast would send a hook in depths where it couldn't be seen. The river had few trout in it, but there were two kinds of bass, one a spinier smallmouth bass that sheltered among the larger underwater rocks, and the other a more svelte largemouth variety built for fighting the currents. I caught many of the smallmouths, but only Paul David ever got a legal largemouth.

When I was about thirteen I decided that what we really needed for fishing success in the river was a boat, and since there was no prospect of anybody giving me one, it was clear that I had to build it myself. I knew nothing about boat building other than that it needed to not leak. Building anything with curves in it was far beyond my skill level, so I conceived a sort of punt with straight sides and back and sloped front. If it wasn't for the bow design, the boat would have essentially been a shallow wooden box with seats in it.

I built it in our carpenter shop. First I framed it out with two by threes. Then I cut pieces of plywood for the bottom and sides. I painted thick black roofing tar onto all the joints between the frame and the plywood and then nailed the plywood in place. I framed out supports for three rows of seats and made them with flat boards. Then I painted the whole thing inside and out with battleship gray primer.

Now we were ready for launch, but there was a problem. The boat was so heavy that Paul David and I could barely move it by ourselves. I had meant to try it in the brook first, but we decided it would be too much work to get it there and we had to go straight to the river with it. So I badgered Papa incessantly until he agreed to help us. We put our roof rack on the car, and with Papa on one side and Paul David and me on the other we managed to hoist the boat into place and tie it down.

Once at the swimming hole in Brookline, getting our craft to the water was a new challenge. To get down to the beach, we'd drive across the iron bridge to the Brookline side, after which the road turned hard right and ran parallel to the river. Two hundred feet after this turn a sandy little dirt road on the left doubled back to an open space where people parked their cars. But this place was at the level of the bridge, and to get to the water required descending twenty feet along a narrow track that was nearly as steep as a stairway and surrounded by tall bushes on either side. Somehow we grappled the boat down this track and made it to the water.

We put the boat in. It floated! We got in it, and it continued to float! And it barely leaked at all. I virtually glowed with pride at my own craftsmanship.

Now we pushed off into the deeper water, and at this point the navigational shortcomings of my design began to make themselves manifest. I hadn't made oars, but we had the wooden paddle that had been used with Paul David's plastic boat of a few years earlier. Oars would have been better, but the biggest problem was that in the interest of saving myself a long end-to-end saw cut through a sheet of plywood I'd made the beam of the boat be four feet, way too wide for one person to row on both sides. Paddling was impossible without two people working simultaneously and we had only one paddle. Rowing a skiff through the La Brea tar pits with a soup spoon would have produced more headway than the flat prow of this boat allowed. And since there was no keel or centerboard, what little motion a paddle stroke did stimulate tended to be spinning rather than forward motion.

Although the river flow in the pool was leisurely, the little current that it did exhibit proved to be more than we could paddle this sloth-like craft against. I started to panic that we'd drift so far down the river that there'd be no place for us to get the boat out. So as soon as we reached a point shallow enough to stand, we jumped out and hauled the boat over to the shore. If coming down the path from the parking area was hard, going back up was nearly impossible, but somehow we managed. Returning home, we carried the boat behind the barn and leaned it against the wall, where it commenced an uninterrupted and decades long journey of rotting into nothingness. Thus concluded my career as a shipwright.

Parades were a frequent and important feature of every summer. For reasons I don't understand, Newfane never had one, but there were parades in neighboring towns like Wardsboro and Grafton for Memorial Day, Independence Day and Labor Day, and Townshend had a combination parade and rummage sale in early August for no apparent reason other than there was too much time between July 4 and Labor Day. At each parade Papa would get out his marching drum and play with the Grafton band. In retrospect it would seem that populating a drum corps with near octogenarian players wearing reading glasses to allow focusing on a postcard sized piece of sheet music clipped to the rim of a vibrating drum as they concentrated on playing and then asking them to walk in time along the cracked and buckled pavement of the streets in a Vermont town while being hammered by the hot summer sun could only be a plot to improve business for the local ambulance services. But miraculously none of the players ever fell and fractured something or collapsed from a stroke.

Television has helped people become accustomed to thinking in terms of the Rose Bowl or Macy's parades, events requiring planning on the scale of the Normandy invasion and costing nearly as much. Any imagination in this direction with respect to our parades can be dismissed. For one thing, most Vermont towns have a main street of two or three blocks. This places real practical limitations on the length and duration of a parade. Our parades usually assembled in a field behind someone's barn at one end of town. The parade marshal would dictate the order of appearance for each group in the parade. There'd be two marching bands, the Grafton band of farmers, and a high school band. Usually the high school band came near the front of the parade, and the Grafton band was closer to the end. The brevity of the parade meant that the bands didn't need to know more than four songs, so they usually sounded pretty well rehearsed. A handful of veterans representing the two World Wars and the Korean War would provide the real reason for the parade, but following them would be a variety of other attractions with no discernible connection to the given holiday.

For example, here would come the guy who owned the general store. He had given his convertible its annual wash, stuck a few ribbons of crepe paper on it, hung a hand lettered sign for his store on the front and rear, and loaded the back of it with twelve packs of Charmin toilet tissue and other similarly fetching examples of his fine merchandise. Then the fire department would appear driving every motorized vehicle the station owned. The four members of the South Wardsboro chess club would appear. Next maybe Doctor Otis would drive his late 1940s canary yellow Packard behind a chaotic phalanx of people that he'd brought into this world in the Grace Cottage Hospital delivery room. A local farmer would drive a tractor pulling a trailer with a cow on it. A group of matronly women carrying pies would come into view, fronted by two young girls holding a sign announcing a church bake sale.

And so it went for about seven minutes, and then came the part where the marshal would have really earned his pay had any compensation actually been involved. The parade had to be turned around and marched back through the town in the opposite direction. It's easy to trivialize the complexity of this when you're used to being given all the streets of lower Manhattan in which to circle around a couple of helium-filled Snoopy balloons, but when you've got an entire parade featuring not only war heroes, but marching bands, fire trucks, livestock, bakers and chess experts all standing impatiently in the hot sun on a narrow country road just south of Wardsboro, Vermont and you want it to go in the other direction, well, you have a real job on your hands.

But somehow they'd pull it off every year, and after a few minutes while the murmur of anticipatory conversation flowed over the sound of wind blowing through the trees, here would come the parade yet again, with the bands each playing their other two songs, the pie crusts starting to become soggy, and maybe the farmer with the cow not participating because in trying to reverse direction he backed his trailer over an embankment and is now preoccupied with getting his cow out of the beaver pond into which it has been unceremoniously but accidentally dumped.

When the last of the parade passed by, the crowd would fall in to line to follow it. An hour or two of congratulatory hob-knobbing would ensue centered on the successful conclusion of yet another parade, and then usually there'd be some kind of potluck dinner at the Grange or at the church where you'd get big bowls of revolting molasses sweetened Boston baked beans to go with much more welcomed hamburgers, hot dogs and corn on the cob. And we'd all go home stuffed and entertained enough to last the four weeks to the next parade.

Of course, there was more going on in Papa's fertile mind than planning for the next parade. We never knew what new project would come along. There had been a series of sessions in which we gradually built out floors on each storey of our gray barn. In the early sixties, that barn consisted of its frame of eight-by-eight beams, exterior boards, roof rafters, roof boards and sheet metal roof, and floorboards on the ground floor only. Inside was a large open volume interrupted only by the big timbers of the frame. But over a span of several years, we floored a second story and then a third. The normal process for this would be that around eight o'clock on Saturday morning a big lumber truck would arrive and unload a towering stack of planks on the grass in front of the barn. This was the official notice to Paul David and me that, had we had any plans for the weekend, they were now cancelled.

We'd then begin the process of hauling all this lumber into the barn and up to whatever floor it was going to. Any woman will tell you that some men struggle with commitment, and when it came to lumber, our father was in that camp. For all projects involving wood, his goal was to minimize both the cutting of lumber (not to save labor, but because two short boards were worth far less than one long one), and the use of fasteners of any kind, since these damaged the lumber, the whole idea being to make it possible to re-use all the material if this particular project didn't work out as planned.

So he'd figure out ingenious ways to make spacers that would hold floor joists upright without any nails, and we'd lay the floor for an area that was twelve or fifteen feet on a side with almost no use of a hammer. Spanning the big gap between the beams, the joists could exhibit an alarming amount of bounce as you walked across, but as the purpose of each floor was for storage of boxes, a little slumping with weight was OK.

We moved between the floors by climbing up ladders

through small openings in the boards. Once the floor was complete, we'd then start moving boxes of stuff from some other part of the barn for storage on the new floor, squeezing ourselves and the box through the floor opening while climbing the ladder without use of hands, the idea being to free up space for Papa to get at his metal working machines which since Yalta had gradually been buried under an invaluable but inconvenient accumulation of unidentified treasures.

I think Papa genuinely would have liked to be organized, but he fundamentally was just not capable of it. He routinely carried three or four three-by-five index cards in his pocket, neatly lettered with pencil in a font that required a magnifying glass (also ever present in his pocket) to read. The notations were typically reminders of things to do or about where he had put things, but they'd also include grocery lists, commentary about things he saw in the paper, or anything else that popped into his head that was worthy of retaining. What was on the cards would quickly get as jumbled as the things they were supposed to remind him about. And then he would lose the cards or put them in a box that he then filled with unrelated bits and pieces. He'd then find cards he'd written out months previously, but in the meantime he'd have started new ones, so he'd put them all in a pile, and before you knew it there was a stack of three-by-five cards two inches deep, all unreadable with the naked eye, and with no way to tell which was representative of the current situation.

The blank cards had more than one use. As we moved things, he'd investigate what was in each box, and sometimes he'd write a description of the contents on a card, fold it over, and paper clip it to lip of the box. One such card, discovered many years later, was neatly lettered with "Pieces of Rope Too Short to Keep". It's quite likely Papa fully recognized the irony but also knew he couldn't help himself.

Cards used for box labels were typically written in larger lettering using a grease pencil. Before felt tip markers this was the best thing you could do for a label meant to be easily seen. Grease pencils were designed so that as the "lead" ran out, you'd pull a string back one notch along the paper body of the pencil and then unwrap a section of the paper to reveal another quarter inch of lead.

Grease pencils could write on almost anything. Milk cartons were a favorite. As a family, we drank such staggering amounts of milk that it seems almost impossible to imagine today. An old-fashioned dairy delivery truck came by twice a week, on Tuesday and Friday. But they'd converted from milk in bottles to modern half gallon cartons recently, not too dissimilar to what you can still get in stores today, and we'd get so much milk that the top shelf of the refrigerator would be solid milk cartons squeezed as tightly together as they could be, with a few other cartons on the lower shelves as well. A single delivery would easily be something like twenty-five or thirty half gallons, but by the next delivery they'd all be gone, and in fact on the longer Friday to Tuesday period, they'd be all gone with a day to go and we'd have to go to the store to buy more.

As Paul David and I reached teenage years, consumption of milk became so substantial that Papa resorted to an allocation system. After intense negotiation it was determined how many half gallons each of us should be granted with each delivery. When new milk arrived, he used a grease pencil to write the initials of the owner on the carton, so a peek inside the refrigerator would show cartons lettered P, M, PD, S and J, and we were only allowed to consume milk from our assigned cartons. So at dinner the five of us would sit there at our little kitchen table that was only meant for four people in the first place, and each of us would have our own half gallon milk carton right at our elbow, leaving very little space for anything else. I believe that the highest allocation was for S cartons, but these also depleted fastest, and I remember always running out ahead of schedule on Monday and thinking how unfair this system was, and I'd be trying to think of deals I could strike with Johanna, who always ran out last, to pry some of hers away.

But back to the barn – when we finally got to the third floor, it was serious work hauling the lumber up, and the work of laying the joists was a little scary, since in places a fall would be all the way to ground. We'd balance on one of the eight-by-eight frame beams while trying to position an awkward and heavy twelve foot long two-by-eight floor joist to span the gap to the next beam and then put its spacer in place. We'd then move along the beam and get the new joist handed to us. It was dark and dusty everywhere in the barn, but right under the roof it was also really hot, and we'd be working in shorts and no shirt, so pretty soon we'd be as sweaty and dirty as a coal miner.

After a few floorboards were put in place we could stand up to do our work, but now we found something new to horrify us, as tucked between the rounded rafters and the boards that made up the roof there were lots of sleeping bats, and our heads were right underneath them. If you gave the roof a good bang, a groggy bat might drop onto the floorboards right at your feet. That would make you pay attention!

We were given warning that one of the biggest of these weekend projects was about to happen when with no prior explanation a big dump truck showed up in mid-week and left a huge pile of gravel next to the garage. Something was clearly up, and it was bound to be bad.

Sure enough, the next Saturday morning Paul David and I were roused early from our usual habit of sleeping all morning and dragged down to the garage where we were put to work moving everything to the upper floors of the gray barn. We hooked a chain up to the black Plymouth and towed it out back. Having cleared the place completely, Papa had us bring loads of gravel in and we spread it all over the dirt floor. We then built forms for pouring a concrete slab, sawing up all the needed boards and staking them in place, making sure they were level, and leaving gaps for thermal expansion. We puzzled over why this would be done, since despite the obvious advantages of having cars under cover during the winter Papa had never shown any inclination to doing this. But what other purpose could this serve?

That afternoon a huge concrete truck arrived, and after knocking down the low hanging electric wires from the house to the barn, it discharged its load into our forms. We then raked and hoed the concrete until it was fairly flat and screed it smooth by dragging a two by four back and forth across the surface. But still no hint as to why all this industry was being brought to bear on our humble garage.

For the next several days Papa would go out and poke anxiously at the concrete, making sure it was getting really solid and wasn't cracking or splitting. And the following Saturday the mystery was resolved when a huge tractor trailer truck arrived. It had come to deliver by far the biggest metal turning lathe I'd ever seen, and I'd seen a lot more than most kids ever do. If size was any indication, then this particular example was suited for turning propeller shafts for nuclear powered aircraft carriers.

Under Papa's watchful direction, the crew accompanying the truck rolled this multi-ton machine carefully down a ramp from the truck bed to the ground and then, using rollers and planks, grappled it into the garage, where it completely filled a space long enough to park two cars end to end.

Years came and years went, and nothing more was ever done with this lathe. It was never used, never even turned on, and gradually other detritus was piled on top of it until it was almost invisible. Some thirty-five or forty years later, when she had become mistress of the house, Johanna found someone to haul it away for scrap value. But on one of his sojourns Papa had found it on offer second hand and had concluded that it was a value to good to pass up. When opportunity knocks, you've got to be ready to yank that door open.

Living in a place with such low population density makes it essential to have a mode of transportation that doesn't rely on the largess of parents. Hitch hiking was one solution, but bicycles were another key for us, and I was always trying to find ways to upgrade my bike on the cheap. Up to the age of about ten or eleven I had one of those bikes with twenty inch wheels, a banana seat, high rise handle bars, and a big sissy bar in the back. But with only one speed this was no good for riding any distance, and it was geared so that riding up a hill was brutal. I could coast down to Newfane on it, but coming back I was assured of having to walk all the way up the hill pushing it. I needed a better solution, which I decided would be a three speed English style bike with twenty-six inch wheels. I suspect that at this time there were bikes that changed gears with a derailleur, but I'd never heard about them, so to me the three speed was the pinnacle of bike technology.

I started combing the classified ads in the Town Crier for a used one, but most of them cost more than Papa would pay for a car. Finally one day there was one within my price range. I begged Mama to drive me to look at it. It wasn't much to see. The paint was half scraped off it, the tires were flat, and worst of all, there were no brakes. By this I don't intend to convey that the brakes were out of adjustment, that they needed new pads, or that a cable was broken. I mean that this bicycle was not equipped with so much as a single screw, washer or grommet bearing any relevance whatever to the problem of the dissipation of momentum.

In other words, it was perfect, so I handed over my hard earned thirty dollars and went home an excited customer. I stripped all the parts off it and spray painted the frame fluorescent orange, got new tubes and tires, oiled it all up, and I was ready to get out on the road. I considered brakes, but when I saw what they cost, I decided I could do without them. After all, my sled didn't have brakes either, and that had never seemed like much of an issue. So now and then you'd hit a tree. Big deal.

I quickly found out that riding on a gravel surface on this new bike with its skinny tires was a good way to spend a lot of contemplative time on the side of the road trying to get patches to stick to tubes while cars drove by and kicked up a storm of choking dust, so I pretty much confined myself to asphalt from here on. Fortunately the pavement now came to the bridge over Smith Brook a couple hundred yards from the house, so this strategy was feasible.

It seems worthwhile to mention here that when I first came to California in the late 1970s, I used to bicycle to my engineering job every day. After a couple of weeks, a friendly group of fellow employees asked me if I'd like to go biking with them on the weekend. When I asked where they planned to go, it turned out that they were going to take mountain bikes and ride on dirt fire roads. I was horrified. I'd spent my entire youth struggling over washboard and sharp rocks, fixing flats, using an old toothbrush to scrub the slurry of oil and sand out of my chain, and dreaming of rolling down smooth asphalt on paved roads, and these people were going to ride on dirt roads *on purpose* and they thought it would be *fun*? And they'd *paid money* for a bike specially designed to do this? Ha, ha, ha! This California certainly is a strange place!

But we were about to ride down Wardsboro Road to Newfane. The first few times I did this I'd slow down at the top of the mile long hill and listen for any cars. If I didn't hear any, I'd push the bike over the crest. The steepest part was right away, and pretty soon I was going about thirty miles an hour, which, given all the curves, was fast enough to feel pretty sporty even in a car. And the pavement was rife with cracked and damaged asphalt and sudden bumps that could knock your hands off the handlebars and send you crashing off the shoulder and into the ditch.

I flew around the S-curve, roared past the Mannerhopf's yellow house, whistled across the metal bridge, and just like that I was on the flat section leading into the village, losing speed to wind resistance as I came into the settled part of town at a velocity still well above the speed limit. I dragged my feet on the ground to bring the bike to a halt. It had taken no more than ten minutes from our house to the village, and less than two to come down the hill. You couldn't do it much faster in a car. Fantastic!

Subsequently I elevated the process of dragging feet to control speed to an art form. When I started down the hill, I'd stand up on the pedals with left foot down and right foot up. Then, as though I was going to get off the bike, I'd lift my right leg over the seat so I'd be rolling along standing with my left foot on the left pedal, holding the handle bars with two hands, and with my right foot free to drag or not drag as I saw fit. I wasn't that concerned about oncoming cars since they were usually in the other lane, and at the speed I was going it was rare to be overtaken. But there might be some obstacle in the road, or a loose dog might come after me, and I needed to be able to deal with that.

An observant reader might point out that wearing out one of a perfectly sound pair of shoes by dragging it on the pavement to slow a bike down is probably not as cost effective as having brakes. And I'd have to agree with that, but since my parents paid for my clothing the cost of shoes didn't come out of my personal budget. Bicycle brakes did. I'm sure that anyone working in contracts for the Department of Defense will sympathize with this kind of reasoning.

Traffic on Wardsboro Road wasn't much of a threat for bicyclists. I remember on more than one occasion working with Papa on some project out in front of the barn, and we'd hear a car go by. A second car might follow ten minutes later. At this unwanted intrusion Papa would launch into a bitter diatribe about how bad the traffic was these days and how in the past this had been a quiet neighborhood.

But riding on Route 30 was a different proposition. It was the main artery connecting all the small towns across the center of our county to the commercial hub of Brattleboro. By comparison to even the off ramp of an urban interstate its volume of traffic might seem trivial, but there were lots of trucks and commercial traffic mixed in with townspeople commuting to work, schools and shops. I rode it regardless.

Although by now the road had been widened and

modernized from Williamsville Depot to Brattleboro, for the first four miles south from Newfane and most of its entire length northwards it was still narrow, winding and torturous. There was a double yellow stripe painted down the middle as a sort of suggestion that cars should try not to collide head on, and at the right of each lane was a white stripe indicating the boundary of the road on that side. In the daytime a skillful driver could generally fit a sedan between the white and yellow stripes. Except in the more winding sections a pickup truck or a delivery van would fit, too. But dump trucks and especially logging trucks had no chance, and if they came up on you too fast while you were on a bike, well, that could be problematic.

My goal was to ride directly on top of that white stripe so that overtaking cars had as much room as possible to avoid killing me. This wasn't always easy, since the pavement at the edge was often cracked and broken up, and in places the stripe just left the pavement altogether and went across rocks and gravel. In other places a row of wooden guardrails was so close to the stripe that I'd have to worry about hitting my right ankle on them as I pedaled. I learned to ride looking back over my shoulder as much as looking forwards. I knew every spot where the road widened a little and at each one I'd size up the traffic coming behind me. If there were no trucks and no oncoming traffic to prevent cars in my lane from pulling out, I'd sprint to the next wide spot. In some places, the wide spots were so far apart that it wasn't possible to tell what traffic might come before reaching it. In those cases I'd just grit my teeth, hope for the best, and go for it.

In retrospect it's funny that I could be smart enough to be cautious on Route 30 and so reckless at other times. One particular piece of bicycling lunacy happened the day I challenged Paul David to a game of chicken out by the driveway through the field. He was on his feet near the house and I started my bike up by Grout Road so I could build up the maximum possible speed. I came bearing down on him like a freight train, and at the last second what flashed through my head was: "What am I thinking? This is Paul David, the single most stubborn person I know in the whole world. He's *never* going to step aside. I've got to turn!" So I did, but, alas, I had over-estimated his stubborn streak and under-estimated his pragmatic sense of self-preservation. And as I turned, so did he, unfortunately choosing the same direction as I did. I ran right into him and went over the handlebars and face first into the grass, which I hit hard enough to make green streaks across my cheeks that mingled with the blood from abrasions. We both lay on the grass moaning in pain and simultaneously laughing at having done something so stupid and achieving such a ridiculous result.

The loose dog problem also deserves mention in any discussion of biking. Many people had dogs, and it was standard practice to let them roam loose. On the roads where I rode regularly I knew every house that had a dog, and I knew the habits of every dog. Some would ignore me, some would stay on the porch and bark a little, some would come running after me with a lot of bluff and bluster but wouldn't really come close, and some would try to tear me limb from limb if they could only get at me.

The German shepherds were the worst. There were two of them on the way home. The Schneiders had one, but their house was a couple hundred yards down the Wiswell Hill Road turn off, and if I rode hard I'd be beyond his territory before he could get to me and he'd give up. This sprinting strategy was not as easy as it might seem since I'd just finished climbing the hill from Newfane and was already gasping for oxygen, so while on paper it was a sensible tactic, in practice it sometimes could be touch and go. Fortunately adrenalin can be adequate compensation for lack of oxygen.

The big problem, however, was up ahead. On the right side of the road was Fisher's pond, an artificial body of water that siphoned off part of Smith Brook and was used to farm trout. The road made a sharp right turn around the end of this pond, and the Fisher's little red house sat there on the left side, not fifty feet from its porch to the pavement. And on most days, on that porch sat a particularly nasty specimen of the German shepherd breed. I have no doubt it was a descendant of the very worst of Gestapo police dogs.

Now the real problem about the Schneider's dog wasn't that it chased after me. Far more grievous was the fuss it made, which could easily be heard by the Fisher's dog and alerted him that some sort of spy, probably one of those rats from the French resistance, was about to try to sneak past him. I'd come up to the south end of the pond where I could see the house and its porch, and I'd hope against hope that this drooling, semi-rabid, eighty pound canine was locked indoors. Sometimes he was, and then I'd cruise by whistling. But if he wasn't, there was just no getting by unscathed while riding on a bike. I'd have to dismount and, while on foot, use the bike as a shield. The dog would lunge at me and I'd shove the bike at him to fend him off. He'd try to come around the other side, and I'd spin around, always keeping the bike between us. It was like a bullfight, with me executing my full repertoire of matador moves while simultaneously working to make progress up the road as quickly as possible.

At Wilkinson's bridge my carnivorous foe would begin to feel that his supply lines were overextended and he was becoming vulnerable, and, casting a few parting growls and barks over his shoulder, he'd eventually slink back in failure to his porch, whence he'd resume his defense of the Fascist cause on another day. In five more minutes I'd be home, and in a couple more hours my pulse rate would return to normal.

11 ANIMAL FARM

Although our place hadn't been a real working farm for a long time, like many of the other people around we did have some farm animals while growing up, and between these and our exposure to the wildlife around us, it seemed like we were continually immersed in the animal world. And like most kids, we were crazy for any animal interaction we could get.

Starting on the small and innocuous end of the animal world, we always had cats. Although it's hard to beat the semi-deranged playfulness of kittens, adult cats always struck me as being rather characterless and I preferred dogs, or at least, dogs without a Germanic heritage. Johanna was the most enamored of cats and tended to name the ones who became adults in our household. And the cats seemed to like her as much as she liked them, even when she was really small and played with them roughly in ways that would get most people a good clawing. Thanks in no small part to Warner Brothers cartoons, in my memory we had a line of cats answering to Sylvester with as many descendants as there were kings named Louis in the Bourbon dynasty.

It seemed like every year or two whatever cat currently reigned in our house would deliver a litter of kittens, usually in one of Papa's cardboard boxes in the far back of the attic so that we'd have to move everything to get at them. Then for a few months we'd be surrounded by playful kittens chasing after strings, marbles, toy soldiers, ribbons, balloons, and basically anything that could be batted around with their paws. But as soon as they were old enough to be weaned we'd start giving them away, since the market impact of a cat past the ultra-cute phase was pretty low in Vermont. Lots of people in our town drowned kittens at birth to avoid having to deal with them when they got bigger.

Papa was not an animal lover, but he made something of an exception for cats. His affection wasn't sufficient for him to let them stay in the house overnight, however. On the kitchen porch we kept a box stuffed with blankets and with only a modest opening to get in and out, and other than when there were kittens, the cat population was expected to sleep out there in July heat or January cold. The cat could be inside during the evening, but the first step of us going to bed was to put the cat out for the night. This probably had a lot to do with the turnover in the Sylvester dynasty. By today's standards it might seem cruel to make cats spend every night outdoors, but it was sufficiently common then that each episode of the Flintstones cartoon ended with Fred trying to put his pet saber-toothed tiger outside for the night and nobody made any fuss about that.

Our cats were partly pets and partly mouse control devices. We had a *lot* of mice. In the fall when it got cold, the field mouse population would look for a good place to winter, and there's not much better accommodations than a heated house with many rooms filled with boxes of oddments to hide in and cabinets full of food. So late in the year the indoor mouse population would always explode.

For some time it was one of my jobs to set mousetraps, and in December it wasn't unusual for me to put out five or six of them in the evening and have a smashed mouse in every one the following morning, and to have this go on for multiple weeks. Given how many mice we caught in traps, it's not at all clear that the cats were really earning their keep.

Peanut butter or Velveeta were the preferred form of bait.

211

I'd smear the bait on a little tab, pull back the spring-loaded mouse-smashing arm, and hook the little cross piece that held the arm in place under the bait tab. The attachment of this cross piece had to be sensitive enough that the force of a thirty gram mouse licking the bait would trip it, so one can imagine that a blundering hundred pound pre-teenager would frequently knock it loose during handling, crunching his own fingers in the trap and precipitating a torrent of prohibited verbiage that would in and of itself scare every rodent within earshot out of the house and back into the field for the next week.

At one point Mama bought an ingenious trap with six little tunnels radiating out from a central bait chamber. A mouse would crawl up the tunnel toward the bait and a spring loaded wire would garrote him just before he got to it. Clearly Italian engineering, probably Sicilian. I'd sometimes get four or five mice in that one trap alone, and although it possible to accidently trip this trap while handling it, it was designed to make it unlikely that the event would victimize any fingers.

Our first summer in Newfane Mama bought a ewe and her two new born lambs. One black and one white, the lambs were the very picture of cuteness. When they'd nurse from their mother they'd show their excitement by whirling their tails like helicopter rotors. But all three were really shy, and though we were dying to play with them, they were virtually impossible to catch.

Not so much so for King, the German shepherd who as a puppy had given our drive from Connecticut such a pungent turn on that hot summer day. Like a lot of their breed, King was incredibly loyal to our family. He regarded us as part of his pack, but he was insanely jealous of any potential interloper and to others he was frankly as bad as or worse than any of the dogs I encountered later on my bike. In King's view the sheep were most definitely not part of the pack.

King had grown from a puppy to full size during our first

full year in Vermont and he combined the strength of an ox with the recklessness of youth. We had to tie him up outside because if he was loose he was too much of a threat to anybody who might come by to visit. As he grew Papa used increasingly stout chains to secure him to the trunk of an apple tree out in the yard, and eventually King would break every one of them by running at full speed away from the base of the tree. The chain would run out of slack and snap his neck and head back, but the dog was so strong that after a number of these tests the weakest link would eventually give way. After a while Papa hit on the solution of tying him to a springy branch higher up in the tree that would dissipate the dog's kinetic energy more gradually, and he couldn't break a chain when tied like that.

But one day when we were away doing the week's shopping he managed tear himself out of his collar and get free. When we returned home we found both lambs bitten to death and the ewe in the last throes of dying of respiratory failure from the stress of being chased.

I'm not sure if it's true, but local wisdom was that once a dog tasted blood it would want it again, and Papa decided that King was too dangerous to keep. He had Paul David and me go behind the barn and dig two deep holes. We threw the sheep carcasses into one. In the other, we put a big bowl of dog food to entice King to jump in. While he was focused on eating, Papa shot him in the back of the head with a rifle. We then solemnly shoveled the dirt back on top of both graves.

So our first experience with farm animals ended about as badly as it could, but it didn't keep us from trying again. A few months after the burial, Papa came home with two beagle puppies. Beagles are pretty shy by nature, and these were no exception. Papa set them down on the kitchen floor and went to get Paul David and me to see them. When we came to the kitchen there were no dogs. We searched for a long time and finally discovered that they had gone behind the refrigerator and crawled under it in the spaces around the compressor. We had to carefully pull the refrigerator out from the wall to keep from crushing them, but eventually we got them.

There was a female that we named Tramp and a male who became Sparky. Sparky never did socialize. He was always running away or hiding and in a few months Papa gave him to a neighbor. But Tramp was a wonderful, loyal dog and would follow us on walks through the woods, scouting ahead and disappearing on a chase after a small animal, but always returning. Unlike King, Tramp was no threat to anyone and we'd let her roam free. Most of the time she'd be sleeping in the sun on the porch, but she'd also go running in the woods on solo hunting trips when the mood took her.

Within a year Tramp lived up to her name and became pregnant. This was no surprise since almost no one, ourselves included, thought to spay or neuter their dogs, and running free provided plenty of opportunities for canine romance with the neighbor's dogs. Her belly grew bigger and bigger and we were bursting with excitement about the prospect of having puppies.

One day she came trotting up the driveway to the house and we immediately noticed that she was skinny. So she'd delivered the puppies, but where? She was giving nothing away. We'd try to watch where she went, but while we were watching she didn't do anything unusual. Then the minute we dropped our attention we'd notice she was gone. And a couple hours later she'd be back on the porch wanting to come in. It was maddening.

After several days we caught sight of her crawling through a gap in the stone foundation of the barn. We'd never seen her go there before, and we immediately guessed that we'd find the puppies under the barn floor. The only problem was that no person could fit through the hole she'd slipped through. But on the far side of the barn there was a gap in the floorboards big enough to gain entry, so armed with flashlights Paul David and I crawled in and began searching.

It was horrible under that floor. There was so little room

that we had to crawl on our bellies. The ground beneath us was covered with a dry, dusty dirt that, had we thought about it, was probably permeated with the desiccated half century old refuse that had dripped through the cracks between floorboards from the barnyard animals who once roamed above. Unseen spider webs clung to our hair and faces and got into our mouths. In places we'd have to squeeze through a tight fit between a major supporting beam and the dirt, and at times it seemed for sure we'd get stuck.

After about fifty feet of crawling and scuffling we came to where the puppies were. They were all over the place. I had been expecting two or three new arrivals, but in the bad light it seemed like there'd been a puppy explosion and there was no knowing how many there might be. We couldn't even begin to count them. We hadn't brought anything with us to help carry large numbers of puppies out, so we had to crawl all the way back out to get a box. We were so excited that cobwebs and dirt went completely overlooked.

When we finally emerged with all puppies in hand we counted them out: nine of them, all with heads as big as their bodies and eyes closed tight in little slits, struggling around on their stomachs trying to find their mother's belly. Some were all brown, some were brown with a white underbelly, some were black with white feet, and some were a mottled mix of colors. We brought them up to the carpenter shop, made a nice comfortable den for them with a big box stuffed with a quilt, and settled them in. The arithmetically gratifying quantity of nine meant there were three each for Paul David, Johanna and me, and we quickly divided them up and assigned them names.

That summer was a riot as the puppies grew to be able to run around and chase after us. We'd lie down on the ground and a swarm of puppies would immediately engulf us, crawling all over us like the Lilliputians over Gulliver and tickling us with their little paws until we couldn't breath from laughing so hard. We'd walk across the field to the brook and behind us there'd be a stream of puppies, some walking with a purpose, others stopping to wrestle with their brother or sister or getting distracted by a passing butterfly. They'd walk cautiously but clumsily along the edge of the water, occasionally slipping and falling in and then spluttering up onto the shore for a good shake out.

I think I might have been ten or eleven that summer. An unknown inspiration made Paul David and me decide to begin building our own getaway habitation down by the beaver dam on Kenny Brook. It was a dry year and the water level had fallen to where much of the area that was normally under water behind the beaver dam was exposed. The deeper original brook channel still had water in it as it snaked through multiple curves across the exposed mud flats.

We brought axes, saws, hatchets and hammers and began building. First there was a footbridge across the channel. Then there were ladder rungs that we nailed to the trunks of larger trees so we could climb into their upper branches where we built platforms to sit on. More bridges followed, then little stockade forts, and finally a flagpole with a painted pillowcase for a flag. We called it Mudtown, and every afternoon we'd force our way through the scrub brush down to the brook followed by a rabble of curious puppies, and we'd work on expanding our creation. At the end of the afternoon when Mama called for dinner we'd look like troglodytes covered with mud from head to foot. So we'd get sent down to the far tidier Smith Brook with a bar of soap and a towel each and take a much needed bath to get presentable for dinner. Of course the puppies were all as filthy as us or maybe worse, so we'd toss them in the water and watch them paddle desperately to shore, with noses just above water and eyes bulging out of their heads in alarm at the novelty of swimming, and also washing a little of the mud out of their fur in the process.

By the fall, the puppies were starting to get to be big and they had voracious appetites. Mama and Papa were thinking ahead to the idea of having ten energetic dogs in the house through the winter, and realized something had to be done, so they placed a classified ad to sell them for a few dollars a piece. To prevent any appearance of favoritism, the ground rules were that when someone came to look they would choose which puppy they would take and we'd keep the last dog left.

Every time someone took a puppy it felt like a family member was driving away for good; a horrible, empty feeling. Eventually we were at the point of having Tramp and two puppies, and the next buyer who came told Mama that he'd take a puppy but he'd also really like Tramp since Tramp was a purebred beagle. The last dog standing was a puppy who had been one of Paul David's original three. He had named her Grizzly because when she was small and had a puppy's pug nosed face and pudgy body he thought her coloring made her look like a grizzly bear cub. She looked nothing like that now, but the name remained.

Grizzly would be our family dog from then on. She was a great companion who loved just being around us but wasn't fussy or demanding. Having been with us from birth she was tightly bonded to our whole family and had no interest in other dogs, and she'd snap at any dog that came near.

Every morning, winter or summer, we'd open up the kitchen door and Grizzly would release an entire night of stored up energy in a sixty second burst that would carry her like a shoulder launched missile across the lawn, through the tangle of underbrush leading to Kenny Brook, and then half way to the top of Newfane Hill. Her goal was to find something to chase, and when she did she'd begin howling in a way that carried for miles. She had different howls for different quarry, generally with the volume and desperation of the howl being in proportion to the size of the cornered animal.

Lots of the time the animal in question was just a squirrel or a chipmunk, but at times there'd be a skunk, and she'd come back reeking. In this day and age when the annual budget for my spaniel's haircut far exceeds spending on my own grooming and we feel like we're neglecting him if we go two weeks without a washing, it's amusing to think that in those times we almost never bathed Grizzly. Once in a while when she got skunked we'd take her down to the brook for a cleaning, but at other times we'd just have her stay outside until the smell subsided to the point of tolerability.

Urban dwellers are often well accustomed to having dogs skunked, but porcupines are a little less familiar. And they're far worse. We could tell when the morning's adventure involved a porcupine because the howl of excitement would turn suddenly to a cry of intense agony, and shortly thereafter Grizzly would arrive back at the house, whimpering with pain from a face full of quills. There's a myth that porcupines throw their quills, but this is silly. What they can do is to swing their tails, and if a dog's face is in the way, the swipe of the tail buries the quills into it. And sometimes the dog shoves his face into the porcupine to try to bite it and gets quills in its face with no effort exerted by the porcupine whatsoever. The quills are coated with a layer of fine barbs that prevent them from coming out once they've penetrated the skin, so removing them is agonizingly unpleasant.

Today people take their pets for chemotherapy and hip replacement surgery, but it never even crossed our mind to go to a vet to take care of the quills. We removed them ourselves the way everybody else we knew did it for their own dogs. We'd get Grizzly to lie down on the ground and we'd position a double tined hayfork over her neck and push it into the ground deep enough to pin her head down and (mostly) immobilize it. We'd put a rug over her body and I would sit on it to hold her still while Paul David used a pair of pliers to pull the quills out. The key to minimizing the pain was to pull the quill straight out with as little side-to-side wiggling as possible, but with a dog doing everything possible to avoid this crude surgery, it wasn't always easy, and she'd let out the most pitiful cries as each quill came out.

The odd thing about this was that she didn't learn about porcupines after the first time. She got hit several more times over the next few years. And it's not like she lacked the ability to learn quickly, either. For example, in her first year she used to chew on everything that was left lying around, destroying boots, shoes, gloves, and whatever she could sink her teeth into. But when we got into December all this chewing stopped like someone had flipped a switch. We didn't know what happened, but we weren't going to complain.

Early January came and it was time to take down all the Christmas decorations. Outside the house we had a tree with colored lights, and there was an extension cord running out to it. When we began to pack it up, we found it was riddled with teeth marks, including some that left exposed copper wiring. An educated guess might be that Grizzly's change of heart on chewing might have had something to do with the state of this cord.

But the worst of the porcupine incidents was one where she had been hit below the chin. The quills went through the underside of her mouth, through her tongue, and into the roof of her mouth. I can't begin to imagine how painful this must have been. But horrible as it was, a couple days after we removed the quills she'd always seem perfectly happy. The resilience of dogs can be amazing.

Having seen the pain they inflicted on Grizzly, we tended to give porcupines plenty of space when we saw them around the house or in the woods. But the day I looked out the kitchen window and saw a mother porcupine followed by five little babies walking across the lawn under the apple trees I had to throw caution to the wind. I ran into the woodshed and grabbed a fishing net, the kind that looks like a tennis racquet only with a net in place of the strings, and ran out after them. By the time I caught up the mother and one baby were up in an apple tree, but there were still four babies on the ground and I deftly scooped them all up.

It always surprises me today how many of these kinds of events there were and how rare it was that I had any well thought out plan. The script for these adventures always seemed to go something like this:

Act 1: Catch one or more wild animals
Act 2: Um, hmmm, not sure what to do here

For example, we'd be walking down the road and there would be a big snapping turtle working his way to the other side. These beasts always struck me as a most inappropriately named species. *Snapping* is a term that suggests speed or quickness, and there was no element of either of these attributes about a snapping turtle. Had we been foolish enough to stick a finger near their mouth they would have *never* snapped at it. Instead, the turtle would have thoughtfully placed its jaws above and below the finger, and then contemplatively closed them in a gradual, vice-like motion that at some point in the next three or four seconds would sever the finger from the hand. I will grant that this might be unsettling, but it's nothing like *snapping*.

So our approach was to find a good solid stick about an inch in diameter and two feet long, and we'd try to persuade the turtle that it was a particularly succulent and tasty finger. The turtle would eventually succumb to our blandishments and clamp onto the middle of the stick. Then we'd each grab an end of it and carry the turtle to our house, hanging by his own teeth. They could be quite heavy, these turtles, and exactly what we expected to do with one once we got it home is unclear. Certainly having a crazed dog jab-stepping in excitement around a turtle that could crush its nose is a poor combination.

But let us return to the porcupines in the net. After some thought, I brought the babies into the woodshed and put them into a wooden crate on the floor. I tried touching them gingerly, and unlike their prickly parents they were soft and furry feeling. For a lid I put a piece of plywood on top of the crate and a brick on top of that, and I went in the house to finish breakfast, hoping that some form of inspiration would strike me.

So it was with some surprise that twenty minutes later I

looked up from the table and saw the mother porcupine again crossing the lawn, and again accompanied by five babies. But this time they were further ahead of me and by the time I had the net all were way up in the upper branches and out of my reach. Were my four baby porcupines up there? I went back to the woodshed to check, and there was my crate with a big hole chewed right through its side by the mother. A jailbreak, clean as can be, and right under my nose.

Grizzly had a special voice when she found a deer. Under most circumstances a deer could easily outrun her and the barking would end fairly quickly. But one January morning when she ran out there was a real hard crust from freezing rain that had fallen after about two feet of powdery snow. The crust was easily strong enough to support Grizzly's thirty or so pounds, but a deer's small hooves concentrated its weight so it would fall through. Under these conditions there was no way a deer could get away.

We heard Grizzly start baying up on the hillside and it didn't let up. Paul David and I pulled on boots and coats and took off after her. As we went the direction of the sound shifted and moved down the hill toward Smith Brook. We were also plunging through the crust with each step and couldn't move much faster than the deer Grizzly was chasing, so it took us a while to catch up. When we did, we found Grizzly frantically leaping along the ice on the bank of the brook, and a small deer was in the water trying to get under the ice for protection.

We chased the dog away and plunged into the water to rescue the deer. Unless it is well below freezing for a long time, brooks usually don't freeze solid everywhere. The faster the water runs the less likely it is to freeze. Ice forms in a shelf around rocks in the brook, and since the water level is constantly going up and down depending on how much melting is happening, these shelves can be stranded a foot or more above the level of the water. When there are several rocks close together the shelves can join together creating a suspended roof of ice over fairly large areas. The deer was trying to force its way for protection under a shelf of this sort, first to escape from the dog and then from Paul David and me.

So we waded in to the bitter cold water, reached under the shelf and pulled the deer out. She was bleating pathetically with the kind of sound a young lamb might make, and her legs were cut and bleeding from falling through the crust. She seemed exhausted and resigned to her fate and didn't fight us, so with Paul David carrying her front quarters and me her back, we brought her back to the woodshed at our house where we dried her off with towels. We gave her water and fed her some of the grain we gave to our steer. Meanwhile Mama had called the game warden and he suggested we should just let her go, so we did, but not before locking Grizzly in the house where she remained for the rest of the day to give the deer plenty of time to get well away.

There were a lot of deer around, and while getting to catch one was unusual, for the most part we weren't that impressed by them. On the other hand, raccoons represented possibly the very pinnacle of the animal kingdom. It started with Fess Parker playing Davey Crockett and subsequently Daniel Boone in two different TV series through most of the sixties. Parker always had a coonskin cap with a raccoon tail hanging down the back of it. In my view that hat was miles cooler than any fashion offered up by swinging sixties Carnaby Street, and I would have killed to have one.

One day I was pushing the mower up Wardsboro Road to one of the lawns I needed to mow, and, lo and behold, on the side of the road lay a dead raccoon, hit by a car not long ago. I had no idea how you would skin such a carcass, but to me the key element of the hat was the tail, and all I needed to do to get that was slice it off with my pocket knife, so I did. The fur was incredibly soft and the alternating black and brown rings were gorgeous. It would for certain go down as the find of the summer.

When I got home I pinned the tail to the wall next to my bed, where I would lovingly admire it for the next several weeks. Then one day Paul David and I were engaged in one of our regular bouts of rough housing, wrestling each other to the floor and each generally trying to make his counterpart as miserable as possible. At some point in this I decided that if I rubbed the raccoon tail in Paul David's face when we wasn't expecting it that he'd find it especially annoying.

So I grabbed it off the wall, and when I did maggots fell out of it all over me. I almost jumped out of my own skin from the horror of it. Of course, a real raccoon hat is made with a cured and tanned pelt, whereas the attachment end of my uncured and untanned tail was basically just rotting dead raccoon and thus a perfect place for a housefly to lay its eggs. The larvae hatched from these were all hidden on the side of the tail facing toward the wall, so until I yanked it loose I had no idea what was going on back there. But I can tell you that I threw that tail straight out the bedroom window faster than you could blink.

Beyond the glamour of coonskin hats, in the late sixties there was a Walt Disney movie called *Rascal* featuring a raccoon that some kid adopts and they have all kinds of exploits together. Rascal is a paragon of cuteness, charming, clever and fastidious to the point of washing his food before he eats it. His boy partner in crime gives him a lump of sugar to eat and, in a devastatingly adorable scene, Rascal is completely baffled when the lump dissolves and disappears when swished through the water, looking at his empty hand as if to say: *I just had it here. What happened?* So it can perhaps be understood that after attending this movie our interest in raccoons rose from an already heightened state to a level that bordered on religious fanaticism.

I sometimes wonder that Walt Disney hasn't long ago gone bankrupt from class action lawsuits brought by parents whose kids have done pathologically moronic things while trying to emulate what happens in their movies. There must be hundreds of thousands of children dead, maimed, psychologically impaired, or at the very least stricken with rabies, all because they tried to copy something Hayley Mills did on the big screen that could never, ever happen in real life. On at least a dozen occasions Paul David and I avoided joining their ranks by the narrowest of margins. *Rascal* would inspire another.

Shortly after seeing the movie we found tracks from a raccoon that was coming around the house at night and up on the kitchen porch where it could eat whatever cat food was left behind. We figured if we could only capture it, this animal would instantly recognize the benefits inherent in becoming a tame pet just like Rascal. So Paul David devised a trap using a metal crate intended for milk bottles. He turned the crate upside down, put a heavy rock on top of it, and propped up one side with a flimsy stick. He put a plate of cat food under it for bait, confident that this would be irresistible. I was dubious and told him that traps like that only worked on TV and would never work for us, but Paul David was undeterred and left it for the night.

Next morning he got up early to check if he had any luck, and skeptics be damned, the milk crate had fallen down and the raccoon was trapped under it. After puzzling briefly about the next step, Paul David slid a small piece of plywood under the crate to make a floor and then lifted crate and raccoon and carried them indoors, putting them in the small bathroom off the library. He then closed the bathroom door and excitedly went upstairs to get me to come see his handiwork and eat a slice of humble pie for having ever shown any doubt.

But when we came downstairs there was a sound emanating from the bathroom like it was being demolished for subsequent renovation. The raccoon had escaped from the milk crate and was now desperately trying to get out of the bathroom, leaping at the windows, tearing down the curtains, and clawing big chunks out of the door.

We knew that to control the damage we had to get him out of there quickly, but we had to be sure he would go directly outdoors. There were several rooms to pass through on the way to the door at the kitchen steps, and if he took a wrong turn and went upstairs, he might destroy half the house before we got him out. So we closed all the doors that could lead in the wrong direction and left those open on the path to the outside. I got as far out of the way as I could, and Paul David stood a little behind the bathroom door and opened it really quickly. Our would-be Rascal shot like a shell from a cannon out the kitchen door and disappeared, having demonstrated that his counterpart from stage and screen was a raccoon of much more genteel breeding than our local variety, and that we probably ought to leave him and his friends alone.

Our next domestic animal after the sheep disaster was a young steer we named Dusty, mainly because he was. You'd give him a friendly whack on the side with the flat of your hand and a big puff of dirt and dust would rise from his hide, the result of lying on the ground chewing his cud while thoughtfully working out the solutions to problems in particle physics every afternoon. The idea was to have him for about eighteen months and then slaughter him for beef.

Dusty arrived in the spring as a calf about the size of a Shetland pony. Rather than trying to fence in our field for him, we fitted him with a big leather collar and tied him to a heavy iron stake that we drove into the ground with a sledgehammer. Throughout the next day he'd eat every blade of grass he could reach right down to the ground, leaving a close cropped circle interrupted only by a half a dozen cow pies.

In the evening, we'd go out to feed him some grain and move the stake so he'd have a fresh plot of grass for the next day. This work mostly fell to Paul David, but sometimes I'd tag along and maybe help carry something. Paul David would take the grain bucket out with him and leave it just unreachable outside the circle. If I was feeling helpful, I'd join him to go down to the brook with a pair of big five gallon buckets and fill them with water. We'd come staggering and sloshing up the embankment with these and set them near the grain.

Then Paul David would place the grain bucket just within the circle where Dusty could start to eat it. Grain was catnip as far as Dusty was concerned, and he'd go head down in the bucket for as long as anything was left in it. While Dusty was thus engaged, Paul David would hustle over to the stake, work it back and forth until it was loose enough that he could pull it out, and then re-position it so that the next day's grazing circle would just touch today's at a tangent point. Then he'd hammer the stake back into the ground. We'd put the water buckets at the edge of the new circle so that Dusty couldn't wrap his rope around them and spill them over, move his salt brick to where he could reach it, and the chore was done.

Of course all this bovine activity was taking place right in the middle of the same field we used for baseball, and there were numerous consequences for the game as a result. There is nothing quite like racing full bore in bare feet after a fly ball, eyes focused skywards, and stepping in a fresh cow pie. The effect is quite like those old cartoon scenes where Bugs Bunny drops a banana peel in front of an antagonist. All traction is instantly lost, and the would-be fielder goes flying posterior over anterior into the grass, which, if he is especially unfortunate, is graced with further cow pies that add insult to injury. Then the ball hits the ground with a thud within half an inch of the supine fielder's head, and two runs score before he has a chance to reflect on what has just happened.

After this, he begins to notice a ripe odor, and on further contemplation realizes that it is coming from his foot, which is smeared up to the ankle with agricultural byproduct. Major league baseball Rule 402.3 states that this circumstance necessitates calling time so that the player can go to the brook and wash away the offending offal before play resumes, and of course we are nothing if not sticklers for the rules.

A common misconception is that cow pies get their name only from the circular format in which they are generally presented. This is part of the story, but it hides the inner truth, which is that, much like a pie meant for human consumption, cow pies also go through a baking process. When first created they are soft and wet, much like an uncooked pastry. But as time goes by, perhaps the first day in the sun, they develop a crispy outer crust concealing the richness buried inside. Left to bake for a week, they eventually cook all the way through and become hard and dry throughout, much the way our mother's pie would have had she forgotten to take it out of the oven before leaving to play a couple rubbers of bridge with some friends in Putney.

Each of these stages of pie baking presented a different hazard for the outfielder. The fresh pie has been discussed already. The fully baked pie was unquestionably the least problematic. It is true that its rough texture compared unfavorably to grass as a surface for athletic events, and it would often cause a stumble by virtue of being an inch or two higher than the rest of the field, but overall it was no more than a minor hazard. A relative lack of odor was another significant factor in favor of this variety.

On the other hand, the partially baked pie with the outer crust was particularly unpleasant, mainly because the first contact felt reassuringly firm and might have misled the fielder into momentarily thinking that he was dealing with the fully baked variety. However, this misperception was generally very short-lived. Milliseconds, perhaps. Then the crust would break through and the foot would plunge into the molten interior. The experience from this point onwards was typically identical to the uncooked pie scenario discussed previously.

At no point in the baking process was it especially easy to gather up cow pies. One can imagine that there was little enthusiasm for gathering any pie that was not fully baked. But generally by the time all softness was out of a pie, grass would have grown through it from underneath and thus would root it to the ground with a hold that wouldn't easily let go. So we tended to leave the pies out on the field. The resulting fertilizing effect made the grass grow richer and greener than it ever had previously.

In the winter things were more difficult. Then Dusty had to stay in one place in the barn. We fed him a combination of grain and hay from bales that we bought from the local farm supply store. But for the most part there was little chance for him to get outside. With no sun to dry it, his pie product piled up in his enclosure and had to be shoveled out the back of the barn every day. Here it formed a big frozen mound, pungent even in the winter cold and positively asphyxiating in the spring when it began to thaw. We shoveled this manure into wheelbarrows and mixed it into the soil in the vegetable gardens. Delightful work if you can get it.

When the second autumn of Dusty's career came around it was time to slaughter him. Mama found a man in Dummerston who would do it for some of the meat. This fellow was so poor that he didn't own a car, and we had to drive to his place and pick him up. His house looked like it hadn't been painted since the Teapot Dome scandal, and there was junk like rusting washing machines and parts of cars piled up everywhere around the outside.

He led Dusty by his rope out to the corner of our garden near the apple trees and put a pan of grain on the ground in front of him. As Dusty bent over to eat it, the man gave him a tremendous blow on the top of his skull with a big sledge hammer. Dusty's legs crumbled underneath him and he collapsed in a heap, dead as a doornail.

I suppose that today most parents would have done everything they could to avoid having their ten year old child watch a spectacle like this, but events of this kind were common in Vermont. I was even younger when King had killed the sheep and Papa had shot him. I understood from the start that we were raising Dusty for meat and that this was how it was going to end, and I was fascinated to watch the butchering process first hand. Readers who get queasy at this sort of thing might want to skip a couple of paragraphs.

The first step was to get as much blood out of the animal as possible. The man used a big sharp knife to slit the throat, and the heart, which continues to work reflexively for a little while, pumped a huge pool of blood out of this cut and into a dishpan, saving it so Mama could make a batch of her, um, *legendary* (yes, that's the right word) blood pudding. Then the man cut off the head. Getting the entrails out quickly without their contents contacting the meat is a key part of the process, and he slit open Dusty's belly and in short order had a huge mound of intestines and organs lying on the lawn. Later it would be my task to dig a big hole and bury most of this mess, and in the process I punctured the guts with a shovel blade. I don't think I had an especially weak stomach, but the smell that came from inside was enough to make a grown man cry for his mother and I came within an inch of losing my last four meals over it.

Showing a little humor in the midst of this ghastly process, the butcher tied off the upper end of the bladder and then blew into the lower end, inflating it like a balloon until it was all stretched out in a big round ball. He tied off the lower end and hung it in the tree, where over the next couple days it dried into a leathery bulb.

Once all the organs were out the butcher hoisted the carcass to hang by the hind legs from a strong branch on an apple tree. He then cut the hide off. When freshly removed this was soft and pliable and seemed like the sort of thing an Algonquin would use to line the floor of his tent, so in a decision of remarkable stupidity we had the man put this untanned hide in the attic above the carpenter shop, where in a few days it became as stiff as a sheet of plywood. It was too big to get back down the stairs, so we just left it there until a few years later when we tore the entire floor apart as part of a remodeling effort that turned the woodshed and carpenter shop into rooms for Trollhaugen guests.

The butcher then hung the carcass from a beam in the woodshed to age in the autumn cool. His day's work completed, Mama drove him back to his home. A couple days later while I was in school she went and picked him up again and he butchered the meat into all its various cuts.

Mama ground much of the meat from poorer cuts into hamburger using a hand-cranked grinder, and all the meat, ground or whole, was wrapped in a heavy waxed paper and stored in a big outdoor freezer sitting on our porch.

In the next few months we were treated to the entire buffet of beef related delicacies. Blood pudding and liver, of course, but also brains and tongue. I know I ate more beef in the next year than at any point in the rest of my life. I think that when we had finished it Mama decided she'd had enough of beef on the table and cow pies on the lawn, and we never raised another calf after that.

We never had a milk cow, but when the Mullers gave their place to their daughter, she and her husband did, and on a couple of occasions when they were away they paid me to milk it in their absence. The process of hand milking a cow is an activity that will cause you to think twice about whether eating dairy products is all that smart, and it really makes you wonder why anyone would have their own cow when the store down in Newfane has such nice milk in refrigerated plastic bottles for only a few dollars.

You start by getting the cow into its bay in the barn and give it some grain or hay to help keep it focused on something other than what you are doing. You will immediately notice that this bay has several differences from the sort of surgically cleaned area you would prefer to have in an area used to handle food intended for human consumption. For one thing (and, to be perfectly frank, once you have this one thing no other things are needed and the entire discussion can be closed), as in any place inhabited by livestock, there is, and I am sorry to be indelicate here, cow shit on just about everything. The vast majority of the milking process relates to maintaining separation of the milk product from the rest of this environment.

The separation begins by washing down the milk bucket and disinfecting it with iodine. Next is cleaning the cow's udders, which you are hoping to take from a state of complete filth to a surface that you'd willingly eat from. This cleaning begins with warm soapy water (too cold or too hot and the cow reacts much the way you would if someone used the wrong temperature to wash your own personal parts) and finishes with an iodine wipedown that in theory kills the majority of lethal bacteria on the critical areas.

Next, you wash your hands with warm water and soap, sit on a milking stool next to the cow, speak soothingly to her to try to keep her in the mood as much as possible, and if your diversionary tactics appear to meet with success, gently take hold of a teat in each hand, forming a ring around the top of it using the thumb and index finger. Then you squeeze one finger at a time from the index finger down to your pinkie, which pumps the milk down the teat and out. The first couple pumps should be aimed onto the floor since they're not very clean, but after that you shoot the milk into the bucket. You repeat the squeezing until the teat starts to look flabby and empty and the flow tapers off, and then you're done.

It sounds reasonably straightforward, but there are many kinds of problems that can arise. While the causes are diverse, most of these problems conclude with the cow either lifting a hind leg and putting it in the milk bucket, or, for cows possessing lesser sophistication and skill, merely kicking it over. Either of these outcomes require you to start the whole cleansing process all over again. Alternatively, the cow might choose to kick you personally instead of the bucket. This saves cleaning, but might result in a lost tooth or a concussion.

The most likely offences that bring this to happen are: squeezing too hard, squeezing too fast, pulling on the teat, or most commonly, not squeezing the fingers in the proper sequence. The sequence seems easy, and for the first four or five times it is, but if you're inexperienced as I was, your hands quickly tire and then you start to close all four fingers at the same time. Sensitive cows find this treatment offensive and will soon let you know.

But you can be squeezing like a well oiled machine and

still have everything go wrong. The cow might finish her grain and get bored. A horsefly might bite her. She might not care for the tone of the sweet nothings you are whispering in her ear. I never got anywhere near what I'd call experienced at milking, but to me it was a raging success if I finished the one cow in half an hour and half the milk that came out of her ended up being usable.

Livestock needed hay, and you could buy it from a farm store as we did when we had sheep or a steer. I also helped our neighbors out with gathering their own hay, which was much less expensive but replaced cash with sweat equity. They didn't have much of a hayfield themselves, but they paid the owner of a farm down on Route 30 for the right to mow their field and take the resulting hay. They gave me a few dollars to help load the bales onto a truck and then unload them into their barn. This was brutal work. The August sun was intense so we worked shirtless and you'd walk alongside the truck as it slowly made its way up and down the field, grabbing bales off the ground and throwing them up to a guy on the truck who would then position them in place. Of course we were all dripping sweat and this quickly blended with straw and pollen falling off the bales as we tossed them over our heads and made every inch of skin itch like mad. When the truck started getting full it was serious work to throw the bales up to the top of the pile, which was easily ten or twelve feet off the ground.

Then we'd get a fifteen minute reprieve as we'd tie the load down and drive a couple miles back to their barn, but now we had to throw all the bales up onto the second floor through a door designed for this purpose. A few hours of this work and you'd be so tired that, in the unlikely event that your appearance made any difference to you at that point, you couldn't have raised your arm to comb your hair.

These same neighbors also had a goat. I failed to see any upside in goat ownership. The goat would try to eat just about anything, edible or not, and could be counted on to destroy something it wasn't supposed to get into on a nearly daily basis. What's more, for reasons that only God and perhaps some evolutionary scientists understand, goats have brains wired to make them want to butt things. Where the pleasure lies in smashing your head into a solid object escapes me, but a goat certainly enjoys it.

If there is a goat around, you have to be cautious about turning your back, and bending over is about as foolhardy a move as you can make. If you did that, our neighbor's goat would hit you so hard that, as Southside Johnny once said to Lee Dorsey, when you woke up your clothes were out of style.

If you were facing the goat, you had a chance. He'd stare at you and get this weird sort of cross-eyed look on his face that made you know he was coming, and then he'd charge. With quick reaction you could grab his horns and prevent a crunching impact, but this was like having a tiger by the tail. Having his horns held made the goat want to butt you twice as badly, so as soon as you let go, he'd come right at you again. Sometimes he'd appear in our yard, and the only thing to do was to drag him by the horns all the way back to where he belonged and lock him in the neighbor's barn.

For a teenage boy the goat was a danger only if he caught you not paying attention, but for a younger child or an older person without the quickness or strength to grapple with him, knowing he was ready to charge wasn't enough and it could really be scary. I came home from school once and found Mama up in an apple tree with the goat waiting for her to come down. He'd hit her once already and she couldn't get back to the house without risking a second hit. I'm not sure what happened to the goat, but I suspect eventually our neighbors reached the same cost/benefit analysis conclusion that I did and got rid of him.

Today Johanna has more animals at the place than we ever did as children. Growing up we typically had only one major animal at a time. First we had sheep, then when they were gone we had Oscar the pig, then Dusty the steer. But Johanna simultaneously keeps a flock of chickens, geese, ducks, about half a dozen pigs, and an equal number of sheep, and she slaughters and butchers the animals herself, all the while holding down a full time job as a teacher. From my now urbanized perspective this is all quite amazing to observe.

12   THE OUTSIDE WORLD

The world we saw on the TV news seemed to me like it was a long way away. For the most part I just hoped we'd be left alone in all the chaos that seemed to be out there. Not to minimize the issues that the world faces today, but it sure seemed a whole lot scarier in the 1960s where tensions between the US, Russia and China made the threat of all out nuclear war alarmingly real.

My awareness began with Kennedy running against Nixon. There was a lot of talk of communists, and I remember Mama reading a woman's magazine with an advertisement for a canned food of a sort that I've forgotten, but I do remember that the brand was Red Devil. The ad had an image of a fiendishly crimson colored demon trailing a forked tail and holding a pitchfork. He was temptingly holding out a can of the product on offer, and I asked Mama if that was what a communist looked like, because, after all, the politicians on TV were always carrying on about the red devils.

Images come quickly after this. Men go into space; Mercury, Gemini and Apollo programs in rapid succession. The Cuban Missile Crisis. JFK killed. Goldwater vs Johnson. Tonkin Gulf. Dominican Republic. Selma. The Tet Offensive. Assassinations of Martin Luther King, Jr. and

RFK. Johnson withdraws and Humphrey loses to Nixon. Student unrest. Kent State and Jackson State. Nothing changed in Newfane, but elsewhere it seemed like everything was changing.

The civil rights movement began to be big news about the time we moved full time to Vermont. There had been one African American boy in my class in Connecticut, but in Vermont the closest thing we had to a minority group was anybody who was Catholic, and nobody really noticed them all that much. It was really hard for a Vermont kid to understand the passions in the whole race issue. Why did the southern whites hate the blacks? Why did blacks riot? Why would someone kill Dr. King when he seemed like such a good man? Not understanding it made things a lot more worrisome.

Then we'd constantly hear about what was wrong with college aged kids. They took drugs, they were unpatriotic, they protested, they had long hair, they listened to horrible music, they were dirty, and on and on. Of course the reporters didn't spend much time interacting with young people to find out why they did what they did, and on the few occasions when they actually did talk to kids, they'd usually pick wholesome, straight laced types who felt the same way as the newscasters.

My Newfane school classmates all had pretty short hair. When I was in eighth grade in 1967, a time when the Beatles had taken to looking remarkably like the pictures of Christ's disciples that were hanging in our local Congregational Church, one slightly rebellious kid got sent home from school because his hair touched the collar of his shirt in the back. But high school was more tolerant and would be an odd mix of future farmers, greasers, straights, and trendier kids aspiring to be hippies.

But the issue that towered over and influenced everything was Vietnam.

I think Mama came to an understanding that the war in Vietnam was a bad idea faster than the vast majority of

Vermonters. Not that she needed a lot of material for arguments with Papa, but I remember them dueling over Vietnam at the kitchen table while Paul David, Johanna and I fidgeted in our chairs and tried to figure out which side we should be on. In about a year, though, Papa came around to Mama's point of view, too.

As the war dragged on, understanding it started to become more urgent as Paul David and I began to realize that in just a couple years there was a very real chance of being drafted and sent to fight in the jungles of the Mekong Delta. In 1969 the military implemented a new draft system that matched a lottery number to each birth date in the year, with the lowest numbers drafted first. Paul David turned eighteen in 1970 and had a lottery number of forty. The draft call-ups were in groups of fifty lottery numbers, which made his forty for all intents and purposes the same as having number one. The idea that my brother, who just a couple years previous had been building Mudtown with me and Johanna, could be forced to go to a war where he'd shoot at and be shot at by Viet Cong in southeast Asia was appalling. To this day I believe that it's a barbaric act of national cowardice that we ask kids under the age of twenty to bear the brunt of fighting in our country's wars, and it should be no surprise to anyone that so many veterans of Vietnam and other wars are homeless or psychologically shattered when they have been sent into an environment like that at such a young age.

Mama thought Paul David should go to Canada, but he felt this wasn't fair to the others who went, so he went to the recruiting office near Albany where he was given a physical. He was luckily disqualified after his medical exam showed that he might have a blood disorder that indicated a kidney problem. And when it was my turn for a lottery number, I drew a ten, but by then the draft had been stopped and I was at no risk of being chosen. But every teenage male of that period worried about Vietnam all the time. There was no escaping it.

13 GETTING OLDER

In my high school years I had no idea what the next phase of life would be like, but I knew I did want to go to college and would be devastated if I didn't make it. I saw how hard people worked in Vermont and how little they had for their efforts. I'd tasted it myself from all the different odd jobs I'd done to earn pocket money and build the start of a nest egg to pay for college. Even before I got to high school I would think of how I didn't want to be laboring away outdoors in the cold of winter or the heat of summer, and it was clear to me that the path to this was to find a way to work with my head and not my hands.

In the high school guidance councilors' office there was a rack full of brochures with titles like: *So You Want To Be A Teacher*, or *A Doctor*, or *A Chemist*. I flipped through a few of these until I hit one entitled *So You Want To Be An Electrical Engineer*. It said you should be good at math and enjoy solving practical problems. It's quite likely that there was no one in our entire county who could have told me anything more about electrical engineering than this, but it sounded about right for me. So in the five minutes it took to read that pamphlet, I chose the career I'd spend forty years working at.

On graduating from high school in Brattleboro I went off to study engineering in Massachusetts. During this time I would come home in the summer to earn some of the money to pay for the next year, borrowing the rest. On getting a master's degree I moved to Tucson and enrolled in a doctorate program at the university there. I arrived in mid-June and it was over a hundred degrees every day from then until I decided that life in the Sonoran desert was too big a change for a Vermont boy, and I quit school, moved to San Diego, and got my first professional job.

Mama and Papa finally got divorced around the time I left New England, and Mama moved back to Norway for a while. But in the early seventies she'd been diagnosed with leukemia, and both the symptoms and the treatments were getting more severe. She returned to Vermont for her last year or two, house sitting for friends when they traveled or renting a small apartment. Somehow the acuteness of her illness had never really penetrated my consciousness and although there was really no reason I should have been taken at unawares, when she died in 1980 it felt like a complete surprise to me. I had foolishly assumed the existence of parents as a constant, and to my regret was proven wrong.

Although he was fifteen years older than Mama, Papa seemed invulnerable. I'd call him regularly from Tucson to see how things were going. One day when I was on the phone with him I thought to ask how Grizzly was. She'd have been a pretty old girl at that point, fourteen or fifteen I guess. There was an unsettling quiet from the other end of the line, and I asked, "What's wrong?"

Another hesitation, and then Papa said defensively, "Well it's all easy for you kids. You run off to school and then move away completely, and I'm left here with this dog that I have to take care of. It got to be too hard to do. So I shot her."

Well, that was a bit of a conversation stopper. But to be honest, I shouldn't have been surprised. My father came from another era, where a dog was often considered as a farm implement and security device, and if it stopped having utility, you did what you had to do. You might be fond of it, but you could be fond of a car, too. He didn't have any particular attachment to dogs in general or to Grizzly in particular, and it wasn't like I hadn't seen him do this sort of thing before. And he was right that Grizzly had been our dog, not his. But I was surprised he didn't have just a little bit of a soft spot for her.

When I tell friends today that Vermont was a conservative place in the 1960s, they don't believe it. But it's true. What has made today's Vermont so liberal is an influx of energetic, vocal and affluent people from outside of the state. They'd come on a ski holiday and be overwhelmed by the romantic charm of the place. They'd see a house for sale in the middle of a village that looks like something from a Norman Rockwell painting, and when they'd find it cost about a quarter of the price of a one bedroom apartment in Manhattan, they'd go: "Nice! I'll write a check". Some of these houses are used for vacations, and some for retirement, but forty years of these kinds of transactions have had an irrevocable impact. The village in Newfane is a ghost town compared to what it used to be. The houses are all still there, many with remodeled and upgraded interiors, and for the most part they're maintained much better than they were in the sixties, but usually no one is home and the streets where people once were out walking all the time seem deserted. But it could be even worse, and the proof is thirty-five miles up Route 30 from Newfane. Here all the homes in the center of the once charming town of Manchester have been converted into outlet stores where on the days that their desk-trained muscles are so sore that they need a day off from the slopes, the ski crowd shops for brands they could just as easily get in their local mall back home in New Jersey.

Many people with real local roots have been priced out of the villages and full time residents now are more likely to be found living out the dirt roads where they've built an ugly ramshackle cabin on a lot carved out of the woods. While it is true that the native Vermonters have been influenced by the opinions of the imports to become much more liberal themselves, it seems unlikely this would have happened without the influx.

But there's still a divide. The newcomers who do settle on a full time basis often have an expectation for schools and other services that can clash with the budget realities of ordinary Vermonters. From time to time the national news carries a segment on the quaint town meetings in places like Newfane, usually accompanied by a talking head blathering on about how these meetings represent grass roots democracy in action. What they never seem to get is exactly how these meetings can create conflict at the most personal level. When a motion comes up to spend a hundred thousand dollars on school refurbishment, every resident in the meeting can quickly determine how many hundreds of dollars it's going to cost them in taxes this year. These kinds of questions can cause great bitterness between people when there is large variability in the economic status of the voters.

In the mid 1990s, the British pop group Pulp recorded an insightful song called "Common People" in which the struggling singer is befriended by the naive daughter of a wealthy tycoon. To prove her compassion, she wants to live like the common people, but the singer makes the point that she can never really understand, because if at any point she decides it's not what she wants, she can call her dad and he'll come take her back to the world she came from.

I sometimes think that Vermont is like that now. There's one group of people who see the Vermont life through a romantic lens, but it's largely a fantasy for many of them. They can pay for people to shovel their walkways and roofs, mow their lawns, and paint their houses. But if they get tired of it, they can sell their house and go back to the life they know best.

Most native Vermonters don't have that option. In both emotional and economic terms Vermont roots are deep and are not easy to pull up. Salaries are low, and the financial logic that makes it easy for an urban professional to buy a Vermont house works in reverse when a Vermont native wants to leave the state. And the kinds of skills necessary to make a living in Vermont often don't translate well elsewhere.

A story from my summers working at Townshend Dam highlights this divide. My boss was a man named Roy Norman, a man who almost certainly had no more than a high school education but was resourceful enough to manage the operation and maintenance of an entire flood control dam with only the help of a ragtag team of seasonal workers and college kids off for the summer. It never occurred to me then, but Roy did a phenomenal job planning out tasks for his crew. Every day we did something useful from an incredibly diverse menu of tasks including emptying trash cans, maintaining restrooms and mowing lawns in public areas, maintaining signage, painting and repairing dam-related buildings, cutting weeds and brush growing on the face of the dam, greasing the cables and testing the motors that controlled the flood gates, scything the grass on the roadsides, inspecting and maintaining the log boom that kept recreational boats out of the spillway, filling potholes in roads on the dam property, lacing out fallen trees, maintaining dam-owned vehicles and equipment, and of course, in a flood, controlling the flow of water from the dam. He orchestrated these efforts like the professional manager he was, keeping his unskilled, minimum wage team focused and motivated. He was rational, reasonable, and not terribly excitable. If you knew to look for it, you could tell when something really bothered him because he'd pull on the pipe he always smoked just a little harder than normal.

The dam was built with a narrow public road about half a mile long across its top. The road was unstriped, and oncoming cars could pass on it when they met, but just barely. One day Roy sent three of us – two college grads and me in my second year – with a machine used for painting road stripes and asked us to put one down the center of the dam.

Well, how hard can that be? You see road crews out painting stripes all the time, and they seem to just drive along and produce a perfect stripe in no time. On the rare occasion that the stripe isn't exactly where it ought to be, people comment about how the crew must have been drinking, on drugs, or suffering severe marital problems to do such a bad job.

So the three of us, John, Gene and I, are standing on the dam with this painting machine, which is a little bigger than a standard snowblower but with a place to hold a five gallon bucket of paint, a sprayer nozzle pointing a couple inches above the ground, two big wheels in the back and two smaller ones in the front, and a handle to push it. We looked down the road and, perhaps surprisingly, we had the sense to realize that making the line straight might not be all that easy. So I came up with what seemed like a bright idea: we'd get some roofing nails and some blue plastic ribbon we had back in the maintenance garage, and we'd use a tape measure to find the center between guardrails and hammer a plastic marker into the asphalt to give us a guide every five or six guardrails along the road. Then we'd just push the sprayer to connect the dots and get a perfect result.

At this point I should say that when you turned from Route 30 onto the dam road, at first you crossed a hundred foot long iron bridge suspended some eighty feet above the emergency spillway. This bridge was only wide enough for a single car, so we weren't meant to paint it. After the bridge, the road widened a bit, turned slightly to the right, and descended to where it passed the entrance to the dam's gatehouse. From there it was dead straight and dead level across the rest of the dam. We started placing our markers at the Route 30 end, dragging the sprayer with us so that once we reached the far end we could paint as we walked back. On the return trip, every step of the way as we painted we focused intently on going straight ahead to the next marker.

Just as we got back to the bridge and shut the spray off, we met Roy coming across it in a black Corps of Engineers pickup truck. He stopped right at the end of the bridge at the top of the rise, where the view across the dam was perfect.

We walked up to the truck and he rolled down his window.

"How's the job coming, boys?", he asked.

"We just finished!", came the reply.

"Have you looked at it?"

So we turned and looked at what we'd done for the first time, and from our superb vantage point we could see a white stripe wobbling its way off seemingly to the horizon, and looking for all the world as though it had been painted by a crew that had been drinking, on drugs, or suffering severe marital problems.

Roy took two very long firm pulls on his pipe, shook his head, and muttering "You goddamn college kids...", drove back to the maintenance garage. And to this day, every time I see a highway crew painting road stripes, I think they deserve to be paid much better than they are.

But the point of this is that Roy was truly a very capable man. When one of the summer workers drove a huge bucket loader into a boggy section of ground and sunk it in muck to where its body was sitting on the mire and its wheels were at least four feet underground, Roy was able to size up the situation quickly, figure out a plan for how to get it out, and then make it happen. I doubt anyone I know in San Diego could do this. I know I couldn't. There's a real intellect required to solve problems like this that doesn't translate into the test scores or diplomas that urban dwellers are likely to rely on to measure smarts. And when people who have that intellect see people with the test scores and diplomas floundering, it's little wonder their reaction is something to the effect of "you goddamn college kids!"

I had a conversation a while ago with a conservative friend who lives in our nation's capital and earns a very good salary as an executive. He's a deacon in his church and no doubt regards himself as a compassionate man. He was complaining about social security and saying that he thought our country should do away with it. I replied that there are a lot of people for whom there is no other source of retirement income, and his view was that such people were lazy and needed to learn how to work for what they got. This irritated me pretty badly, and I gave him some examples of Vermont people who work very hard but have no access to 401k accounts and make barely enough to get by. My friend replied that these people had made their choices and they should have left the state for something better. Now that's compassion for you.

America is mostly urban now, but oddly a large number of urban residents want to feel that a big part of their character is a reflection of rural values, values that they often misinterpret and don't understand very well. Marketing agencies certainly recognize this, and it explains, for example, why auto companies market trucks with four wheel drive to southern Californians who are likely to never once use more than two. I was baffled when the SUV craze started because in Newfane in the 1960s, driving a four wheel drive vehicle meant you lived way out a dirt road where you truly needed one, and that usually meant you were at the lower end of an already low economic scale. So to me a car like a Jeep or a Suburban was anything but a status symbol.

But real rural values aren't about romance. They're about having less and making do with less, not sweating the little things as much, maybe not competing as ruthlessly, enjoying a warm sunny day more because they don't happen as often, and laughing over past misfortunes like getting stuck in the mud or spinning off an icy road. Rural people aren't necessarily better or worse than people elsewhere. Some of them are lazy and they quarrel and drink too much and take drugs and have kids out of wedlock and commit crimes and wreck their cars and cheat others just like some urban people do. But also as with urban people, a great majority are fundamentally sound and if there is a path leading to a good outcome they are willing to work hard to follow it. On the other hand, rural lives have different constraints and this makes people behave a little differently. There's value in understanding this before taking hard positions like my Washington friend.

For me, I have roots in both worlds, which might not be saying much since it could easily mean that I don't really understand either. Should they read this, Paul David and Johanna may well think I'm pretty cheeky – and sometimes way off base – to talk about what goes on in Vermont at this point. It's certainly a long time since I lived there, but in a lot of ways my experiences growing up in Newfane color almost everything about how I live my urban life today, sometimes for better, sometimes for worse, but always in ways that set me just a little apart from everyone else.

ABOUT THE AUTHOR

Steven Gardner was born in 1955 in Townshend, Vermont. He grew up in the town of Newfane, the county seat of Windham County in the southern part of the state, where the stories in this book take place. He studied electrical engineering, and after completing his bachelor and master degrees he enjoyed a long but recently completed career in a variety of high tech companies in San Diego, California. As a sideline to his profession, he also wrote extensively about rock and roll music for a variety of magazines, and plans several books on that topic in the not too distant future. He currently lives in San Diego with his wife Mary.

If you enjoyed reading these stories, please leave a review on Amazon. This will help lead others to the book.

www.shgardner.com